M000313379

...ALWAYS A FAN

...ALWAYS A FAN

MIKE RESNICK

WILDSIDE PRESS

...ALWAYS A FAN

Published in 2009 by Wildside Press, LLC.
All rights reserved.

Contents

Consider Mike Resnick—

by Tony Lewis

Ah, but which Mike Resnick? There are many Mike Resnicks—all subsumed in the same person. I have no intention of writing a formal biography; you can find a good one at Mike's website:

<http://www.fortunecity.com/tattooine/farmer/2/>

There is Mike Resnick the writer—SF, fantasy, detective, dogs, non-fiction, movie scripts . . .

There is Mike Resnick the editor—SF, Africa . . .

There is Mike Resnick the anthologizer—commissioning original SF . . .

There is Mike Resnick the former collie breeder and exhibitor . . .

There is Mike Resnick the doting husband and father . . .

There is Mike Resnick the convention fan . . .

There is Mike Resnick the Guest of Honor . . .

There is Mike Resnick the costuming fan . . .

There is Mike Resnick the fanzine fan . . .

There is Mike Resnick the good friend . . .

Are you starting to get some idea of what this man is like and what a wide range of interests and accomplishments he has. The annoying thing is that he does all of them so well.

Most of the science fiction world knows Mike as a professional writer. Or, as SF fans put it, a "filthy pro"—more a term of endearment and envy than derision. Not only a professional author but a damned good one and a damned successful one. A list of his novels, stories, and articles would be quite long. In fact, his bibliography page lists 126 novels, 2 screenplays, and an amazing 204 pieces of short fiction. This will be out of date when this book first sees print.

As an editor and anthologist, one of his major achievements has been encouraging and coercing good fiction from new writers—believe me, I know. Mike believes this is his moral obligation to "pay it forward" in honor of those who helped him; you can't really pay it back.

Mike started going to conventions in the early 1960s as a fan. Now, as a world-recognized award-winning pro, he still considers himself to also be a fan and takes part in a number of fannish activities at the conventions; in this he follows in the footsteps of E.E. Smith, Gordon Dickson, and Hal Clement—and those are some footsteps to fill.

In addition to attending conventions as a fan, pro, and program participant, Mike's been guest of honor, emcee, and toastmaster at a number of SF conventions—the most important of which, in my biased opinion, was Boskone 28 in 1991.

Mike—and his beautiful wife Carol—were active in costume fandom when it was first burgeoning. They've won awards at the World Science Fiction Convention masquerades. Mike made a point of capping the cost of their costumes; he believed—and still does—that imagination and humor will do more for you in the long run than money.

Now, this is how Mike loses money: he writes for fanzines. Fanzines don't pay much. In fact, most pay nothing at all. In the past, some fanzines have even asked their authors to help collate and staple the zine. Of course, in today's high-tech world, everything is done automatically by machine, or failing that, by hands-on work of fans. Every time Mike writes a fanzine article or essay, that time could have been spent earning fantastic amounts of money from books or screenplays. What the hell. Mike knows where he came from and is proud of it. It's all family, after all.

Here, in this collection of essays—from convention reports to obituaries—you will mostly see Mike as fanzine fan but other aspects will pop up in subtle ways. Look for them; it will greatly increase your enjoyment—that's what this book is all about.

— Tony Lewis
Natick, Massachusetts
March 2009

Foreword

Well, I *did* promise you a decade ago in *Once a Fan...* that if I was still around ten years later, I'd see you in the pages of *...Always a Fan.*

Not much has changed. I've written a bunch of novels and a bigger bunch of stories, I've won a few more awards and lost a lot more, I've gone blind in one eye (which, to the dismay of some critics, has not hindered my productivity), I've finally gotten a high-speed connection for my computer but I still steadfastly refuse to own a cell phone, I've signed a few Hollywood deals and have not yet seen a feature film based on my work (though there have been some short ones), I've collaborated with 12 more writers, I've been the science fiction consultant for a line of books (BenBella), I've been the executive editor for *Jim Baen's Universe*, and I've attended about seventy conventions.... which is to say, nothing much has changed. I still consider myself a fan who happens to make his livelihood by writing science fiction, I still support the fanzines and the small presses whenever I can, and I still feel like the luckiest man alive to have spent a life in science fiction and fandom.

And I am sure I'll still feel that way ten years from now, when I collect another decade's worth of fannish writing for *Still a Fan.*

— Mike Resnick

I don't remember quite when I started writing up my Worldcon diaries, but they've become very popular. Most have appeared in Guy Lillian's *Challenger*, and over the years I seem to have written up a few other cons as well, such as DragonCon and the Nebula Weekend.

Well, why not? The Worldcon is invariably the highlight of my year. I look forward to it like a kid to Christmas, and no matter how poorly it's run (and some are run pretty poorly) I always manage to have a wonderful time, while simultaneously lining up my work for the coming year or two.

Part I

Conventions

Chicon IV

Chicon IV, held in 1982, was the first of three Chicago Worldcons to use the Hyatt as its headquarters hotel. It was a wise decision; the Hyatt has proven to be the best Worldcon hotel on the circuit, capable of containing all the myriad of events and ceremonies within its friendly confines, and attached to a number of other venues by underground walkways.

The Guest of Honor was A. Bertram Chandler, and since he was an Australian this was the first chance many fans had to meet him. The always-popular Kelly Freas was the Artist Guest of Honor, the legendary Lee Hoffman was the Fan Guest of Honor, and Marta Randall was the Toastmaster (and did it so well that she was Toastmaster again for Chicon V.)

The masquerade was still a huge draw back then (they've gotten a lot smaller in the past couple of decades, in number of costumes if not the size of the audience), and the Hugos were well-attended and went off without a hitch. The Dealers' Room was immense, close to 300 tables, and the art show featured almost all the major artists in the field. The multi-track programming wasn't quite as fragmented and complex as it has become, the movies were well-chosen and very popular, and the party suites were filled every night. The famous fannish video, *Faans*, starring a bunch of Midwestern fans, was shot at various spots around the hotel; I especially remember one scene where a ton's worth of fans did a song and dance on one of the Hyatt's indoor balconies/walkways.

This was the first Chicon in 20 years, and a lot of fans who'd never been to the Windy City before got to sample its many wonderful restaurants, as well as visit the Field Museum, the Art Institute, the Museum of Science and Industry, the Lincoln Park and Brookfield Zoos, and the city's plethora of used-book stores. Most fans arrived a few days early, and many stayed a day or two past Labor Day.

I had four or five books out in the previous year, and found myself on a number of panels, as well as being a masquerade judge. This was the last convention where I was able to spend any serious amount of time as a fan rather than a pro—these days Worldcons are almost about entirely business for me—and for that reasons I have very fond memories of it. You'd wake up, make your daily tour of the Dealer's Room and the Art Show, attend a couple of selected panels, visit with friends, dine like a king, catch the Hugos or masquerade or whatever the evening's main feature was, and party all night. Wasn't anything wrong with that back in 1982; won't be anything wrong with it at the next Chicon either.

ConJose Diary

Wednesday, August 28, 2002: Uneventful flight from Cincinnati to San Francisco, which is to say, I slept for all 5 hours of it. The ConJose web page had warned us that a door-to-door shuttle from the San Francisco airport to the Fairmont Hotel in downtown San Jose was $34.00—but they never asked for the group rate, and it turned out that each extra member of a party was only $5.00, so while everyone else was avoiding the shuttle, we got there for less than half the price of a taxi. (Usually we get to Worldcon on a Monday or Tuesday to spend time with all our fannish friends, since once the con starts I'm a working pro, but because we were touring Monterey after the con with a bunch of them, we decided not to show up until Wednesday.)

We'd gotten a call the night before from Debbie Oakes, who was co-hosting the CFG suite, that it was in room 905, so naturally we asked for the 9th floor. And got it. In the new tower. Which meant that every time we wanted to go to the suite we had to take an elevator down to the ground or second floor, walk across to the *old* tower, and then take an elevator up to the 9th floor. On the other hand, there were no parties in the new tower and it was quiet as a tomb. Never a wait for elevators, either—until they started breaking down.

While Carol unpacked and took a nap (she *doesn't* sleep on planes), I met Janis Ian and we registered and went over to the dealer's room. It wasn't open to the public until Thursday, but 39 years after my first Worldcon, I am not without my resources.

The convention center was a couple of blocks from the Fairmont. Not a terrible walk, but we'd packed and dressed for 72-degree days and 55-degree nights, and a few of those days the temperature hit 90. And, like last year, I managed to bust a big blood blister, this time on the big toe of my left foot. Didn't hurt, but since I've been a diabetic for the past five years and I'd kind of like to go to my grave intact, I medicated and bandaged it twice a day. (I've *got* to remember not to wear new shoes to Worldcons.)

On the way back, Janis and I stopped at the Fairmont's bar for soft drinks, and ran into George R. R. Martin and Terry Prachett. Strange feeling to be the only guy at the table who *wasn't* a Pro Guest of Honor at an upcoming Worldcon (2003 for George, 2004 for Terry).

As usual, I had a bunch of books coming out from small presses timed to coincide with Worldcon—and as usual, even though I handed in the manuscripts from 8 to 10 months before the cons and proofed them a few months in advance, one (*With a Little Help From My Friends*, my collection of 26 collaborations with different writers, from Farthest Star) was in the huckster's room when the con began, one (*The Science Fiction Professional*, from Farthest Star) made it Friday, and one (*Once a Fan . . .,* from Wildside Press) never made it at all. Given that any specialty press can reasonably expect to double their sales on a sub-1500 print run by getting it out in time for the whole of Worldcon, I have never understood why they can't seem to manage. (I remember that at Chicon VI, in 2000, I had 5 specialty press books due out for Worldcon; 2 showed up Friday, 2 Saturday, and one never. Go figure.)

While greeting old friends and buying and autographing books, I found out that my friend Charles Sheffield wasn't the only major sf writer currently suffering from a brain tumor. It seems that Robert Forward also has one, and isn't expected to last to next year's Worldcon. And this year we've already lost Damon Knight, Ray Lafferty, and two of my very close friends, Jack Haldeman and George Alec Effinger.

Saw Jack Chalker riding around on one of those motorized scooters. I assumed it was because of his arthritic knees, but he explained that a couple of times in the past month he'd become so short of breath that he couldn't walk, and was waiting for the results of some medical tests.

Not a good year for longevity *or* health.

We picked up Carol and met Tony and Suford Lewis, Rick Katze, and Debbie Oakes for dinner, and went to the Inca Gardens. Nice food, mediocre service, and horrible management (it took them 40 minutes to compute our check, and I still don't know if the tip was included. Asking them didn't help; they only spoke Incan or Peruvian, whichever is more obscure.)

Went back to the hotel, visited a bit, hit the LA party and a couple of private parties, and went to bed relatively early—about 2:00—since I knew I wouldn't be getting much sleep the next few nights.

Thursday, August 29: Carol took one look at the menu posted outside the hotel's "cheap" (compared to its other restaurants) coffee shop, discovered that a glass of orange juice was something like $9.00, and decided we were eating elsewhere, which was fine by me, since on those rare occasions I'm up before noon all I have is coffee anyway. She found a charming little outdoor area maybe 200 feet from the hotel, outside the Knight-Ridder building, where she had some juice and rolls, and I injected a little coffee into a vein. Then I went off to the con, and she and Debbie Oakes and Cokie Cavin began touring those San Jose sights and landmarks that were, well, tourable.

Val Ontell came up to me and invited me to be Guest of Honor at Con-Dor, a February convention in San Diego. Leave snow-covered Cincinnati and spend a few extra days visiting the San Diego Zoo and

Zoo Park and maybe do a little whale-watching? Tough call. Of course I accepted.

A new audio company, Audio Literature, sought me out and suggested that they wanted to do a little business. I sent them some suggestions after I got back home, and we'll see what's what. Audio Frequency, the audio "magazine" that records the Hugo nominees for Best Short Story, was there, and had asked to record my reading—but I never saw them. I think they sponsored a party in the SFWA Suite one night. (Want to lose me? Go to the SFWA Suite. I promise I won't follow.)

Ran into Caz—Camille Cazedessus, Jr.—the Burroughs fan (and 1966 fanzine Hugo winner) at a dealer's table. He's the guy who published my first fanzine articles and fiction just about 40 years ago, and introduced me to fandom (well, the Burroughs variety, anyway) and Worldcons. Said hello to all the book dealers, most of whom have been friends for ages, signed a bunch of books, then went off to do the first of my panels, something titled "The Future of Africa." I didn't think it sounded all that interesting, but we filled a huge room to overflowing, and indeed I was the only panelist who hadn't spent most of my life as a full-time resident of either Zimbabwe or South Africa. I am a pessimist about Africa's near future—say, the next half century—but my opinion was positively upbeat compared to those who'd been living there lately.

I had to go off to do a pair of print interviews, and then a radio interview. Janis joined Carol and me for dinner at Stratta, an Italian restaurant right next door to the Inca Gardens. (Why? Because the Inca Gardens ladies' room was out of order the night before, and they had to use the one at Stratta, and as they walked through the place they decided they liked the looks of the dishes.)

CFG (Cincinnati Fantasy Group for the uninitiated) almost always has a 5-day hospitality suite at Worldcon, and this year was no different. But I didn't get to it right away, because Terry Bisson had written a radio play called "The Hugo Nominee," and had enlisted me, Janis, Lucius Shepard, Nancy Kress (before Charles developed the brain tumor and they had to cancel out of Worldcon), and four or five other pros to appear in it Friday night, and the only chance we had to rehearse was in the Fairmont lobby at 8:00 Thursday. It went rather well, and I must admit it played a lot funnier than it read.

Then it was nearing 10:00 Thursday night at Worldcon, traditional time for the Babes For Bwana party (formerly yclept the Resnick Listserv party . . . but it's not limited to the Listserv. Any CFG member, indeed just about any pro or fan I know, is welcome.)

Once again Gordie Meyer (Mr. Obscura Press) graciously donated his suite, and Christy Harden-Smith served as cook and hostess. We really laid out a hell of a spread, topped off, like last year, by chocolate fondue. By 10:45 we had quite a crowd, and then the belly dancers showed up, just like last year, and entertained for maybe an hour, by the end of which a lot of the Babes (and non-Babe Ron Collins) were tentatively attempting the ballet de belly themselves. Julie and Linda, the dancers, stuck around and gave a repeat performance at about 1:00, after which Bart Kemper and I borrowed their swords and gave a brief fencing demonstration. The door to Gordie's suite was literally across the hall from the door to the CFG suite, so each party kind of slopped over into the other—and Bill Cavin, the God-Emperor of CFG, remembered to bring his video camera, so this year we've got the dancers and some of the party on video.

At some point Susan Matthews, who has the most delightful and distinctive giggle I've ever heard, showed up, and we agreed to collaborate on a story in the next few months. (Time to start stockpiling stories for *With a Little More Help From My Friends*.)

The party finally broke up around 3:30, and I stayed an extra hour or two, talking a little business with Gordie and a couple of other editors. Finally got to bed about 6:00, par for the course at a Worldcon.

Friday, August 30: Got up at 9:00. Showered, medicated and bandaged the toe, and went off to meet Shayne Bell for coffee. We'd collaborated on a funny Mars story for *Mars Probe*, and were in the middle of collaborating on a serious novella when tragedy struck—Shayne lost someone very dear to him—and we put it on the back burner for a few months. Now we're back on the track, and we hope to finish it by year's end.

I went right from coffee with Shayne to lunch with Bob Silverberg. Since he knows his way around San Jose—he lives an hour away—I left the choice of restaurants to him. Well, we wandered and wandered and wandered, as we discovered that each restaurant he fondly remembered had been torn down or sold. Finally we ate at what I consider a typical California restaurant—they seemed to specialize in parsley-and-grass sandwiches—but we had a very pleasant visit for maybe an hour and a half. He had come straight from the SFWA meeting—I attend once a decade, and since I went in 1998 I felt no obligation to go again this soon—and he related some of the silliness that passed for serious debate, enough to make me think that once a decade is probably a little too often. Then he was off to a panel, and I had to go be photographed by *Locus*, which is replacing all their black-and-white files with color shots.

I had a midafternoon kaffeeklatsch at the Hilton, which was attached to far end of the convention center. For the second year in a row, they supplied neither coffee nor pastries—not even the usual weak coffee and stale donuts—but Joe Haldeman and I had side-by-side rooms, and we filled them. As usual, I brought a bunch of giveaways—*Santiago* and *Hunting the Snark* cover flats, color Xeroxes of some foreign covers, leftover trading cards from Chicon—and we had a pleasant enough hour. Then I spent another hour autographing at the Asimov's booth while Gardner Dozois tried to raise a little money on the side by selling kisses to me. When that didn't work, he hit upon a far more lucrative proposition: pay him and I *wouldn't* kiss you.

Now, all during the day, Terry Bisson or ConJose committee members had been approaching me and all the other performers in Terry's play to give us a never-ending series of schedule changes. It seems that Patrick Stewart (is that his name? The bald guy in the Star Trek show) was going to be at the con for an hour, and we were scheduled to follow him, but he kept changing the times he'd be there, and as more con members found out about it they kept changing the venue. Originally it was in the Imperial Ballroom of the Fairmont, then in the Civic Auditorium, then the Ballroom again, then the Auditorium again. We were first scheduled to perform at 8:00 PM, then 9:30, then 7:45, and so on. Just before I left for dinner, I was told that the final, set-in-stone, never-to-be-changed-again schedule was that we would perform at exactly 9:15 PM at the Auditorium (though all the signs advertising us at the Ballroom were never removed and a lot of disgruntled con members showed up there.)

We went to dinner with Harry and all the Turtledoves—wife Laura, daughter Allison, daughter Rachel, daughter Rebecca, and Janis Ian. Harry and I agreed to collaborate on a story for a Lou Anders anthology later this year, but I spent most of my time talking to Laura, who is the one person in science fiction who knows as much (or probably more) about the musical theater as I do. I've been trading audio and video bootlegs with her for a couple of years now. Recently she picked up an extra job creating the weekly trivia quiz for Fynesworth Alley (a small company that makes CDs of off-Broadway and truly obscure musicals.) We ate at the House of Siam, the one truly outstanding restaurant we found in San Jose.

Then, at 8:30, Carol and Janis and I walked over to the auditorium, where we would be performing at 9:15. And walked in. And heard something remarkably like "The Hugo Nominee" coming from the direction of the stage.

Right. They changed the time *again*. Whoever was in charge of scheduling—probably a former elevator Nazi—walked up to Terry when Patrick Stewart had finished and told him to put his play on. He explained that most of his actors were still at dinner, since they had told him the play would go on at 9:15. He was then told that he had five minutes to start or they were canceling it. So he got a bunch of volunteers from the audience—Dave Hartwell took my part, John Douglas took Janis', and so on—and they gave a not-wildly-impressive stone cold reading. I was just as happy to sit in the dark and relax, but Janis was annoyed and I'm told that Lucius was furious.

Then it was off to the DAW party. It was private, for DAW authors only, and I'm not a DAW author—but I did edit four anthologies for DAW this year, so I didn't have any trouble getting in. Ran into Marty Greenberg, and briefly discussed a couple of new anthology proposals with him. Someone from Indianapolis walked up and invited me to be the Guest of Honor at a new and as-yet-unnamed convention to be held in January of 2004. They laid out quite a spread at the party, and I ate enough pastries to last for the weekend. Then I dropped in on the Japanese and Boston parties, went to a couple of private parties and Gordie's suite, and wound up, as usual, at the CFG suite, where I stayed until maybe 4:00, talking to old friends.

Saturday, August 31: I dragged myself out of bed and managed to meet Betsy Mitchell, the relatively new head honcho at del Rey Books, for breakfast at 10:00. Well, she had breakfast; I had coffee. I'm still officially a del Rey author, though I haven't given them anything since *Kirinyaga*, and they seem to have decided that it's time for me to sell them something else. I don't know what'll come of it, but it was a pleasant meeting/breakfast.

I went from there to the convention center, where I led the Fan History tour. It was a nice exhibit, with a couple of dozen Hugos from different years, a bunch of giveaways and program books from each Worldcon, even a photo display, and we just went down the line while I told anecdotes about each item. As usual, it was the single public performance I enjoyed most. This was my third year in a row of leading the tour, and I hope they'll ask me again next year.

Then I had to race back to the hotel for lunch with Marty Greenberg. Well, officially lunch; in point of fact the coffee shop was still serving breakfast, and I was almost awake by then, so I had some eggs Benedict, always my favorite breakfast wherever I am. Janis, with whom I am editing the big-budget *Janis Ian's Universe*, joined us, we discussed future anthologies with her and ways to promote the current one—possibly with a signed, numbered hardcover shrink-wrapped with a CD of all the songs the writers are basing their stories upon—and Marty told me he'd be hitting the DAW ladies with a couple of my proposals on Sunday and would let me know which they bought (if any) at the Hugo ceremony.

Trudged back to the con center—and by now I was really getting tired of that two-block walk, and the fact that from time to time they turned off the escalators to save on electricity (or so the explanation went)—and joined Joe Haldeman, George R. R. Martin, and Patrick Neilsen-Hayden for a panel titled "I'm Still a Fan," in which 3 multiple-Hugo-winning authors and the guy in charge of Tor's science fiction program tried to convince a skeptical audience that we really were fans. Then I spotted Fred Prophet in the audience, and announced that a former Worldcon chairman (Detroit, 1959) was sitting among them, and that all 4 of the panelists knew who it was and were long-time friends of his, and would the audience members who knew please raise their hands—and in that huge audience, only Paula Lieberman and Gay Haldeman knew Fred. Then Rusty Hevelin wandered in and took a seat, and I announced that I could also spot a former Worldcon Fan Guest of Honor (Denver, 1981), and that again, all the panelists knew who it was and had been his friends for years, and did any audience member besides Gay and Paula know who I was referring to? The answer was No. I had Fred and Rusty stand up and introduced them, and our fannish *bona fides* were not questioned again for the remainder of the panel.

I had a few minutes to talk a little business with Warren Lapine and John Douglas, and then I had to do the "official" autograph session for an hour. After that I stole a few more minutes to talk some business with Mark Olson and other powers-that-be at NESFA Press, and then I had a panel called "The Horsey Set," composed of five lady writers who own, ride and love horses, and good old Mike, who wrote a weekly column on horse racing for over a decade but happens to think that horses are among the dumbest creatures that God made. I did get to explain the interesting economics of the sport—Seattle Slew was valued at $160 million in the late 1980s, and this year Storm Cat will service over 100 mares at a fee of $500,000 per service—and I managed to introduce the audience to George Alec Effinger's wonderful story of the one-legged racehorse who was ten yards from winning the Kentucky Derby when he broke his leg . . . but for some reason the panel was scheduled at 5:30, and like most of the panelists I had to leave early because of a previously-scheduled business dinner.

In my case, it was with Carol and Eleanor Wood, my agent for the past 19 years. Eleanor's more than an agent. She's a friend, who has gone to Egypt with us (and just decided to come to the San Diego convention and visit the zoo and zoo park with us in February), and once our business was taken care of, we spent a couple of hours just visiting. And since we'd liked it so much the previous night (and no one seemed to recommend anything else with any enthusiasm), we found ourselves back at the House of Siam again.

We weren't going to walk over to the Civic Auditorium to stand in an endless line to see the masquerade, so I decided to watch it on closed-circuit TV in the CFG suite. Then I found out that for the first time in years no part of the con, not even the masquerade or Hugos, were on closed-circuit, so to this moment I have no idea who won or if the costumes were above or below average. (Sometime Saturday people began calling the con "Nolacon II without the French Quarter.")

Carol stayed at CFG, and Eleanor and I went up to the Tor party, where I ran into David Brin, Kage Baker, Gene Wolfe, Stan Robinson, Jim Kelly, Orson Scott Card, and a number of other writers I hadn't yet seen. (Jim was really upset that I hadn't brought along my tux for this year's Hugos. I explained that I only wore it on years I thought I had a chance. As it turned out, I think he was one of only three writers with a tux—but then, it was California.) I asked David how many kids he was up to now. His classic answer: "One human and two boys."

I got to visit a bit with Beth Meacham, my long-time Tor editor (18 years and counting) and for a change I found Tom Doherty inside the suite rather than gasping for fresh air in the hall. All the Tor writers were busy doing business with all the Tor editors, so I signaled B. J. Galler-Smith and Tom Gerencer to join me and got Tom, who was feeling expansive and loves to talk business, to give them the equivalent of a condensed college course on publishing and distributing science fiction.

I went down to the Japanese party, hit the Boston party, looked in at the Columbus party, stopped by CFG for awhile, and then went back to Tor to talk a little business with a couple of foreign editors who had asked to meet me there at 1:00 AM. I also found Joe Siclari and we spent some time discussing a book project we've been putting together. Then it was back to CFG until about 4:00, and off to bed.

Sunday, September 1: For a change there were no business breakfasts on the schedule, so Carol and I wandered over to the Tech Museum and had a very nice, very quiet breakfast. As usual, it felt like the only occasions we got to spend any time together at a Worldcon were during meals. It didn't used to be like that—but I didn't used to be a pro who lined up his work for the coming year at Worldcon.

I had a panel with Rob Sawyer and a couple of others on "Genetically Engineered Pets" at 11:30. Rob had to leave early for a lunch appointment. Dull panel; I envied him.

I had to sign for half an hour at the SFWA table at 1:00, and then at 1:45 I did a reading. For the second year in a row, the Worldcon programmers didn't give us an hour—it was 30 minutes at Philadelphia, which was ridiculous, and about 35 or 40 minutes here, which wasn't a hell of a lot better, since it meant you couldn't read a novelette or even a longish short story. I read "Robots Don't Cry," which will show up in *Asimov's* next year, and was pleased to see a few tears show up on audience cheeks. And B. J. Galler-Smith cried so much that I had an almost unbearable urge to stop reading, put the story down, and just watch her.

Then it was 2:30, time for my hour's signing at Larry Smith and Sally Kobee's table, and, just like last year, I'd made an arrangement with Linda and Julie, the belly-dancers (their third member wasn't here this year) to perform right next to where I was signing. (Last year Larry, who could reasonably expect to sell maybe one Resnick book an hour at a Worldcon where I was in attendance, sold about $600 in the hour that I autographed and they danced.) After 20 minutes I was afraid it was a one-time phenomenon—they had sold only a single $20 trade paperback—but then everyone started buying, and they did about $400 worth of business the next 35 minutes . . . so yes, the belly dancers will be back again next year, not just at the party but at the autographing.

I picked up another Guest of Honor gig—they asked me not to mention it until they announce it officially—and then Janis and I went off to be interviewed on television by Donna Drapeau, who had done a fine interview with me at Chicago and had interviewed the two of us at Philadelphia (but some jerk in the studio had inadvertently erased it before it could be shown.)

Then the Albacon crew, where I'll be Guest of Honor in less than a month, took Carol and me out to dinner, and we got back in time to change into somewhat better clothing (I wore a jacket, but for the first time as a Hugo nominee I didn't bother with a tie).

There were three elevators in our tower, which had worked to perfection all week, but on Hugo night two of them chose to break down, and it took maybe fifteen minutes to catch the other and take it down to the ground floor. We picked up Janis, who was our guest, and went to the Hugo reception, three hot blocks away at the Hilton. I was glad we'd eaten; unlike Philadelphia, they didn't lay out much of a spread.

About 8:00 they marched us across the street to the Civic Auditorium. I've been to steambaths that weren't as warm. People started sneaking out after ten minutes, and kept it up all night, which beat the hell out of staying and fainting. Even Janis, who performs under hot lights almost every night, couldn't take the heat and left before the Hugos were announced.

Tad Williams was the first (male) Toastmaster in a quarter of a century not to wear a tux, which made me feel a little less conspicuous.

Evidently no one had tested the equipment, because the Toastmaster's microphone wasn't working for the first few minutes. Most people were so uncomfortable in the stifling heat of the auditorium that they didn't even notice.

The late Martha Beck, who died this spring, was posthumously awarded the First Fandom Hall of Fame Award. Very deserving; she lived for fandom, and it would have been one of the true highlights of her life. It brought back all the visits we'd shared and all the cons we'd gone to together.

Then our dear friend Pat Sims won the Big Heart Award, and you can read about all the other winners in my annual Hugo Ceremony report for *Chronicle*. There were some major upsets, foremost of which was Gardner Dozois losing Best Editor for the first time in a decade. I think we could clearly see the results of massive electronic voting this year, in that electronic editors (Ellen Datlow) and publications (*Ansible*) beat the traditional favorites/winners.

And yes, for the record, I lost both the Best Short Story and Best Related Book Hugos, both to worthy winners, though not to the ones I had expected to lose to.

I never did run into Marty Greenberg again, though I later got an e-mail telling me which anthology we had sold to DAW. Jaime Levine, who has just taken over Betsy Mitchell's old spot at Warner's, walked up as we were leaving the Hugos, introduced herself, and suggested that we might do some business together. Sounded good to me, and I'll be getting back to her as soon as I catch up with all the other commitments I seem to have made in San Jose.

Since the elevators weren't working in our tower, and there was an hour-long line for them in the party tower, Carol and I sat down with Eleanor Wood in the Fairmont's lobby and ordered some much-needed cold drinks. (I had my first beer in a decade, to show you just how warm and uncomfortable I was. Usually I only drink it in Africa, where it's safer than the water.)

At one point Connie Willis walked up to thank me for offering to write her biography for this summer's DeepSouthcon program book— the committee forgot and had someone else do it—and to assure me that it wasn't her idea. I told her that I wasn't upset at all . . . but she wanted to make sure, and in the process mentioned that she would be happy to write *my* biography if I ever asked—and I stopped her right there and told her she could do it for Albacon next month. So I'm going to be written up by the dreaded Female Person From Colorado, to whom I have lost 86 Hugos (well, maybe only 73, but it *feels* like 86.)

While we were there, we signed another couple of get-well cards for Charles Sheffield, and wished him a speedy recovery for yet another video camera. It'll take all his energy just to go through all the cards and videos he receives this week.

I skipped the Hugo Losers party—I simply couldn't get to an elevator. Carol and I went to CFG for awhile. Then she went back to the room, while I ran into Bill Fawcett. I can't remember what party we were at, but it was so crowded that we went back down to the lobby—it was after midnight now, and it had emptied out somewhat—and started bringing each other up to date on what we'd been doing. And while I wasn't looking for any assignments, he came up with one for a non-fiction book he's editing with my old pal Brian Thomsen that looks like so much fun I'd have done it for free. And his wife, Jody Lynn Nye, extended an invite through him for me to write for an upcoming anthology of hers.

Sleep deprivation finally started catching up with me, and I went to our tower, waited for the one functioning elevator, and actually flopped into bed at about 2:15, maybe the earliest I've been to bed at a Worldcon this millennium.

Monday, September 2: Had another photo session at 11:00 AM, then went off to my final panel, "Creating Anthologies," which had a lot of anthology editors on it—me, Ellen Datlow, Patrick Neilsen Hayden, maybe a couple of others—but whenever I'm on one of these anthology panels, I keep wanting to suggest that they just get Marty Greenberg to do a Q-and-A with the audience and be done with it, since he's behind about 90% of the anthologies that get published in this field, even when his name's not on the book.

Then I bade the convention center farewell, made that 2-block walk for the last time, and went off to lunch with Carol, Gardner Dozois, Susan Casper (who seems to be recovering quite well from her quadruple bypass last spring), and Janis Ian. Gardner seemed to be taking his Best Editor loss quite well; at least, he knew not to complain in front of a guy who has now lost 7 Hugos in the past three years. When we were done we wandered into the gift shop and ran into Greg Benford. Greg and I exchanged some market and restaurant info for a bit, and then he, Gardner and I started going through all the toys and playing with them while our ladies waited in annoyed silence.

Since a bunch of us were staying in California to visit the Monterey Peninsula, Debbie Oakes, Bill Cavin, Carol and I, who would be splitting the driving, took a cab to the Hertz corral at the airport, where we had reserved a Windstar van, and drove it back to the hotel.

CFG had agreed to let Janice Gelb use our suite for her 25th Anniversary in Fandom party from 1:30 to 5:30 PM, provided CFG members could attend, so we spent part of the afternoon there. Rich Lynch got me to promise to write an article for *Mimosa #30*, which he and Nicki swear will be their last issue despite all their Hugos . . . and with *Lan's Lantern*, another of my favorite fanzine markets is dead, it looks like I'll be doing a lot of my future fan writing for a pair of new fanzines, Michael Burstein's *Burstzine* and John Teehan's *Slight of Hand* . . . plus old standby *Fosfax*, and of course Guy Lillian's *Challenger*, which I really think deserved the last two fanzine Hugos.

Carol and I went out for dinner with Janis, who seems to have become a member of the family—kid sister, older daughter, we haven't figured out which, but we're very comfortable with her—but all the restaurants were closed, and we wound up back at the Fairmont's Grill, where you could get a perfectly acceptable $18.00 meal for only $40.00.

Carol stayed at CFG until maybe 9:30, then went off to pack. I stayed until about 2:30, had a pleasant visit with Karen Anderson (Poul's widow), whom I hadn't seen in years, teased the hell out of Stephen Boucher (who seems inadvertently to have become the Chairman of the Australia-in-2010 bid), passed a little time with Rick Katze and John Hertz, saw Mark Irwin (a long-time fan with whom I actually won a bridge tournament when we were both high school students back in the Pleistocene), and finally went back to our own tower, where the elevators were working perfectly now that the con was officially over.

Tuesday, September 3: Got up about 9:00, and while Carol finished packing, Debbie and I drove Dick Spelman and Roger Sims to pick up their rental car. Then we wasted half an hour trying to ship my largest suitcase home—UPS didn't have a big enough box—before we found out that the Fairmont had a shipping service and had boxes of all sizes.

By 11:00 we were ready to go. Carol, Debbie, Bill and Cokie Cavin, and I all piled into the van with our luggage. Pat and Roger Sims and Dick Spelman went into the rented car. Adrienne Gormley, who lives in San Jose and spent Monday night at her house doing her laundry, drove out by herself. The eight of us (everyone but Adrienne) stopped at a Marie Calendar's for lunch—I'd never heard of it, but I've been assured that it's a national franchise specializing in great pies—and about 2:00 we reached the Pacific Gardens Inn, a row of large wooden cabins, in Pacific Grove, halfway between Monterey and Carmel.

Only one problem with the inn: it had such a primitive phone system that I couldn't connect to the Internet. I had 93 auctions closing on eBay that evening, and I had promised a lot of editors, collaborators, and fans to send a lot of stuff . . . but after messing around trying to log on for a few hours that night, I had to admit it couldn't be done and everyone from successful bidders to anxious editors would just have to wait until I got home a few days later.

Since we still had a goodly part of the afternoon left, and were on Daylight Saving Time, the nine of us loaded up the van and car—I don't think we ever took Adrienne's truck anywhere—and went off to see the fabled Seventeen Mile Drive, which cost $8.00 to enter, and was worth it. Everyone else got to see the seashore and birds and seals, and Roger got to see the Pebble Beach Golf Course. (So did I, though I couldn't spot the 17th hole. Too bad; I was actually curious to see what it looked like. Some years back I wrote a story, which has appeared in half a dozen magazines and books, and indeed just won a Prix Ozone in France, called "How I Wrote the New Testament, Brought Forth the Renaissance, and Birdied the 17th Hole at Pebble Beach.")

Roger decided that he wants to live there and play Pebble Beach every day, so I picked up a real estate listing magazine and found him a home: right on the golf course, 5 bedrooms, $20 million. That's $4 million a bedroom. I used to write in the sex field during my starving-writer days, and even *I* can't think of $4 million worth of things to do in a bedroom.

We ate dinner in Monterey at a restaurant called The Fishwife. Very nice seafood (though I got the impression that *every* restaurant in all three towns served very nice seafood, and just about nothing else.)

Six of them went off to play Wizards, a card game that has never interested me. Adrienne, who recently became an Active member of SFWA, and I talked a little science fiction while Carol read, and then I started catching up on lost sleep. I crashed at 9:15, and never budged for 11 hours.

Wednesday, September 4: We had coffee and Danish at the inn, then went down to the Monterey wharf, got onto a boat with a marine biologist and maybe 20 other customers, and went whale watching. I slept for the first hour, but I woke up in time for The Sighting—and what a sighting it was! In an area where 99% of the whale sightings are humpbacks, we found ourselves in the middle of a pod of blue whales, and that's as big as animals on this planet have ever gotten to be. (Comment by the biologist: "Here's a little one. Only about 70 feet long, barely 55 tons.") Unbelievable, to be surrounded by half a dozen of these hundred-foot behemoths. To the best of my knowledge no whale ever attacked a man; any whaler who died was killed *after* they'd harassed and harpooned one of these huge creatures that seem perfectly willing to live in peace and harmony with everyone and everything—and even then they were killed because the whale destroyed the whaling boat in its crazed attempts to escape. You have to wonder just how badly we really needed oil to light the lamps of New England, or why we couldn't have just killed a few trees to light the place up.

A number of different dolphin species, including one incredibly rare one that seemed to thrill the hell out of our marine biologist, raced playfully alongside the boat at different times. Their speed and endurance is remarkable. We were going full speed, and they paced us for the better part of a half hour before losing interest.

When it was over, we went back to the inn, grabbed some lunch, and then I went out book-shopping with Carol, Dick, Debbie and Adrienne. (There are more than half a dozen second-hand bookstores along Lighthouse Drive, the main drag in Monterey.)

By dinnertime we were all getting a little tired of seafood (except me; I don't eat anything with scales. Ever. Which means I never get tired of it) so we found another Marie Calendar's at a shopping center about 8 miles away and had dinner there. Then, just like the previous night, almost everyone went off to play Wizards, only this time I didn't even stay up to talk science fiction with Adrienne. I was in bed and asleep by 10:00.

Thursday, September 5: We had coffee and Danish at the Inn, then drove to the world-famous Monterey Aquarium. I've been to Tampa's state-of-the-art aquarium, to Chicago's huge, remodeled Shedd Aquarium, and to the brand-new Cincinnati/Newport Aquarium—but Silverberg, Benford and George R.R. Martin were right: this is much the best. And while they have huge tanks filled with sharks and tuna, and they have a fascinating otter exhibit, and they have tons of other stuff, Silverberg was also right about the most fascinating exhibit: believe it or not, it was the jellyfish display. It is so colorful, so beautiful, and (especially) so other-worldly that I can't imagine a science fiction writer not being able to come up with half a dozen alien species after seeing it.

The aquarium had a very fine restaurant, and we had lunch there. Then we drove to Carmel. Fascinating little tourist town, filled with stores selling the most useless and expensive trinkets you ever saw. Two stores were devoted entirely to Christmas decorations. In California. In September. Dozens of art galleries, selling unknown artists for unbelievable prices. But the architecture was charming, and the whole town was within a few blocks of the ocean. Parking was all-but-impossible. (We had been warned that even the hotels didn't provide parking, which is why we chose to stay in Pacific Grove.) City Hall, where Dirty Harry used to preside a couple of years ago, has a grand total of six parking spaces, four of them reserved.

After we'd walked around for an hour to get the feel of the place, I decided to do what I love doing in new and scenic upscale areas, and that was to drive down a number of side streets and residential lanes and get thoroughly lost and just look at all the houses and landscapes and views that aren't on the tourist trail. I've done it everywhere from Fairfield County in Connecticut to Barrington Hills in Illinois to Boca Raton in Florida, and I've always enjoyed it—and since I had the car keys, I announced that I was going to do it here. So everyone piled in, and as it was too early for dinner, Dick and Pat and Roger followed in their rented car.

And it was the highlight of the day as far as I'm concerned. After we'd gone up and down winding roads past 3-and-4-level houses built into the hills, many with gorgeous bay views, I came to something called Ocean Drive, so I turned on it, and we spent the next half hour driving along the ocean, passing one $15 million mansion after another, with some of the most stunning views I'd ever seen. (The smells were also stunning, in a different way. Not many places stink quite as badly as the Northern California seashore. Carol assures me that it's because of all the sea life—live seals and sea lions and otters and birds, and dead fish and fish parts washing up onto the shore—and that it's the sign of a healthy ecosystem. I never said it wasn't healthy; I just said it stinks, and I stick by it.)

For dinner, we decided not to go too far afield, and we found a delightful place in Pacific Grove right on the waterfront called The Tinnery. Then everyone went back to the inn for more Wizards, and I actually stayed up reading until maybe 11:00.

Friday, September 6: We all made the airport on time. I slept for the whole 150-minute ride. Then, since we were there three hours early (Bill and Cokie's flight left ahead of ours), I slept for another hour. Then we boarded the plane and I slept for another 5 hours.

By the time we got home I'd made up just about all the sleep I lost at Worldcon. Just as well. There were 974 e-mail messages waiting for me. I stayed up all night Friday answering them, and got done at 3:15 PM Saturday. At 3:30, our mail lady drove up and delivered the 11 days' worth of mail that had been on hold while we were gone. Three huge baskets' worth.

I know why I go to Worldcons. What I wish I knew is why I ever come back from them.

Torcon 3 Diary

Tuesday, August 26, 2003: I wasn't looking forward to this day. I hate long drives, and we had rented a minivan so that we could drive to Toronto with octogenarians Mary Martin and Margaret Keifer and also with Debbie Oakes, who was recovering from some fractured vertebrae suffered in a car accident.

We'd rented a 7-passenger minivan after ConJose last year, spent a few days driving around the Monterrey/Carmel area with five passengers, and found it quite crowded. In fact we had to ship some luggage home rather than stuff it into the van. So when I paid for the van Monday night, I noticed that it was parked next to a much larger 8-passenger minivan and wondered aloud rather wistfully how much more it would have cost. The girl at the counter just shrugged, said no one was renting the 8-passenger vans anyway, and gave it to me for no extra charge.

I had spent the prior week making audio cassettes filled with things Carol and I loved that I thought would please at least some of the passengers—the original Second City Players, a number of professionally-read science fiction stories (some of them not even by me), old radio shows, and the like . . . so of course the van didn't have a cassette player, and at the last minute I had to hunt up a batch of CDs instead.

We left at 9:15 in the morning, caravanning with Bill Cavin and four other passengers in *his* minivan. Carol and I had planned to drive in two-hour shifts, but I felt so comfortable I just kept driving, even after we stopped for lunch near Detroit. I was still driving when we reached the Royal York at about 7:15 that night, the longest uninterrupted driving stint I'd ever done. (Carol and I were used to driving four and five hours at a stretch from the days when we showed collies. Every time we'd stop for coffee or lunch or to use the facilities, the dogs would wake up and have to be walked, so we learned to go hours and hours without stopping.)

The Royal York was exactly as I remembered it—a large, elegant lobby, friendly staff, wildly expensive main restaurant, and the smallest rooms this side of my guest closet. We unpacked and then, accompanied by ten other people, we walked a couple of blocks to Shopsy's, which was heralded by all the guide books as the best deli in Toronto. Turned out to be the worst meal we ate all week. Ran into Bob Silverberg and Karen Haber there; Bob and I were still trying to coordinate our schedules at that late date so that we could have our annual lunch together . . . but we attacked it with less enthusiasm than usual, since we always try to eat at a deli, and dinner at this one hadn't been encouraging.

CFG (the Cincinnati Fantasy Group) always takes out a hospitality suite at Worldcon, and this year was no different, especially since we had 25 members there. But the suites were so tiny and so overpriced for what they offered that instead we took facing executive bedrooms, each of them capable of holding maybe eight guests on sofa and chairs. In all honesty they were totally inadequate, but the suites the hotel offered for twice the money weren't any better.

I was scheduled to give Janis Ian away at her wedding the next afternoon, and since I'd never met her spouse, I popped over to their room to do so, and stayed to visit for maybe half an hour. Then it was down to the lobby to greet old friends who were starting to arrive, and finally off to bed at a relatively early 2:30.

Wednesday, April 27: We woke up about 8:30 (maybe six hours earlier than usual for me), went down to the Epic—the hotel's upscale restaurant—and had breakfast with Pat Snyder and Janis, who were being wed a little later in the day. Then, in the company of some CFGers, we took the subway to the Bata Shoe Museum.

That's right: a museum dedicated to nothing but footwear. And absolutely fascinating. From the earliest caveman foot coverings to the shoes that were made for Chinese women who'd bound their feet, to wooden clogs, to moonwalking boots, the museum was filled with every imaginable kind of shoe. There was a celebrity room where you could see the shoes that Gene Kelly wore when he made *Singing in the Rain*, shoes that Astaire and Rogers danced in, Michael Jordan's first pair of Air Jordans, Pierce Brosnan's latest 007 shoes, the memorable boots Elton John wore in *Tommy*, the shoes Maury Wills wore when he stole his 100th base, a pair of Shaquille O'Neal's size 22's, and hundreds more. There was a room that displayed nothing but the bride's wedding shoes down through the ages and from all across the globe. There was a room with Canadian footwear from prior centuries, mostly made from the skins of animals. And the nice part was you could do the whole place in under two hours.

We took the subway back to the Royal York, got into our flowery shirts (the wedding party was told to dress Hawaiian), and walked a mile to City Hall, where we signed as witnesses and joined a little wedding party composed of Janis and Pat, Carol and me, Dave Axler, George R.R. Martin and Parris McBride—and the *New York Times*, which got wind of it and sent both a reporter *and* a photographer.

We walked back along a different street, window-shopping all the way, and registered at the convention center. No one tried to stop me from entering the hucksters' room a day early. (Maybe they were desperate for the business; after selling 300 tables at each of the last three Worldcons, Larry Smith was unable to sell even 90 at this one. The art show was even smaller compared to prior renewals.)

Then, at dinnertime, we were joined by the Boston Mafia of Tony and Suford Lewis, Rick Katze, and Paula Leiberman, plus a few CFGers, and we went to the Movenpick Marche, about a block from the Royal York, Fascinating place, with an enormous selection; you visited a little kiosk for each specialty—steaks, seafood, crepes, pizza, whatever—and had whatever you wanted cooked to order, then brought it back to your table. Same with the desserts.

So yeah, I broke my diet, and no, it wasn't by accident. I'd been on it since the first weekend of May—I started it the day after the Kentucky Derby—and I'd lost 66 pounds by August 26. I knew I couldn't stay on it with the sumptuous meals that (I hoped) the various editors would take me to, so I just made up my mind to go off it for six days. I have to admit that I enjoyed the hell out of those six days; I don't feel even the slightest trace of guilt.

We got back to the hotel at perhaps 8:30, and spent the rest of the night hitting the bid parties to meet our fannish friends, and now and then I'd go down to the bar, grab an iced coffee (I don't drink) and meet my pro friends. (A lot of them don't drink either, but until the pro parties open up each year, most of them hang out in the bar.)

CFG was starting to attract a fannish crowd, but since it was so small and cramped, most of them filed right back out and spent their time at the competing Los Angeles and Kansas City parties, which had enormous suites (and, doubtless, enormous hotel bills.) I wound up spending the last couple of hours of the evening/early morning talking to Joe Siclari, Edie Stern, Jay Kay Klein and Rick Katze in one of the Los Angeles suites. (They had two huge ones and a couple of smaller ones as well, all clustered together.)

Thursday, August 28: We got up at 8:30 again, this time to grab coffee and go to the Toronto Zoo, accompanied by the newlyweds, plus Pat and Roger Sims and some more CFGers. Carol and I are zoo buffs, so much so that we even went to zoos in Kenya and Malawi after touring the game parks—and we both agree that the single most impressive zoo exhibit we've seen in our lifetimes is the gorilla pavilion at the Toronto Zoo. It covers quite a few acres, and is (I hope) a harbinger of things to come at all zoos.

There were a number of other indoor pavilions as well, doubtless so they'd have someplace to display the animals during the brutal Canadian winters, and whoever designed them all was underpaid no matter how high his salary was.

I had hoped to spend the entire day at the zoo, and indeed had told the Program Committee not to schedule me on Thursday. So of course when the preliminary schedule came out (so close to the con that changing it was almost impossible) they had me on two Thursday panels. I told them again that I was going to the zoo and to reschedule me. So they compromised and put me on only one Thursday panel.

I just love the Torcon 3 Program Committee.

We got back at 3:00, at which time I parked the car in the convention lot for $13 Canadian a day, rather than return it to the Royal York, which was extorting $30 a day. Then I went inside and shed my (figurative) fannish beanie and donned my (equally figurative) pro hat for the next three and a half days. I took a quick tour of the tiny art show, spent a little more time in the hucksters' room, and finally went to my 5:00 panel, a totally typical Humor in Science Fiction discussion, made bearable by the presence of Esther Friesner and Tanya Huff.

At six I met Carol and my agent Eleanor Wood—we were celebrating 20 years as Man and Agent, having entered into our licit relationship at the 1983 Baltimore Worldcon—and we went to dinner at Canyon Creek, a surprisingly good basement chop house somewhere along the two-block walk from the Royal York to the con center. And I did something at dinner I have never done at any meal at any convention in my life: I signed a contract right there on the linen tablecloth. (It was for a new Widowmaker book, plus reprints of the first three, and Eleanor had been negotiating it for a few weeks, but it was still a unique experience to actually *sign* a contract at a con rather than just negotiating one or promising to sign it when it was ready. Made me feel like a Real Writer. I hope no one minds all the salad dressing on Page 4.)

Then it was back to the hotel. I think they had a Meet The Pros party after opening ceremonies, but no one officially announced it and like most pros I never go to it anyway. This was the night that Josepha Sherman and I discovered the Charlotte suite, where they served the most delicious chocolate fondue you can imagine. Just about all the bid parties—Charlotte, Seattle, Los Angeles, Columbus, Kansas City, and Japan—were open, so were the con suite and the CFG rooms, and there were a number of private parties as well, which is to say that by Thursday night the convention was going full speed. (The SFWA Suite didn't open until about 2:00 AM, but it was just around the corner from my 7th floor room, and because of the convenience I found myself visiting it a little more often than usual.)

I kept running into Bob Silverberg, and we got so much visiting done that we decided to put off lunch for a year and try again at Boston, when our schedules might mesh a little better. (I'd offered to drag myself out of bed on yet another morning, but he considered the prospect of facing me at 8:00 AM before I'd injected any coffee into a vein and promptly— and wisely— decided against it.)

Friday, August 29: At noon I had a panel on Travel As A Research Method. It consisted of Jo Sherman, Elizabeth Moon, Samantha Ling, and a moderator, a young girl who defined herself as a writer though she has yet to sell a word, and who completely dominated the discussion despite her lack of travel *or* writing experience.

When the panel was over I wandered over to the huckster room, met Stephen Pagel of Meisha Merlin Press, and went to lunch with him and his art director. They're in the process of transforming themselves from being a small press to the big leagues—they were the ones who bought the new Widowmaker book—and they couldn't have given me a nicer dessert then when they told me that Donato Giancola, who had painted the original three Widowmaker covers for Bantam and whose work I love, had agreed not only to paint the cover to the new Widowmaker book but to do brand-new paintings for the three Widowmaker reprints as well. (I named a star after him in the third book. I wonder if that had anything to do with his decision?)

After lunch I ran into Nick DiChario and his parents, spent a little time visiting with them, and then Nick joined me as I went off to do my 4:00 PM reading. I'd told a number of people that I would be reading "Travels With My Cats," which I think is one of the two or three best stories out of the couple of hundred I've written, and I was really disappointed to see the small turnout I got—maybe six or seven people, tops. When I left the room at 5:00, I bumped into B.J. Galler-Smith and Ann Marston, who had said earlier in the day that they were going to come to the reading, and asked them why they had skipped it. They insisted that *they* hadn't skipped it, *I* had, that they sat in a room with maybe 40 or 50 people waiting for me to show up and read and I never did.

OK. Originally the Program Committee scheduled me for a 30-minute reading. I told them that was unacceptable, that whichever of my upcoming stories I read, I needed more than 30 minutes. So on Sunday, a day and a half before I left, they e-mailed me that I was to read from 4:00 to 5:00 in room 206D. I never thought about it again. But on Friday morning, the committee, as it did every day, passed out a correction sheet with all the new venues for the program, and on that sheet I was to read in some other room. Basically, if you got your information from the convention's web page, you went to the room where I read. If you got it from the daily correction sheet—the committee handed out the pocket program on Thursday and immediately told everyone to ignore it—then you went to the room where I didn't read.

I just love the Torcon 3 Program Committee.

At 5:00 I went over to the *Stars* autographing. *Stars* is the major anthology Janis Ian and I co-edited for DAW Books, and we had a special signing with all the authors who were in attendance. It was the first time all weekend I'd managed to see Joe Haldeman or Rob Sawyer, but we didn't have any time to visit because there was a seemingly endless line of people wanting those books signed. (It stopped only when every last huckster ran out of copies.) And, since it involved Janis Ian, two Toronto papers and a Toronto TV station sent people to cover it, and even *Publisher's Weekly* sent someone to write it up. I usually give out a couple of interviews at Worldcon; at this one I gave out 6 to the press and 2 to television, and only one didn't lead off with either "How did you meet ***Janis Ian***?" or "What's ***Janis Ian*** really like?"

The session broke up at about 6:30. I went back to the Royal York, met Carol, and we went down to the DAW suite, where we joined Betsy Wollheim, Sheila Gilbert, and everyone who had worked on *Stars*, including my good friend Marty Greenberg (who was the guy who actually sold the project to DAW Books.) When we were all assembled we walked through the underground mall a couple of blocks (I read somewhere that it's seven miles long), emerged in some skyscraper or other, took the elevator to the top floor (the 54th, as I recall), and entered Canoe, which, if it isn't the finest restaurant in Toronto, is surely in the top three. Best meal we had all weekend, and while Carol spent most of her time visiting with Betsy, Marty and I put our balding heads together and worked out a number of projects—most of them, surprisingly, having nothing to do with anthologies—that we plan to do together. (He had inadvertently left his medication back in Green Bay, not surprisingly didn't feel all that well as the weekend progressed, and left the con a day early. I heard from him the day after we got home, and he's fine now.)

We got back to the Royal York a couple of minutes before 11:00, just time enough for me to get to our room and pick up an envelope that contained three of my upcoming stories. You see, when I thought I was only getting half an hour to read, I made an arrangement to do a private reading in B.J.'s and Ann's suite at 11:00 PM Friday. I even contacted the Babes For Bwana Harem Division (which is to say, Julie Mandala and Linda Donahue, the belly dancers who regularly perform at the Babes For Bwana parties and at my autograph sessions) and got them to agree to serve as halftime entertainment between my stories. And just because the Program Committee relented and gave me an hour (well, actually, they gave me two hours, both of them at 4:00 on Friday), I saw no reason to cancel the reading *or* the dancing.

And for a private reading, I'd have to say it was pretty public. I think at one time we jammed about 35 people into that suite, and the belly dancers certainly kept them there between stories. We finished at about 1:00 AM, and I stopped by Pat and Roger Sims' room, where Leah Zeldes was throwing a party to celebrate her 30th year in fandom.

Then I went up to the Tor party. It still had quite a crowd, but both my publisher, Tom Doherty, and my long-time Tor editor, Beth Meacham, had already left. Still, I got to see a lot of friends I hadn't connected with yet, and pick up a couple of assignments to write stories for upcoming anthologies, and I was pleased to see that my jacket to *The Return of Santiago* and my daughter's jacket to *The White Dragon* were both prominently displayed on one of the walls.

The rest of the night was just a matter of making the rounds of the 6 bid parties, the Tor party, the SFWA Suite, and CFG. I found Walter Jon Williams, who's the head of SFWA's Anthology Committee, and volunteered to work on it. (I think my exact words were: "Can I join your gang?") He said I could if President Catherine Asaro okayed it, and since we're old friends and collaborators, I knew she would . . . but I had a chance to ask her five minutes later, because as I was walking from one party to another at about three in the morning, I passed by her room, and was confronted by our gorgeous president in her nightgown. Some noisy group had awakened her and she was standing rather groggily in the doorway, trying to figure out what had happened—so I took the opportunity to volunteer, and she took the opportunity to mutter an affirmative before going back to bed. I seemed to continually run into members of the Resnick Listserv—B.J., Ann, Toby Buckell, John Teehan, Guy and Rosy Lillian, a number of others—and finally toddled off to bed at about 5 in the morning.

Saturday, August 30: I got to sleep late—well, late for a Worldcon, anyway—for the second day in a row. Skipped the SFWA meeting as usual, woke up at 11:15, and made it to Larry Smith's table for my noon signing, where the belly dancers were waiting for me. It was a repeat of the last couple of years. For 20 minutes I thought I'd made a mistake; they drew hundreds of people, but everyone took photos and no one bought books. Then they began buying, and again I think Larry did about $450 to $500 worth of Resnick sales in my allotted hour.

We treated the newlyweds—Pat and Janis—to lunch, and then I joined a very small and informal meeting of the anthology committee in the Royal York's lobby. They've got some nice projects coming up, not the least of which is an anthology of translations of foreign sf stories that Jim Morrow is overseeing.

At 4:00 I went to my kaffeeklatsch, half-expecting to find that the venue had been changed, but a bunch of people were there and we had a pleasant hour. I passed out signed cover flats to a number of upcoming books, signed trading cards from Chicon VI—I still have maybe 200 of them left—and answered questions about current and forthcoming projects.

Then I met Carol and Beth Meacham for dinner at Epic, the hotel's very fine and even more expensive restaurant. Beth's another one I talked into the Medifast diet; she's lost 50 pounds in 3 months and changed her hair style, and I literally walked right by her without recognizing her. Her husband is down over 70 pounds in the same time period. This is some diet, let me tell you.

Then it was off to the Hugo ceremonies. Spider Robinson did a much better Toastmaster job here than he had done in Orlando back in 1992, and the movie excerpts were thankfully only about 30 seconds each, rather than the interminable ones they tend to show at these things. Rob Sawyer had a night to remember: his *Illegal Alien* won the Seiun (the Japanese Hugo) for Best Translated Novel, and then, about an hour later, his *Hominids* won the Hugo for Best Novel. I'll be writing the ceremony up in detail for *Chronicle*, and the results are available all over the internet, so there's no sense going into them here. There were no major surprises: Gardner Dozois won the Gardner Dozois Award (Best Editor), *Locus* won the Locus Award (Best Semiprozine), Bob Eggleton won the Bob Eggleton Award (Best Artist), and Dave Langford won the Dave Langford Award (Best Fan Writer).

Then it was off to the parties. Most of the bid parties were closed, except for Columbus and Glasgow, since the votes had already been counted (and the 2006 Worldcon was won by Los Angeles, where the Anaheim Hilton remains the best party hotel on the Worldcon circuit— as opposed to the best overall hotel, which is Chicago's Hyatt). Ace gave a huge blast right after the Hugos, Boston hosted the annual Hugo Losers Party, Glasgow held a party, Calgary (which is hosting the 2005 Westercon) had a very nice party, and the ASFA (the American Science Fiction Artists guild) had a pleasant and reasonably uncrowded suite. I did a little business here and there, and went to bed at about 5:30 AM.

Sunday, August 31: I had asked the Program Committee not to schedule me before noon. Ever. So of course they gave me a 10:00 AM panel on Sunday, something titled "A United Africa," which is somewhat less likely to occur than, say, riding a flying pig from Cincinnati to Minsk. There were a couple of Africans on the panel, along with Steve

Stirling, and everyone agreed that it was an asinine proposition. For this I had to walk over to the convention center on four hours' sleep.

I just love the Torcon 3 Program Committee.

When the panel was done, I ran into CFGer Jeff Calhoun and we wandered over to one of the coffee stands, where I got my morning dose of caffeine.

Then I went to my official autograph session (i.e., no belly dancers, plus it was late in the con, two reasons why I had less books to sign than at Larry's table). Carol and I had hoped to have lunch with Jo Sherman, but I was on display at 10, noon, 3 and 4, and she was on panels at 11, 1 and 2. I hung around the hucksters room (why do I spend so much time in the hucksters room when I buy so few books these days? Easy. It's where you find readers as opposed to watchers), signed from 2:00 to 3:00 at the SFWA table, and at 3:00 I showed up for a panel entitled "Dying is Easy; Comedy is Hard," with Connie Willis, Terry Pratchett, and Esther Friesner. I think there have been maybe 70 funny books published in the science fiction field in the past 20 years, and the four of us are probably responsible for half of them. We drew a huge audience—my guesstimate was 500 to 600 people, the most I've ever seen for a panel—and had a great time being funny rather than instructive.

Then, the moment the panel was over, I had to show up for another one, the Kelly Freas Retrospective Slide Show, with Joe Haldeman and Howard Waldrop. Kelly was supposed to have been there, but he broke a hip the week before Worldcon, it required surgery, and he had to stay home—a hell of a way to spend your Worldcon Guest of Honorship—and Alex Eisenstein took his place.

So there we were, all ready to do the slide show. Only one problem: no slides.

Since all of us are Kelly's friends and have known him for decades, we decided to kill some time by telling mostly funny stories about him while a committee member went looking for the slides. He returned after we'd ad-libbed for about 40 minutes to announce that he couldn't find any slides and it wasn't the committee's fault, that we panelists were supposed to supply the slides. It was the first any of us had heard of it, and indeed I doubt that any of us except perhaps Alex possessed even a single slide of Kelly's artwork. So much for the Kelly Freas Retrospective Slide Show.

I just love the Torcon 3 Program Committee.

We met Steve Saffel, my editor at del Rey, in the Royal York and then took a cab to Toronto's Greek Town, where we had dinner at Ouzeri, which had been touted to us by Rob Sawyer and other residents as the best Greek restaurant in town. I can't imagine there were any better ones; Ouzeri was just a cut below Chicago's Greek Islands, which is the best there is.

During the meal Steve mentioned that Eidos, which owns the Lara Croft character, had approved my manuscript—I'd done the first novel for the game, as opposed to the movie, franchise during the summer; it's set it Africa and Paris and is known unofficially around the del Rey office as "The Slightly Fictionalized Resnick Travel Diaries"—and that the book would be coming out in December. Evidently the numbers—which is to say, the pre-publication orders—look very good, always music to an author's ears. Steve also told me that his grandfather was Armand Denis, the African traveler/adventurer/zoo-animal-collector. I have some of Denis' books, and more to the point, I have a DVD of his rarest film, *Wheels Across Africa*, which was made in 1936. I'm having it copied for Steve, who's never seen it.

The Science Fiction Book Club held its 50th anniversary party on Sunday night, and since I've sold them so many books I felt obligated to attend—and wound up enjoying it more than any other party all weekend. Somewhere around 1:00, as I was making the rounds and dropped in for the third or fourth time, I found myself with SFBC's Andy Wheeler, Jo Sherman, Jim Minz (my daughter's new editor at Tor), and former SFWA President Paul Levinson. Paul decided to tell a joke; none of us would let him get two lines out before criticizing it. He was still trying to finish it at 2:30, when I left to check on the other parties once more.

One of those other parties was in the SFWA suite, where *Asimov's* and *Analog* threw a party for Stan Schmidt, who was celebrating his 25th year as *Analog's* editor. Very crowded party, very good cake.

Baen Books also threw a party, hosted by Toni Weisskopf and, in Jim Baen's absence, by Bill Fawcett, with whom I've done a number of projects in the past. We wanted to talk, but it was too crowded the first few times I dropped in. Finally, at about 2:45 in the morning, we were able to put our heads together in a corner without being overheard and actually got some business done.

I kept making the circuit of the pro parties, plus Los Angeles, Columbus, and CFG until it was almost 6:00. Then I went to bed and read for a bit, and finally fell asleep when the sun started shining into the room.

Monday, September 1: Carol had remarked a couple of times during the year that she hasn't enjoyed recent Worldcons as much as the Good Old Days when I was just a fan and didn't have to do any business, that for the past ten or twelve Worldcons it seemed the only time she saw me once the con started was at dinner, so I made up my mind that at this

Worldcon we'd spend more time together. As I mentioned earlier, we went to the Shoe Museum (and the wedding) on Wednesday and the zoo on Thursday. And since the Program Committee had evidently figured I would be ready to kill them all by Sunday night, they left me totally unscheduled on Monday. So we had lunch together, just the two of us, and then, joined by Beth Meacham and a couple of CFGers, we took the Hippo Tour. This consisted of getting into an amphibious bus, spending an hour or so riding past all the most interesting sights and buildings in Toronto while a guy with a microphone at the front of the bus gave us some history and anecdotes about what we were seeing, and then plunging into the lake, where the bus became a boat and chugged around the shoreline. Fascinating trip; I wish we'd taken it earlier in the con.

Carol and I are Honorary DiCharios. Nick and I have collaborated on so many stories that we actually produced a book of them a couple of years ago (*Magic Feathers: The Mike and Nick Show*, if anyone cares), and Carol and I couldn't be more fond of Nick's parents if they were our own. As soon as we learned that they were coming to Torcon, we set Monday night aside to have dinner with them, and enjoyed ourselves thoroughly. (Nick's dad is also going on The Diet. I seem to be a walking advertisement for Medifast, so I had Ralph Roberts, who not only publishes Alexander Books and Farthest Star, but is also a Medifast representative, send me about 40 business cards as a diet rep, not a publisher. Anyone who asked about my weight loss and expressed any interest in going on the diet themselves got a card; I came home with only 6 left.)

There wasn't much in the way of parties. The con suite was too crowded to turn around in, so a few of us went up to B.J.'s and Ann's suite (where I had done the reading on Friday night) and spent some time there. Then, as with just about every Worldcon, I wound up in what passed for the CFG suite, stayed until 5 in the morning, and went to bed just before the alarm clock went off.

Tuesday, September 2: I dragged myself out of bed about 7:30, helped Carol finish packing, grabbed some coffee, retrieved the van, drove back to the Royal York, picked up our passengers, and drove home. Took about 10 hours, including pit stops and lunch.

Came home to learn that our 17-year-old cat hadn't died while boarding at the vet's (we half-expected her to). There were over 700 e-mails waiting for me, a pile of mail about 25 inches high, and sitting on my desk as I write this is the little notebook I always take to Worldcons. In the front it has the room numbers of all my friends and professional contacts. Shortly after that it has a list of all the party and bidding suites, then a list of private parties in a code no one else can read (just in case I misplace the book and someone picks it up), then a list of all my panel and autograph assignments as well as a list of all my luncheon and dinner engagements, followed by a list of the dozen or so restaurants, with phone numbers and addresses, that we've culled from various guide books.

The very last thing in it is a list of all the things I've promised to send editors, writers and fans. As I look at it right this moment, I still have 27 things to send, so this seems a proper time to close.

Was it a good Worldcon? Not very.

Did I enjoy it anyway? I always do.

Am I looking forward to the next one? Like a kid looks forward to Christmas.

Noreascon IV Diary

Tuesday, August 31, 2004: Met fellow CFG members Mary Martin, Debbie Oakes and Jeff Calhoun at the airport, and we all caught the same flight to Boston. (I might as well confess that I am wildly in love with Mary, our retired octogenarian plastic surgeon who was good friends with Heinlein and Clement—and won the 1966 Worldcon masquerade—and I intend to marry her just as soon as I work Carol to death.)

CFG (the venerable Cincinnati Fantasy Group, for the uninitiated) always takes out a hospitality suite at the Worldcon. Those of us who had been to the three prior Boston Worldcons—or any of them, in fact—remembered the Sheraton's elevators with horror, and we all wanted to stay in the Marriott . . . but when we priced the suites, we found we could get essentially the same suite at the Sheraton for $225 a day less, which meant we could keep it open for seven days, Tuesday through Monday, rather than the usual five. We're not exactly a party and not exactly private—we don't turn anyone away, but we really don't want three thousand strangers coming by for food and drinks—so we never advertise the suite. If you know enough trufen, you'll find us. Anyway, for that reason, we prefer a non-party floor, and then we try to block a number of CFG members and friends around the suite to act as a noise buffer. Worked beautifully this year; the suite was at the end of the corridor, and I think the friends of CFG had every room between the suite and the elevator. (And, surprisingly, the elevators caused no problems at all this time around.) I can't recall an evening that there wasn't a hot game of Wizards—a bridge-like card game for six players—in the smaller parlor.

We got there in early afternoon, unpacked, got our name tags and printed material—Guy Lillian outdid himself editing the program book—and checked out the mall, which was wildly impressive. Nothing had been enclosed 15 years ago at the last Boston Worldcon; now you can walk blocks in enclosed, air-conditioned comfort. (I still remember getting rained on walking from the Sheraton to the Marriott in 1989.)

The Sheraton's rooms were on the small side, though nowhere as near as claustrophobic as the Royal York's at last year's Torcon 3. The suites, on the other hand, were spacious and comfortable. I am told that the Marriott had closed-circuit TV and you could watch the Hugos and masquerade in your room; the Sheraton had no such luxury. To our surprise, the Sheraton's elevators worked perfectly all weekend, a vast improvement over the last three Boston Worldcons. On the other hand, the Sheraton may be the only four-star hotel in the country that doesn't have a restaurant open after 3:00 PM.

We met NESFAns Rick Katze and Tony and Suford Lewis for dinner, along with some CFG members and the Florida contingent of CFG (Dick Spelman and Pat and Roger Sims, who had all moved to Orlando from Cincinnati.) The one place where a crowd of 15 or 20 could always get a table without a reservation was Marche, which was as enjoyable an exploring-and-eating experience here as it had been at Toronto, where we first encountered the Canadian-based chain.

I watched the Governator give a rousing speech to the Republican convention, concluded that the Democrats will never agree to a constitutional amendment allowing naturalized citizens to run for the presidency as long as he's alive, then hung around the lobby for a few hours after dinner greeting old fannish friends, because as always I metamorphose into a pro by Wednesday night and don't change back into a fan until late Monday, and most of my friends are fans. Ran into Paula Leiberman, my annual shadow at fannish parties, for the first of maybe thirty times during the con. I went to bed early (for me, anyway) at about 3:00 AM because we had to get out of bed pretty early in the morning. (By definition, if the sun's in the eastern half of the sky, it's too damned early . . . or else it's the end of a long writing day.)

Wednesday, September 1: Got up at (ugh!) 8:30, dressed, couldn't even face coffee that early in the day, and met Bill and Cokie Cavin and Jeff Calhoun in the lobby. We hopped a pair of cabs and drove down to the harbor, where we met CFG's Orlando contingent, plus Sue and Steve Francis (the Louisville branch), and we all boarded a boat and went off to bother whales. Saw a pair of minkes, some humpbacks, and a finback during a three-hour trip.

After we got back to the hotel Carol and I went off for lunch, and then I spent a couple of hours scouting out the huckster's room, which didn't open officially until Thursday. It was large—300 tables—and impressive, with more book dealers and less junk (i.e., non-books) than usual. I bought the one book I hadn't been able to find all year—John Clute's *Scores*—and picked up a couple of fannish items I was totally unaware of. Then, since three of my program items were in the Sheraton rather than the Hynes Center, I went back there to find out exactly where they were located and bumped into Josepha Sherman, who was doing the same thing.

Then it was time for dinner. I went up to the room and got Carol, who had cheated and taken a nap, and we went down to meet Glenn Yeffeth, the publisher of BenBella Books, and his managing editor. I've been his science fiction editor for the past four months, and have gone a bit overboard, picking up about a dozen titles in that time. (He's a small press; these will last us through mid-2006.) Before I'd become his editor he'd bought the reprint rights to my Oracle Trilogy, and I got to tell him that I'd optioned them to Intrinsic Value Films a couple of weeks before Worldcon. His eyes lit up with dollar signs, and I then had to explain that that merely lowered the odds against their becoming a movie from a google-to-one down to maybe fifty-to-one (but not before I suggested they'd sell even better with some Bob Eggleton covers, and he agreed to talk to Bob about it.) I don't ordinarily like Thai food—too spicy, and I don't like heat, either temperature or flavor—but this was a wonderful meal, properly cool and (Carol would say) bland; the restaurant, for anyone who's going to Boston and is interested, is the Chili Duck.

Spent most of the evening back in the CFG suite. Donna Drapeau, Toby Buckell, Herb Kauderer, Steve Silver and John Teehan had shown up at the con; before the night was over, so had Bob Faw and Linda Kelly. We got word that Gardner Dozois had shattered his shoulder in a car accident, had already undergone surgery, and wouldn't be attending; and that Barry Malzberg's wife Joyce was in the hospital and Barry also wasn't coming.

I absolutely hate being reminded that we don't all live forever in perfect health, especially since I'm now 62. (How can I be 62? I remember every detail of Discon I from 1963—fridathe people, the meals, the program items, even the wallpaper. It was just a year or two ago, wasn't it?)

Thursday, September 2: Had breakfast with Bob Sheckley. We've been good friends, collaborators, and constant correspondents, but this was actually only the second time we'd met in person.

Since Gardner was unavailable, that freed up a meal. Bob Silverberg and I always try to have lunch together at Worldcon, but we hadn't been able to mesh our schedules this year . . . and suddenly we were both free until 3:00 PM, so we popped over to an oyster bar he knew. While we were eating we decided to collaborate on a non-fiction anthology. I've bought stories from Bob, and he's bought from me, but this is the first time we've ever worked together, rather than for one another.

At 3:00 I moderated the panel that was the most fun of the con . . . hell, of the last half-dozen cons. Fred Pohl couldn't make it, but there was Harry Harrison, Phil Klass (a/k/a William Tenn), Bob Silverberg and me, telling funny stories about the giants of science fiction who are no longer with us. This included the stories of how John Campbell presided at his own funeral; how Ted Sturgeon and his wife, devout nudists, would invite couples over for dinner and greet them in the altogether; how Randy Garrett always stiffed worshipful new writers with huge dinner checks; and on and on. I hope to hell someone was tape recording it.

(Most of the panels were filled, but this one drew Standing Room Only and spilled out into the corridor.)

At 4:30 I signed at the SFWA table, and I moved over to the Wildside table to sign from 5:00 to 6:00. Then I went up to the room to relax for an hour, and Carol and I walked over to the Marriott lobby, where we met John and Kim Betancourt and went off to dinner at a Persian restaurant, the Rialto, across the Charles River; best meal of the convention. During the meal I sold John the anthology Silverberg and I had decided to put together, and asked what I could do for the next issue of *Adventure Tales*, the pulp reprint magazine that had run an article by me along with all the old pulp stories in its premiere issue this summer. He said that it was still a reprint magazine, but he would make an exception if I would write a Lucifer Jones story for each issue. (You want to become my lifelong friend? Ask me to write about my very favorite character, the Right Reverend Honorable Doctor Lucifer Jones.) It was all I could do not to pick up the check for dinner.

So we returned to the hotel at maybe 10:30, just in time for me to grab a handful of stories and go to the Rhode Island suite, where Donna Drapeau and her gang had invited me to come do a reading. I like to rest a bit between stories, so like last year I invited the Harem Division of the Babes For Bwana—Linda Donahue, Julia Mandala, and any other belly dancers they could round up—to provide the entertainment between stories, and as always they came through with flying colors. Well, shimmying colors, anyway. And not to be outdone, the Rhode Island ladies (and one incredibly graceful guy dressed in a spacesuit and a grass skirt) performed some hula dances. I don't think the thing was publicized much beyond my Listserv, but Bob Eggleton and a number of others showed up and seemed to have a pretty good time. Adrienne Gormley also read a story, and Donna read a story by the late Robyn Herrington that I'd bought for one of my anthologies; it turned out to be the last story she ever wrote. Wonderful party, and I hope they'll invite me again, if not at Glasgow, then at Los Angeles in 2006.

I stopped by the SFWA Suite, talked to a number of pro friends I hadn't seen yet, went down to the spacious and well-run con suite, and stopped in at the bidding parties. Columbus and Japan shared the same large suite, which seemed counter-productive to me. Back in Chicon V in 1991, Louisville entered the Worldcon with a substantial lead for 1994, but Winnipeg caught and passed them in the five days of the con by the simple expedient of importing a chef and catering service and dishing out some great food. If someone had done that here, the fans would never have known which side was responsible or who was striving so hard to please them and win their votes.

I wound up the night at the CFG suite, where CFG members kept arriving—Joel Zakem, Steve Leigh, Frank Johnson, member emeritus Mark Linneman, others—and I stayed until maybe 5:30 in the morning.

Friday, September 3: My schedule was really getting busy now. I ran into Laura (my daughter, who very likely outsells me these days) on the way to the hucksters' room, met Stephe Pagel, the publisher of Meisha Merlin, and we went out for an early lunch. I had just turned in *A Gathering of Widowmakers* to Stephe two weeks earlier, and I spent half the meal begging for a Donato Giancola cover and the other half hitting him with a 3-book proposal—one reprint, one new novel, one collection, all related—that I think he'll be making an offer on once he runs the figures later this month or next.

Then, at 1:00 PM, I stopped by to introduce and watch "Metal Tears," the 40-minute movie made by Jake Bradbury from my Hugo-nominated story, "Robots Don't Cry." Jerry Bradbury—Jake's father and the film's producer—had sent me a DVD a week earlier. I was enjoying the hell out of it for the first ten or twelve minutes when the damned thing froze, so I was really eager to see it all the way through. They started running it . . . and it froze again. They put in a different DVD and the same thing happened. But it had worked on Jerry's laptop, so finally they tied the laptop into the projector and it worked perfectly, and it was clear that the audience loved it.

It's a wonderful effort, and stayed far closer to the original than I did when adapting *Santiago* and *The Widowmaker* for Hollywood. The robot, the alien, and the older version of the narrator were excellent, and the younger version was at least adequate, and you can't get much better than that for a $6,000 film. (To give you an example: $6,000 buys approximately one-third of a *second* of *Van Helsing*, the biggest turkey of the summer.) I'm incredibly flattered that they chose my story to film, and equally pleased with the way it turned out. Contractually it's an amateur project, so they can't sell it or charge people to watch it . . . but I hope they take it on the convention circuit and let people get a look at it. It's worth the effort.

At 2:00 I had to rush off to a panel about what would have happened if JFK had lived. I looked at the audience, composed mostly of people who hadn't been born before he was assassinated and who worshipped him because the press worshipped him. I explained that he was a multi-millionaire from a wealthy and politically-powerful family, he had a brother who also held considerable political power, and that the hallmarks of his brief presidency were tax cuts, an aggressive foreign policy (he was elected because of the mythical "missile gap"), and military intervention overseas (Cuba and Vietnam). Pause. Then I pointed out that if he were alive today with those credentials, his name would be George W. Bush. Kinda got the audience thinking.

At 3:00 Greg Benford and I autographed at the *Asimov's* table, which seemed to be taking the transition from Gardner Dozois to Sheila Williams very well. (So was I. I sold Gardner the last story he bought as *Asimov's* editor, and I sold Sheila one of the first she bought.)

At 4:00 I was on a panel promoting a new science fiction imprint, Pyr Books, owned by Prometheus Press, which has been around for ages but never published any fiction before. Lou Anders, the editor, was there. So were a couple of artists, and a pair of writers. (I was there because I was in the process of selling him some books. Gardner was scheduled to be there, too, having sold him an anthology—but he was still laid up in the hospital back in Philadelphia.) I especially liked one of the artists' work, and requested him for the first novel I do for Pyr —and got him.

Then Carol and Xin, Lou's lovely Chinese wife, joined us and we went off to the Kashmir, an Indian restaurant, for dinner. I had my usual korma—I don't do spicy, ever—but Carol, who loves hot food, tells me her meal was excellent, which means it probably stopped just short of melting the enamel on her teeth.

We got back in time for the Retro Hugos. I still can't get over that list of novels—*Farenheit 451*, *The Caves of Steel*, *Childhood's End*, *Mission of Gravity*, and *More Than Human*. Can you imagine any other year when *The Space Merchants* couldn't make the final ballot? Bob Eggleton did a very competent job as the emcee, and Terry Practhett and Phil Klass, the pro Guests of Honor, and Jack Speer, the Fan Guest of Honor, took turns interviewing each other.

I went off to the *Asimov's/Analog* party in the SFWA Suite, ran into Tony Lewis, and learned that NESFA Press had agreed to buy a book Joe Siclari and I have been assembling for years and which I had proposed to him Tuesday night.

There were parties galore this night—*Asimov's/Analog*, a Tor party up on the top floor (where I visited with my del Rey editor, Steve Saffel, and never found my Tor editor, Beth Meacham), a Norwescon party, Columbus and Japan bidding parties, an sff.net party, a Glasgow party, an ASFA party (that's the science fiction artists' group), tons of others. When I stopped in the Japanese party the second time, someone there who works for Hayakawa's science fiction magazine handed me a contract for the Japanese rights to my short story, "Stanley the Eighteen Percenter." I hit them all, pro and fan parties alike, checked in at the CFG Suite, hit 'em all again, and wound up at CFG at maybe 4:30 AM.

Saturday, September 4: I dragged myself down to the coffee shop at (yucch!) 10:30 AM, where I met my editor from the Science Fiction Book Club, Ellen Asher, who wasn't a hell of a lot happier to be up in the morning than I was, but it was the only free hour we both had. She had purchased *Down These Dark Spaceways*, an original anthology of six futuristic hard-boiled mystery novellas, from me, an assignment I'd gotten at Torcon 3. I delivered the book during the summer, and hit her with some more proposals. There's one she claims to be anxious to do, but I gather we're going to wait to see the initial orders on *Down These Dark Spaceways* before we talk price. Just as well; I'm too busy to do much on it right now anyway. After that, we spent the rest of the meal talking horses. She's the ride-em-and-love-em type, like Judy Tarr and Beth Meacham; I'm the I-love-to-watch-them-race-but-they're-the-dumbest-critters-God-made type, like Josepha Sherman and Barry Malzberg. We found a common ground at 11:29 and had to leave at 11:30.

At noon I was on yet another African panel, made more satisfying by the fact that it was (I think) the first time I've ever been on a panel with Laura, who has brought me fame if not fortune as Laura Resnick's Father. Other than that, there wasn't anything said that hasn't been said at the last thirty such panels. This one was limited to Africa; usually it's about the Third World and is the one place I can count on meeting Lucius Shepard in the course of a Worldcon.

The second it was over I raced a couple of (indoor) blocks through the enclosed mall to the Marriott, where I spent half an hour visiting with Marty Greenberg. I had given him eight or ten anthology ideas to pitch, and as I write this the results aren't known yet. (They vary wildly; our best year we sold 5, in 2001 we sold 4, a couple of times—including last year—we sold none.) Toby Buckell joined us after a few minutes, and he and I went back to the Hynes at 1:45.

At 2:00 I had my kaffeeklatsch. This year Boston decided to have kaffeeklatches for the teetotalers among us, and literary beers for the drinkers. I hope the beer folks got a little something to drink; I never saw any coffee until I asked a thoughtful committee member to find some for me. (Now that I come to think of it, this was probably the sixth time in the past eight years that the kaffeeklatch neglected to provide kaffee.) As always, I came equipped with giveaways—autographed covers, autographed matte paintings from one of the early and never-made versions of *Santiago*, autographed trading cards from Chicon VI (leaving me only another 300 to give away over the next quarter century before I run out of them).

At 3:00 I had lunch with Scott Pendergrast of Fictionwise.com. He mentioned a project he and his brother Steve had wanted me to do back in 2001, before we all got too busy, so we're going to take another crack at it this winter or next spring.

From 4:00 to 5:00 I finally got up to the art show on the third floor of the Hynes. It was magnificent. The regular show had some fine work by Michael Whelan, Bob Eggleton, Donato Giancola, Don Maitz, and others—the usual superstars—plus some excellent upcoming artists . . . but the highlight was the Retrospective Art Show, with magazine and book covers and paintings from the 1950s and earlier by Kelly Freas, Ed Emshwiller, Virgil Finlay (my all-time favorite), Alex Schomburg, and more. Great show, second only to the Alex Eisenstein collection at Chicon VI.

At 5:00 I moderated the best-attended panel of the con. It was devoted to Jack Williamson, and featured his friends, his collaborators, his agent—a stellar line-up that included Fred Pohl, Dave Hartwell, Eleanor Wood, Scott Edelman, Connie Willis, Melinda Snodgrass, Stanley Schmidt, Larry Niven, Jack Chalker, Michael Swanwick, and I'm sure I'm forgetting a couple. What made it unique was not just the line-up, but the fact that Jack was tied in by phone from Portales, New Mexico—at 96 he doesn't travel to Worldcons any more—and his comments were fed into the speaker system so everyone in the huge room could hear. I think it was a great idea; why wait until one of our giants dies before we pay tribute to him?

Carol had spent the afternoon on a trolley tour with Laura. She took the trolley back to the hotel, while Laura opted to walk. She joined Eleanor Wood (my agent) and me and we went over to the Hugo reception, while Laura showed up there maybe an hour later. Tony Lewis had made an offer on NESFA Press's behalf for the collected Resnick/Malzberg Dialogues that run in every issue of the *SFWA Bulletin*. I ran the figures and told him that we'd need a little more front money before we'd sign. Then Catherine Asaro, the president of SFWA, saw me and mentioned that SFWA would like to publish it, but probably couldn't come up with the advance we'd need. So I found an empty couch, sat Tony and Catherine down together, and told them not to get up until they'd worked out a co-publishing deal. They eventually got up, so I guess they managed; at least Tony tells me they did, and they'll work out the details in the next couple of months. (And do you begin to notice how every deal will be done in the next couple of months rather than the next couple of days? That's why writers get so grouchy at bill-paying time.)

Next we went to the ceremony itself. The reason Connie Willis and I have toastmastered one Worldcon each and Gardner Dozois has never been a toastmaster, despite the fact that we're acknowledged to be among the most entertaining speakers in science fiction, is that we're always up for Hugos, and it's considered gauche for the Toastmaster to give himself a Hugo or announce that he's just lost one. So why did they pick Neil Gaiman, whose short story had won a bunch of polls in the spring and summer and was a lock to make the ballot, as this year's Toastmaster? (Mind you, I'm not complaining about the job he did; he was funny and fine and everything a Toastmaster should be. I'm merely suggesting that if the Toastmaster isn't supposed to be a nominee, someone messed up—and as the ceremony went on, someone messed up even worse.)

Bob Silverberg gave a very amusing and informative speech about the first fifty Hugo ceremonies—he's the only person to have attended all of them. Then came the plethora of lesser awards, and finally the Hugos—which were seriously marred by the fact that the idiot running the slide projector managed to flash the name of the Hugo winner before Neil announced it, and did it with more than one award.

The results are common knowledge by now, so I won't repeat them here, except to mention that I lost yet another one, this time with "Robots Don't Cry." When I saw the tallies later in the evening, I was surprised to see that I'd come in eighth among editors, though I only had four anthologies out (and the major one, *Stars*, was co-edited with Janis Ian), and I even got a handful of votes for best fan writer, which at least shows that *someone* reads these diaries.

After the Hugos Eleanor took us out to dinner, and for the second year in a row I signed some book contracts at a Worldcon meal (after 39 years of *not* signing any). These were contracts for the Pyr novel, to be called *Starship: Mutiny*, and the Pyr collection, to be titled at a later date.

Then it was off to the parties, and I was having such a good time at them that I never remembered to hit the Hugo Losers party. I made it to SFWA, Baen, ASFA, half a dozen fannish parties, and wound up (of course) at the CFG suite, where I visited with Bob Faw until maybe an hour before dawn.

Sunday, September 5: I'd been scheduled to have a late breakfast/early lunch with Barry Malzberg before our panel, but since he wasn't at the con I was able to have a meal with just Carol, a real luxury at a Worldcon.

At noon Barry and I were supposed to do one of our dialogues, a two-man panel following the format of our *SFWA Bulletin* articles. (We agree that God outdid Himself when He made Sophia Loren. After 25 years of close friendship, we have yet to agree on anything else.) So on Saturday I had looked around to find a pseudo-Barry, and lo and behold, there was my old friend David Gerrold. I don't know that we disagree on quite as many things, but we've held a number of very funny insult contests, including a couple for television, and I figured if we couldn't enlighten the audience we could at least amuse it, so I drafted him. It was the one panel that didn't draw a full house, but that's because the con committee had heard Barry wasn't coming and announced in the thrice-daily newsletter that the panel was canceled. (Of course, no one ever thought to relay that information to the other half of the panel.) Even so, we pulled maybe 20 people, and then David cheated by seriously addressing all the questions I put to him.

At 1:00 I did my "official" reading (as opposed to my reading with belly and hula dancers). I read a couple of stories I think ought to make some final ballots—"A Princess of Earth" and "Down Memory Lane," both forthcoming in *Asimov's*—but they are both very sad stories, and a woman I'd never seen before accosted me as I was leaving and castigated me for depressing her, stating that she had previously read the Lucifer Jones books and *The Outpost* and had come expecting to fall out of her chair laughing. I explained that if she'd fallen out of her chair she'd probably have broken something and wound up depressed, and if she was going to be depressed anyway, at least this way she heard some good stories.

At 2:00 I managed to find 45 minutes to take another partial tour of the hucksters room (which is where I practically lived when I was just a fan and didn't do my year's business at these shindigs) and probably spent more time visiting with all the booksellers I'd known for decades than looking at their wares.

At 3:00 I showed up for the official autographing session. Year in and year out the autograph session is held in or next to the hucksters room, so people can buy the books they want autographed and take them right up to the authors. This year, for reasons that eluded all of the pros, it was literally as far from the hucksters room as it could get while remaining on the same floor of the immense Hynes.

I'd signed so many books at all the other tables during the con that I was done by 3:40. So was Nancy Kress, who was signing next to me— but while we were signing we agreed to collaborate on a short story next year.

At 4:00 I wandered over to the Fan Lounge and went through all the fannish memorabilia on display, since I was leading the Fan History tour at 5:00. While I was there they auctioned off a Tuckerization in one of my stories for DUFF, and I got to meet the fellow who will be semi-immortalized. I had just found a table and was relaxing with Joe Siclari, Rich and Nikki Lynch, and Guy and Rosy Lillian when it was time to lead the tour. We began with the previous years' Hugos, and I told stories about most of them (or the cons where they were given out), then moseyed over to the impressive Doc Smith exhibit. Doc was the first pro Carol and I met at our first Worldcon, and I was happy to be able to tell a number of stories—all complimentary—about him. We were working our way through ribbons and program books when the hour ended and I went back to the Sheraton.

The Resnicks—Carol, Laura and me—met the Turtledoves— Harry, Laura, Allison, Rachel, and Rebecca—in the lobby for dinner. (Actually, I call the younger Turtledoves The One on the Left, The One on the Right, and the One Without an R in Her Name.) We went back to the Kashmir where Lou Anders had taken us; very nice food, even the second time around. Harry and I had collaborated on a story we sold to Lou Anders this summer, and will collaborate on a novel in a year or two (we're the only two people in the world with any serious interest in the subject, and we figured two such novels would be one too many), but I suspect the real reason we always meet for dinner at Worldcon is so he can plot to run off birdwatching with Carol (they're both ardent birders), and he suspects that it's so I can plot to run off to New York with Laura (his, not mine) to see endless musical theater performances (she and I have been trading bootleg videos and audios for years).

All the younger generation skipped dessert and headed off to watch the masquerade, and the oldpharts stayed at the table and visited for another hour. (I still don't know who won the masquerade. I do know that people began showing up in the CFG suite at 10:30 and 11:00, complaining that they hadn't yet finished the first run-through and that the emcee was not going to put Robin Williams or Billy Crystal out of business.)

Then it was the usual round of all the parties, with frequent stops back at CFG, and off to bed at perhaps 5:00.

Monday, September 6: One last bit of business and then I was free to be a fan again for what little remained of the con. I had lunch with Chris Roberson, a fine new writer and the publisher of Monkeybrain Books. I had sold him a Lucifer Jones story—I love the title: "The Island of Annoyed Souls"—for an anthology he was editing, and we talked about his bringing the three Lucifer Jones books back into print as trade paperbacks. I don't know what will come of it—he's the newest of the new publishers, and he's just getting established—but it's nice to know Lucifer still has fans. He's my favorite of all my characters, and he'd been in mothballs for eleven years due to lack of interest. Then, suddenly, he's in *Argosy* and Chris' anthology and *Adventure Tales*, and

I imagine Monkeybrain or someone else will reissue the books in the next year or three. Lord knows I've written more important stuff, lots of it—but if I could only write one thing for the rest of my life, it'd be Lucifer Jones stories. I just love them, and I'm grateful that there are once again some editors who feel the same.

And that ended my business for the con. I met Carol and Bill and Cokie Cavin, and we took a ducks tour, an amphibious bus (same thing as last year's hippo tour in Toronto). Our driver had honed his routine, and we got a groan-inducing pun or a joke with long whiskers on it every fifteen seconds for the whole two-hour tour.

Then we went back to the Sheraton and met my Listserv members for dinner—Bob Faw, John Teehan and his lady, Adrienne Gormley, Guy and Rosy Lillian, a number of others—and wound up where we'd started: at Marche, which can accommodate a group like that on two seconds' notice. Carol came up to the CFG suite for an hour or two, then went to the room to pack and turn in early. I hit the few remaining parties, wandered down to the con suite for an hour, then back to CFG, where John Hertz had stopped by, and visited with him until maybe 5:30 AM.

Tuesday, September 7: Carol figured that I'd had about twenty hours sleep in the last five nights, so she very thoughtfully went out, bought some blueberry muffins, and brought them and coffee back to the room before waking me. We checked out, met Jeff Calhoun, took a shuttle to the airport, were joined by Mary Martin and Debbie Oakes, and flew home.

I found 1778 e-mails waiting for me. After I'd painstakingly eliminated the spam, one piece at a time, there were 114 left.

I just love the way technology has simplified my life.

Nebula Diary, 2005

As soon as I arrived on Friday I unpacked my bags, hooked up with my spiritual kid sister Janis Ian, and went out for lunch. Then I spent a few hours visiting with the SFWA members who had already shown up, and after that my agent Eleanor Wood took Janis and me out for dinner to my favorite Greek restaurant in the whole world, The Greek Islands, where I pigged out on saganaki, dolmades, and pastitsio.

Del Rey Books had a very nice reception for this year's Grandmaster, Anne McCaffrey, and I got to meet still more arrivals and spend about an hour with Tom Doherty, publisher of Tor. I visited/partied till about 2 in the morning, and then, since I'd been up since 7 AM and had a breakfast to attend the next day, I went to bed, incredibly early for me at a convention (or anywhere else, come to think of it.)

I dragged myself out of bed at (ugh) 8:30 AM Saturday, got dressed, and shuffled down to the *Asimov's/Analog* Award Breakfast. Even Eggs Benedict (my favorite breakfast on those rare occasions that I have breakfast at all) and a quart or two of coffee couldn't get me too alert . . . but I was sitting at a table with Gardner Dozois, Charlie Brown of *Locus*, and my Surrogate Carol (Janis). Janis asked about some fannish legend or other, and Gardner, Charlie and I spend the next 90 minutes regaling her with one hilarious fannish story after another, and by the time we were done talking and laughing I was as wide awake as I guess I'll ever be before noon. Allen Steele, who won for both Best Novelette and Best Novella, couldn't make it, so I was the only *Asimov's* award-winner who was there in person. I accepted the Best Short Story Award for "Travels With My Cats," and made a short speech, in which I explained that when I was a young man I wrote a young man's stories, filled with action and adventure; when I matured I wrote mature stories, about the serious problems facing all human beings and how we might go about solving them; now I'm an older, gentler man, and I'm writing older, gentler stories about love and yearnings and regrets . . . and the reason I love this field is that over the 40-year period that I've been writing, it has been broad enough and open enough to accommodate every type of story I've wanted to tell. I don't know what kinds of stories I'll be writing 10 or 15 years from now, but there's no doubt in my mind that there'll be room for them too.

I had a very long (close to 3 hours by my watch) lunch with Ellen Asher, the editor of the Science Fiction Book Club. *Down These Dark Spaceways* is being printed this weekend and should be available in 7 to 10 days, and we discussed what projects we might want to do next. My

Surrogate Carol (yclept Janis) passed by the coffee shop, spotted us, and joined us for the last hour.

When I got back from lunch I ran into Bill Fawcett, and picked up a couple of assignments from him, including one for a sequel to *You Did What?*, the book where Ralph Roberts and I collaborated on a delightful African article (and I also wrote a solo one.) And so that it wasn't all take and no give, I offered Bill and his wife, Jody Lynn Nye, each an assignment as well.

I did a little more visiting, got into a jacket and tie, and went down to the Nebula Reception. Since I don't drink I gave my free drink tickets to my friend Jack McDevitt, who was up for Best Novel; Jack is an old Navy man, and as such I knew he'd have no problem at all about using the tickets.

Then it was time for the Nebula banquet. I sat between Gardner Dozois and the <shudder!> Female Person From Colorado, who was up for Best Novella. The food was far superior to the usual banquet fare, and we all had a pleasant time while waiting for the awards. In all immodesty, Gardner, Connie and I probably get nominated for more awards in the field than anyone else, so we were pretty relaxed and we spent an hour or more joking with each other, which loosened up some of the other nominees at the table, who had come in looking like their undergarments were too tight but wound up laughing and enjoying themselves. Neil Gaiman was the Toastmaster, and did a fine job, much briefer—as is usual—than his Worldcon toastmaster gig. Kevin O'Donnell won a special award for service to SFWA, and then Anne was officially inducted into Grandmastership. Next came the awards. *Lord of the Rings* won for best script (huge surprise, right?), and then I lost the short story Nebula to Eileen Gunn, who was either the first or second juried selection ever to win. (The membership chooses 5 nominees in each category, and the Nebula jury chooses one more.) Ohioan Ellen Klages won Best Novelette, and then, before the last two awards, they asked everyone who had been a SFWA member for 30 years or more to climb up on the stage and sing Happy Birthday (not to any person, but to SFWA, which was 40 years old). Then we were asked to each give a funny reminiscence about SFWA . . . and as Fred Pohl spoke first, I looked around, and the only other 30+ year members on stage were Gardner, Joe Haldeman, Ginjer Buchanan, and me . . . and it suddenly occurred to me that Joe, Gardner and I weren't the Young Turks of the field any more. I mean, I thought of Fred as one of the dinosaurs of SFWA, but suddenly here were 4 more dinosaurs, spewing out reminiscences to a bunch of 40-and-50-year-old kids. Just a tad disconcerting.

Best Novella went not to the Female Person From Colorado, or to my (one-time) collaborator, SFWA President Catherine Asaro, but to Walter Jon Williams. Walter couldn't be there; he was still in the hospital, where he had driven himself to the emergency room with a burst appendix. ("Why didn't you call 911?" I asked him when I heard what had happened. His answer: he lives in such a remote, hard-to-find area that he figured he could die before an ambulance found his house, so he saved time—and probably his life—by getting in the car and racing to the hospital.)

Lois Bujold won for Best Novel with the same novel that won the Hugo last summer, which cheered Eleanor Wood up, as the other two nominees from her stable, Catherine Asaro and me, had already lost. (When you see the photos in Locus and Chronicle, you'll know why I proposed that we award a Special Nebula to Catherine's neckline.)

Then it was back to the hospitality suite, when I visited until they closed it up at about 2:30. Then Resnick Listserv members Toby Buckell and Linda Dunn went down to the hotel's lobby with me. We were joined by Dave Hartwell of Tor, who's up for a Best Editor Hugo again this year, and the four of us chattered for another couple of hours.

I managed to get up in time for an autographing at the 3-story Borders right across street from Marshall Field's in the Loop. I think Kevin Anderson, with whom I'm collaborating on a story this week, signed even more books than Anne McCaffrey did. Toby stopped by, and since I had piles of two anthologies that he was in, I had him sign his stories as long as he was there. Then I bade SFWA and my Surrogate Carol goodbye, caught a subway train out to O'Hare Airport, flew home, kissed the Real Carol hello, and have spent the past few hours trying to catch up on a couple of hundred e-mails.

LACon IV Diary

Sunday, August 20, 2006: Since we were well aware of all the increased security precautions the airports were taking since the London-to-US bomb plot had been discovered a few days earlier, we had Laura drive us to the Dayton airport at 3:00 AM, just to make sure we had time to clear security before our 6:00 AM flight. By my watch, it took the pair of us 54 seconds, total. (We changed planes in St. Louis. We'd been told that we'd have to clear security again. What happened is that we exited our plane at Gate 12, walked 20 yards to Gate 14, and got right onto the Los Angeles flight. Elapsed time: about 90 seconds. So much for security.)

We landed at 9:00 AM Left Coast time, and my cousin Bob Hamburg and his wife Glenda were there to meet us. After a quick breakfast we went to a location Carol's been wanting to visit since it was completed—the Getty Museum. Fascinating place. Maybe a dozen architecturally-striking buildings atop a large hill (or a very small mountain), with extensive formal gardens, and an even more extensive art collection; every inch of every building was filled, and a guard told us that more than half the collection was in storage. The hill was so steep that you parked half a mile away and took a tram up to the museum. Carol and Glenda took the horticultural tour, Bob and I just wandered through the buildings looking at paintings by Rembrandt and Renoir and Reubens and a bunch of other guys, some of whose names didn't even begin with an R.

At around 2:30 we headed south for Anaheim, made the 35 miles in only an hour and a half of freeway driving, and checked into our room. When the LACon committee asked me to edit their *Space Cadets* book in honor of Media Guest of Honor Frankie Thomas, who had played Tom Corbett on television back in 1950 (and yes, I watched it religiously at age 8), they wanted to know what I'd charge. I figured if I charged them a fair price based on their limited print run I'd go broke, and if I charged them a fair price based on my standard fee they'd go broke . . . so I suggested that since they had filled the hotel and doubtless had some comp rooms, they could give me 6 free nights on the 5th (party level) floor. It became 8 nights when they asked me to contribute a story. The room was large, and it had a private balcony, perhaps 12 feet on a side, overlooking Disneyland; every night at 9:30 you could stand there and watch half an hour of the most colorful fireworks display.

We met Janis Ian and her spouse Pat in the lobby, and the six of us went out to dinner. I'd asked Bob to hunt up the best Greek restaurant in the area, and he came up with Christaki's. Great pastitso, very good dolmades, best saganaki (flaming cheese) I've ever had. Interesting belly dancer; not that skilled, but unbelievably beautiful. The four women criticized her dancing; Bob and I just looked and admired.

Bob dropped us off at the hotel, we visited a bit with the CFG (Cincinnati Fantasy Group) members who had arrived on Saturday— Drew and Yvonne MacDonald, Bill and Cokie Cavin, Debbie Oakes— and then, since I hadn't been to bed at all the night before and Carol had only grabbed a few hours sleep, we went to bed before midnight, unheard-of at a Worldcon.

Monday, August 21: I'm collaborating on a novel with Kevin Anderson (our collaborative short story, "Prevenge," appeared in *Analog* during the con), and we had planned to have lunch together and spend the afternoon working. But Kevin was on a book tour for the new *Dune* novel, and while he was in the area, he was at a Hollywood hotel and found out that cabfare would be $125 each way, so we put off the meeting until he actually arrived at the con.

That left lunch and the afternoon free, so we walked over to Downtown Disney. It's pretty small, pretty overpriced, and pretty ugly compared to the lovely, extensive and reasonable Downtown Disney in Orlando. We grabbed a quick and totally unmemorable lunch there, walked back, and Carol took a nap while I went down to the lobby to greet new arrivals. At 4:30 we rented a car—a Sebring convertible, which Carol used to drive before she decided a Jeep Cherokee with 4-wheel drive was more practical on our very steep and hilly streets and driveway—and drove off to meet two of my producers, Ed Elbert and Sarah Black (and their spouses). They currently hold the options to *Santiago* and *Kirinyaga*, and Ed, whom we've known for 15 years, is the guy who got Carol and me the screenwriting assignments for *Santiago* and *The Widowmaker* a few years back.

The restaurant Ed had chosen was La Vie en Rose, which is in Brea, about 11 or 12 miles north of Anaheim. We arrived on time, but there was a call waiting for us that 4 of the 5 lanes of Interstate 5 were closed and the producers would be half an hour late. I started reading the plaques on the wall, and I was still reading them when our party showed up. This place has been voted the best restaurant in Orange County every year since 1993, it gets 5 stars from just about everyone who gives out ratings, it has a certificate calling it the best restaurant in Southern California signed by Arnold Schwarzenegger (as the Governator, not the actor) . . . this is some French country restaurant. Ed and Sarah and their spouses arrived—Ed's wife is a musician who scores movies; Sarah's husband is a screenwriter who's currently scripting a Morgan Freeman film—and we ordered. I had lobster ravioli, mushroom soup in a pastry bowl, duck in orange sauce, and capped it off with an exquisite chocolate soufflé—my first dessert in 3 months. Carol had venison, thereby taking her revenge against the deer who keep invading her garden to nibble on the flowers.

We talked some business, parted company, and returned to the Anaheim Hilton. Oddly enough, not that many people had arrived yet—the previous weekend had seen a Pokemon tournament, and a lot of the kids were still cluttering the lobby, playing their games. We hunted up some friends—mostly old-time fans; I can't remember if we met Darcee Cashman Monday or Tuesday, but I kept running into her all week—visited a bit, and were in bed relatively early (*exceptionally* early for a Worldcon), because we had things to do the next morning.

Tuesday, August 22: I *think* we had breakfast in the coffee shop, but I was too sleepy to remember. Then we drove to the Gene Autry Museum with Drew and Yvonne MacDonald packed in what laughably passes for a back seat in the Sebring, and made it in about an hour. Debbie Oakes and Cokie Cavin went in Debbie's car, and arrived a few minutes after us. Bill Cavin was under the weather and stayed at the hotel.

The Autry is my favorite museum in the LA area, which figures for a kid who was raised up on cowboy movies, and who still has a soft spot in his heart for Hoot Gibson, Ken Maynard, Bob Steele, Sunset Carson, Rocky Lane, and that whole crowd . . . but this time the visit was a bit disappointing. About a third of the museum was closed for renovations and to set up a new exhibit, and some of the permanent collection was out on loan. Still, there was a remarkable display of Colts and Winchesters, a beautifully refurbished stagecoach, gorgeous saddles, Teddy Roosevelt's gun collection, a Buntline special, Doc Holliday's little revolver, Billy the Kid's shotgun, a bunch of exhibits from the B movies (but not the early TV shows; they were in the part that was being renovated, so we didn't get to pay our respects to Palladin, Bret Maverick, *et al.*) Still, it took us 3 hours to get through what they had, plus another half hour in their exceptionally well-stocked gift shop, and then we started driving back to the hotel.

The Autry is about 30 miles from the Anaheim Hilton. We left at 1:30 PM, hardly rush hour. It took us until 3:45 to travel those 30 miles in LA traffic. We'd planned to have dinner at my favorite Southern California restaurant (Babouch—great Moroccan food, you sit on Persian rugs, prop yourself up with embroidered cushions, eat with your fingers, and try not to trip a series of great belly dancers), but it's in San Pedro, another 35-mile drive, and I just didn't want to spend 5 more hours, coming and going in traffic, so we turned in the car after 23 hours and 51 minutes so as not to pay an extra day, got hold of Tony and Suford Lewis—our dinner companions—and told them we were eating locally. Lawrence Person, editor of *Nova Express* and my guide whenever I'm at Armadillocon in Austin—joined us, and we had a nice, if unexceptional, dinner at a nearby sort-of-Mexican restaurant.

Adrienne Gormley showed up Tuesday, and very graciously loaned Carol a laptop for the duration of the con. I had a bunch of eBay auctions closing, and Joel Zakem let me log on with his computer on a few different nights long enough to transfer the money from PayPal to my bank account.

By Tuesday night most of the bid suites were opened—Chicago, Denver, Columbus, Australia, Kansas City and Montreal—and I managed to hit all of them. Carol missed the first few—she watched those fireworks every night that she could—and then joined me. As with every Worldcon, it was the last night before the convention officially opened, which meant that it was my last night to be a fan.

Wednesday, August 23: We had a table with 4 chairs and an umbrella on our private patio, and Carol opted to have room service bring her lunch there. I went down to the coffee shop to meet a pair of Brits, George Mann and his assistant, Mark, who edit the brand-new Solaris line in England. I'd already sold George a novelette, and he wanted to buy some books from me, which is a wonderful way to put me in a good mood. The problem with these diaries is that I write them up right after the cons, and the deals I negotiate aren't complete for months, so I can't tell you what the deal *is*, only that at con's end we thought we still *had* a deal.

I had a quick hour to take my first tour of the huckster's room, which Larry Smith tells me had 247 tables and 17 booths. Then, at 2:30, I had a panel on "Great First Lines." First panel in 30+ years I actually had to prepare for. I mean, how the hell many great first lines can you remember off the top of your head? ("The doorknob opened a cold blue eye and winked," "In five years the penis will be obsolete," "One morning the Pope forgot to take her pill," and out.)

When it was over I went down to the huckster's room to sign at the *Asimov's* table, where I ran into the Female Person From Colorado (a/k/a Connie Willis), who was just finishing her own signing, and finally got to meet her husband, Courtney.

After that I went back to the Hilton, where I did a one-hour reading to a nice-sized audience. I read them a science fiction story that I think has a real shot at the 2008 Hugo, a fantasy story that could have been written by Damon Runyon, and a little, funny, thousand-worder I did for *Nature* Magazine.

I met Carol in the lobby after my reading, and we took a cab to the Grand Californian Hotel—we were running too late to walk—where we met Lou Anders, my editor at Pyr, his wife Xin, his mother, and his 15-month-old son whom I insist on calling Mike Junior. The restaurant was the Napa Rose, every bit as expensive as La Vie en Rose, but while very nice, not in a class with the other one. Had a wonderful two hours—Lou and I have become close friends over the past couple of years—and didn't really talk any business. They're happy with me—I'm the top seller in the Pyr line—and I'm happy with them; they've committed to buy 6 more books. So we just chatted and gossiped, and I played with Mike Junior.

CFG finally got their suite, which they kept open for the next 5 days. We never bid for anything; it's a hospitality suite, open to friends (and by definition, since we never advertise it, a friend is anyone who knows where to find it). SFWA opened their suite, and so did ASFA (the American Science Fiction Artists), both on the 6th floor to avoid a couple of thousand kids trying to crash it.

I had brought along a DVD with three of "my" films on it: *Metal Tears*, Jake Bradbury's live-action adaptation of "Robots Don't Cry" that debuted at Noreascon IV; *Machines Don't Cry*, a computer-animation adaptation of the same story; and the 30-minute condensed backer's version of *The Branch*, famed in song and story as the film that got producer/director Josep Guirao excommunicated from the Andorran church and thrown out of Andorra for 15 years. I left the disk in the CFG suite, and anyone who wanted to load it into a laptop and watch it was welcome to; during the con I saw a number of fans doing so.

I got Drew and Yvonne into the SFWA suite, introduced them to Greg Benford, Pat Cadigan, Gardner Dozois, and a number of other writers and editors, then took them up to the 7th floor where there was a reception for writers and workshop participants, where they met Nancy Kress, George R. R. Martin, and saw CFG member (and the only CFG pro not named Resnick) Steve Leigh, who also writes as "S. L. Farrell."

Everyone kept asking me where Laura was—I suspect she outsells me these days—but she was home recuperating. She'd just spent a few months in Israel for the Associated Press, and got out the day before the shooting started. (Well, before the shooting with Hezbollah; the shooting with Hamas had been going on for a couple of weeks.)

After I left Yvonne charming a bunch of pros, I went to some of the other parties. Ran into Bill Fawcett, and for the first time in years neither of us had anything to sell to the other. Made arrangements to meet next year at DragonCon; I've never been to one, but they offered to fly us there and put us up, so how could I say no?

Ran into Kay Kenyon, and insisted on introducing her to some editors and podcasters who should love her work, then did the same for a couple of other writers. Before the weekend was over, I'd managed to introduce Rob Sawyer, Bob Silverberg, Nancy Kress, Kevin Anderson and Harry Turtledove (as well as Kay) to Steve Eley of Escape Pod, who I believe had committed to buy from all of them by Saturday night.

Eventually I wound up back at CFG, as I almost always do at Worldcon, visiting with Pat and Roger Sims, Dick Spelman, John Hertz, Mark Linneman, Sue and Steve Francis, and other old fannish friends. Pros don't come to CFG very often the way they used to, because the two cultures have diverged, and pros want to talk about the business while fans want to SMOF or talk about what they've read—but I go to the suite to briefly get away from the business end of things, and I'm thoroughly comfortable there.

Thursday, August 24: Bob Silverberg and I always have lunch at Worldcon, and since we both grew up in Jewish neighborhoods and now live in places with no delis (not mediocre or poor delis, but *no* delis) we always try to eat at one. We found a highly-recommended one in Costa Mesa. And Bob was driving down from the Oakland Hills and would have a car.

But Karen (his wife, Karen Haber) took his car to go shopping, so we figured, what the hell, we want a deli, let's take a cab, how much can it be? (Answer: $35 each way. $70 total, so he could have a bowl of matzo ball soup and I could have chopped liver and blintzes. Whoever said science fiction writers are smart?)

We split the cabfare, but Bob had to pay for the meal. And the reason he had to pay was because the LACon committee had asked him to emcee the Guest of Honor speeches on Thursday night and he said, No, get Resnick. The only reason he lived long enough to have lunch is because I thought he'd have a car.

Now, when the committee, on one week's notice, asked me if I'd toastmaster this two-hour shindig, I figured I should get a little something extra for it. Not money; I'm a fan at heart. But I knew my cousin Bob and his wife Glenda were coming by to hear the speeches and attend the private Resnick Listserv party Thursday night, so I said Yes, I will host the damned event, provided you give one-day memberships to Bob and Glenda, which they promptly did. (Well, I also said. "Provided I don't have to wear a jacket and tie, or shoes with laces.")

So while Silverberg and I were seeing the countryside at $3.00 a mile, Carol met Bob and Glenda, saw them through registration, and turned them loose in the huckster room and art show (and they had such a good time that they're coming to Denver in 2008). In the meantime, I had do my official autographing from 3:00 to 4:00.

So I sit down, and Eric Flint comes by to say hello and schmooze a bit while I'm signing, and then Ralph Roberts shows up and sits down next to me to visit, and since he's in a dozen of my anthologies I have him sign whenever one shows up, and I realize at 3:55 that my line is longer than ever. Now, once in a while, I sign an extra few minutes beyond my hour to take care of the stragglers, but this was like nothing I've ever experienced. 4:15 comes and goes, so does 4:30, and the line is *still* long, and I am hoping all my editors are watching, because I am sure I am signing more books in one afternoon than their royalty statements say I have sold in a year. Finally Carol comes by at 5:00 to point out that we have to leave for dinner so I can be back to host the Guest of Honor event, so I tell the last few people to show up at Larry Smith's table Friday and I'd move them to the front of the line.

When we'd gone to ConJose in 2002 we had a couple of meals at a Marie Calendar's, which I gather are commonplace in California but haven't reached the Midwest yet. We fondly remembered their pies, so we asked Bob to drive us to the nearest Calendar's, about 5 miles away, for dinner. Dinner was okay, about the level of a Bob Evans or a Mimi's; the pies were superb.

Then it was back to the hotel, where we showed Bob and Glenda around until just before 8:00, and then moseyed over to the convention center. I stepped out on the stage to check it out, found the spotlight blinding and a notecard I placed on the podium unreadable, and realized I was going to have to do the whole thing off the cuff, except for one part where I had to read off the names of Howard Devore's family. Some guy backstage was nice enough to keep a tally, so I can tell you that in the course of the evening I told jokes about Nancy Kress, Janis Ian, Bob Silverberg, David Gerrold (twice), Gardner Dozois, Connie Willis (thrice), Jim Gurney, Howard Devore, George R. R. Martin, Joe Haldeman, Anne McCaffrey, and SFWA. (It's nice to have friends, even if they're no longer your own.)

LACon lost two of its four Guests of Honor this year—Big-Hearted Howard Devore, the Fan GOH, died a day or two into the new year, and Frankie Thomas, the Media GOH, died a couple of months ago. While I spoke a bit about both of them, it made for a shorter ceremony than might have been anticipated a year ago. Jim Gurney did a fascinating slide show, and Connie Willis, the dreaded Female Person From Colorado, gave a very serious, very emotional, very un-Connie-like speech, which ended with her in tears (and made me decide not to clip her with any zingers after she finished). I thought it went pretty smoothly, and we wound it up in about 95 minutes.

Then it was back to the CFG suite to unwind a bit, and at 11:00 I went down to the third floor, where LACon had thoughtfully provided the Resnick Listserv and its friends with a very nice room. I read a story, then Linda Donahue and Juli Mandala belly-danced, then I read another story, then they danced again, and so on. Adrienne Gormley also read one, and Bob Faw read a sonnet and a short-short. Guy and Rosy Lillian showed up for part of it, so did Drew and Yvonne MacDonald, Jack McDevitt was there for the whole thing (and would *still* be there if the ladies were still dancing), Eric Flint showed up for the final hour. It wasn't a suite or a party room, so there were no couches and no refreshments, but everyone seemed to have a good time, and we broke up after maybe 2 ½ hours.

Bob and Glenda went home, everyone else to their scattered parties went, and I went to the *Jim Baen's Universe* suite, which Eric was hosting. I'd sold him a pretty nice novelette a month earlier titled "All the Things You Are," and he'd asked me to bring another one to the con so he could read it on the way home. I handed him a 6,000-worder titled "The Big Guy"—a science fiction basketball story, except that it isn't really—and instead of waiting to go home, he read it that night and when I woke up there was a phone message that he'd bought it. Which is about the only pleasant way to wake up that I've ever discovered.

Friday, August 25: I dragged myself out of bed and made it down to the coffee shop at the ungodly hour of 11:00 to have my postponed lunch with Kevin Anderson. We spent a couple of hours working out some of the broader details of the novel's outline—Kevin's a guy who likes 60-page outlines, and considering the advances he gets, who can say him nay?—and we'll probably be working on the outline even longer than we work on the book. Hopefully the outline will be ready for submission by mid-December.

Then Kevin and I wandered over to the huckster room, where all the contributors to *Space Cadets*, the anthology I'd edited for LACon IV, were seated at a huge table for an autograph session. There was Connie Willis, Harry Turtledove, Kevin, me, Nancy Kress, David Brin, Greg

Benford, Larry Niven—names like that. And we drew a *huge* crowd, one that kept us there 45 minutes beyond our allotted hour. But there was one guy, I couldn't see him clearly from where I sat, who signed only one autograph the whole time. It was Walter Koenig, who played Chekov on *Star Trek*.. He must have confused this with a Trek convention, because he sat down next to the biggest names in the field, who of course were autographing for free, and had a little sign posted to the effect that he would sign an autograph for a mere $20.00. I wouldn't expect to see him back.

Because of the autographing I was a bit late for the Pyr panel, at which Lou Anders was introducing all his authors, describing their books with fanatical enthusiasm, and showing slides of their covers on a screen. I'd been nagging Kay Kenyon for a year to submit to Lou—I know what he likes—and she finally did, and sold him a 4-book series. This was her first look at her cover; I think her face glowed brighter than the screen. By the time the panel was done I think Lou had made it pretty clear that Pyr is *not* a small press: in his first two years he's published me, Alan Dean Foster, Mike Moorcock, and Bob Silverberg, among others. I've had three different cover artists from Pyr—John Picacio, Stephen Martiniere, and Bob Eggleton—and all three were on the Hugo ballot.

Then at 4:00 I went back to the huckster room for a signing with Janis Ian at Larry Smith's table. And as I've been doing ever since Millennium Philcon, I asked the belly dancers to come and draw a crowd—and as they have been doing every year, they wiggled and jiggled and sold about $400 more Resnick books than I used to sell in that hour before I thought of inviting them to dance. Larry and Sally had brought a large supply of anthologies that had Janis in them, so she was kept busy signing for most of the hour. Linda and Juli drew so many onlookers/buyers than I stuck around autographing for another half hour. I think when the dust settled I had signed about three times as many books at LACon as I'd ever done at any prior Worldcon. I don't know why. My first thought was that I hadn't been out there since the last LACon, but actually I'd been to Con-Dor, just 90 miles south of there, maybe 4 years ago. I guess it'll remain a very pleasant mystery.

We met Glenn Yeffeth, publisher of BenBella Books, and my old friend and recent collaborator David Gerrold, for dinner, and went into the upscale Italian restaurant in the Hilton. We'd been taken there five evenings in a row at LACon III and were thoroughly sick of it by convention's end, but it had been a decade since we'd dined there, and it was a wonderful meal. I'd been editing a reprint line of sf for Glenn for a couple of years, starting in 2003, but it didn't sell as well as his media books (big surprise, right?), and we decided to drop it, which left me free to accept an offer to edit *Jim Baen's Universe* . . . but we remain friends, and indeed I've edited some anthologies for him, and he's reprinting my *Soothsayer/Oracle/Prophet* trilogy. During the meal he announced that he'd spoken to his distributors about the latest anthology we planned to do, and they were so enthused that he now wants to make it a six-anthology series. Which was even more satisfying than dessert (but I had dessert anyhow.)

Never did make the masquerade, though I've now seen photos of all the costumes, and think "Captain Jack Sparrow"—a 6-foot bird in a pirate's outfit—should have been a shoo-in for Most Humorous, Most Creative, and half a dozen other Mosts. Got up to the SFWA suite, where *Asimov's* and *Analog* were having a dessert party, then stopped by CFG long enough to partake of one of the pies—French Silk, my favorite—that the gang had brought back from Baker's Square. Stopped by the overcrowded (as usual) Tor party, got to say hi to Beth Meacham and Tom Doherty, then went to the Escape Pod Party. Stephen Eley has bought six of my stories in the past three months, and has made a firm believer out of me; the first one I sold him was heard by a French producer/director who promptly e-mailed me and bought an 18-month option on it.

Wound up back at the *Jim Baen's Universe* suite, which seemed to be the only non-bidding suite open after 3:00—very unfannish, how early the parties kept shutting down—and visited with the Baeniacs for a couple of hours, then toddled off to bed just ahead of the sunrise, which is the way you're *supposed* to do it at Worldcons.

Saturday, August 26: I had another ungodly early lunch at 11:00, this time with Eric Flint. He'd just bought my story, we had collaborated on an anthology for Baen during the summer, and I had a novel idea that played to both of our strengths that I knew he'd love, so I brought it—and Carol—along. Carol ate and left by noon, Eric decided—no surprise—that he wanted to collaborate on the novel, and we spent the next hour going over some plot points and ideas for sequels, since it should be a relatively easy sell.

Which is just one more reason why I love this field. There are absolutely no uninteresting people in it. Three years ago I'd never heard of Lou Anders; five months ago all I knew about Eric was that he wrote a lot of books, most of them for Baen. Today they're two of my closest friends.

I went to my kaffeeklatsch—they finally served kaffee at one of these things—and passed out autographed dust jackets, cover flats, trading cards from Chicon IV (I still have maybe 200 left), and discussed forthcoming works and answered any and all questions. Lousy venue; we were located maybe 60 feet from the stage of the fan cabaret, with no wall between us, just a curtain. Fortunately there was a lady harpist during my hour; I hate to think of how it would have gone had there been a drummer, or a guy who plugged his guitar into a socket.

I spent the next hour going through the huckster room, signing my books at publishers' tables. Meisha Merlin had brought out a trade paperback of *A Gathering of Widowmaker*, Eric Reynolds had brought out *Golden Age SF*, there was a pile of *The Worldcon Guest of Honor Speeches* to be signed, and so on. The one thing I didn't sign was *Space Cadets*. There were just no more to be had; the limited $75.00 edition was gone by Thursday, and the $25.00 trade was unavailable by Saturday afternoon.

At 4:00 I stopped by the Edge table, which had offered a corner to Rob Sawyer's Red Deer Books, and signed with Nick DiChario. Red Deer had just brought out his first novel, and I'd done an introduction to it, so we signed for an hour. Even signed a few of our collection of 11 collaborations, *Magic Feathers: The Mike and Nick Show*, which was published 6 years ago.

Then it was time to get Carol and meet my agent, Eleanor Wood, for dinner . . . but Carol had picked up a mild stomach virus that morning and opted out, so Eleanor and I ate together. She has been my agent and friend for 23 years now, and I hate to think of where my career would have gone without her. I have explained to her in no uncertain terms that she is absolutely, positively not allowed to retire or die before I do.

After dinner we were joined by Ed Elbert, my producer, and his wife Karen, and we made it to the Hugo Nominees Reception just in time to grab the last of the sweets they'd laid out. (I'd arranged for Ed and Karen to be my guests at the Hugos, as well as Carol and Eleanor—but I'd forgotten that while the committee knew about them, the convention center's security guards didn't. At the last minute I borrowed Bill and Cokie Cavin's badges for them, and returned the badges after the ceremony.)

Connie Willis was the Toastmistress, and Bob Silverberg was her comic foil. The two of them delighted the audience with a routine that ran throughout the ceremony. By now you've all read the results—yes, I lost again, for the 23rd time, which makes my 5 wins seem kind of paltry; I mean, if you couldn't hit .200, you'd find yourself sitting on the bench in the Albanian League. Harlan Ellison presented the short story Hugo and became everyone's main topic of conversation for the next week or two after fellating the microphone, slandering Ginny Heinlein, groping Connie's breast, and otherwise comporting himself exactly like Harlan; this kind of stuff played a lot better 40 years ago.

I took Ed and Karen to the bar for a couple of hours after the ceremony. Then they had to leave—even at midnight they're a 90-minute drive from Anaheim—and I went to the room to check on Carol. She was feeling better, but thought it wise not to eat or party. I recounted the Hugos, and my various conversations, to her, then hit a few suites, went to CFG, found everyone too busy playing this idiot card game called Wizards to visit, so Bob Faw and I went off to visit Baen Books, which had rented out the Presidential Suite for the night. It was for a Jim Baen memorial, but that was over, most of the crowd was gone, and Bob and I sat down and, so help me, we spent the next two hours bonding with Baen's powers-that-be by swapping dirty jokes with Toni Weisskopf and Hank Reinhardt. We didn't break up until 4:30, and believe it or not, it was the most fun I'd had the whole convention.

Sunday, August 27: This was the day of the late-morning Resnick Listserv brunch. We were set to ask for a table for 14, but Bob Faw didn't show up, and Fred Ramsey didn't show up, and Guy and Rosy Lillian didn't show up, and Paula Leibermann didn't show up, and this one didn't show up, and that one didn't show up, and when the dust cleared there was me, Carol, Darcee, Adrienne, Debbie Oakes, and Ralph and Pat Roberts. (You know, Ralph has been one of my closest friends since 1980, as well as my occasional publisher, but this was only the second times we'd ever met in person. Amazing how the computer has changed the art of socializing.)

After brunch Carol decided that she maybe had a 36-hour virus instead of a 24-hour one and went back to the room to lie down and take it easy. I was at loose ends. I'd done the business I'd come to do, with Eric and Baen, Solaris, BenBella, some anthologists and podcasters, and some of my producers. The only other person I'd wanted to see was Ginjer Buchanan of Ace; we'd been working together on next year's Nebula Awards volume, we're old friends, and we'd planned to have dinner Thursday night—but I got a panicky call from her Monday just before she left New York that she'd inadvertently double-booked dinner for that night, and since I knew we'd have access to my cousin's car and not be stuck at a hotel restaurant I said that we'd cancel and meet for a drink . . . and I never saw her the whole convention. I'd given her a proposal and a couple of outlines back at Boskone in February, and I figured if she wanted them she'd have said so, so I just wanted to visit with her and catch up on gossip. And as I was walking out the door of the hotel and heading for the convention center, who should I literally bump into but the elusive Ms. Buchanan. She was looking for someone, and thought he might be in the con center, so I offered to accompany her. "By the way," she said, "I loved your outlines and . . ." and then she broke off to point at some kid in a cute hall costume, and I said, "Ginjer, if you don't finish that sentence in the next 10 seconds there won't be enough of you left to bury." "Oh, I'll be making an offer on it this month," she said distractedly, and went back to talking about the costume.

And *that* is how business gets done.

Now I really had no more business to do, so I went back to the hotel, checked on Carol, went to CFG until dinnertime, found that Carol was finally feeling healthy again, and we went down to the lobby to meet the DiCharios—Nick, Mom and Dad—for dinner.

Then I went to CFG, Carol packed and joined me, and we just hung out till maybe 10:00. Then, since Darcee was driving us to the airport at 2 in the morning, Carol decided to take a nap until 1:30, so I hit the few remaining parties, wound up back in CFG where I ran into Andy Porter, Ed Meskys (who had just lost his guide dog on Friday; that dog had been to more cons that 80% of the attendees), and Fred Prophet.

Monday, August 28: And finally, at 2:00, it was time to go. For once the highway was relatively empty, and Darcee dumped us at LAX at 2:40 AM. Our flight took off at 6:00, we had a 2-hour layover and change of planes in Dallas, landed in Dayton at 5:20, and waited two more hours for Laura, who was caught in traffic right behind an 18-wheeler that jackknifed, to pick us up.

We were exhausted when we got home, but there was one package in the mail that looked so interesting I opened it before I went to bed. It was Jack Williamson's latest novel, published 78 years after his debut novel—and it was dedicated to me (and others). When one of your boyhood heroes does something like that, all the bad stuff—and all careers have some bad stuff—fades away and you feel like you've Arrived.

Maybe one of my dedications can make someone else feel that way in another 15 or 20 years, I hope so.

Worldcon Masquerades:
The First 40 Years

It all began, as so many fannish traditions did, with Forry Ackerman. He came to the very first Worldcon in New York City, back in 1939, and delighted the assemblage by wearing a futuristic costume that would probably have gotten him banned from any Manhattan bar (and dismembered in any working-class Chicago bar, where I grew up.)

But it made a lasting impression, and at the second Worldcon, held in Chicago in 1940, there was a small masquerade.

Now, as we all know, anything that happens twice in a row becomes a Worldcon tradition, and from that day to this the Worldcon has always had a masquerade. For the first couple of decades it was actually a masquerade ball. There was a dance band, and tables, and drinks, and now and then people got up and danced, and every once in a while someone in a costume would walk across a makeshift stage—or simply through an area of the dance floor that had been cleared for it—and at the end of the evening a few winners were announced.

It was pretty informal. But then the costuming bug struck, and costumes began getting more elaborate. Perhaps the first great costumer was Olga Ley, the wife of writer and scientist Willy Ley, who wore a series of stunning costumes in the late 1950s. Another relatively early and always elegant costumer was author/editor Lin Carter, who annually showed up in a gorgeous robe. Lin wore those robes as if he'd been born in them; there was no awkwardness at all. When I asked him about it, he confided that he frequently wore them around the house to get in the right mood to write his fantasy novels.

By the early 1960s a number of fans spent considerable time—weeks, sometimes months—preparing their costumes. Bruce Pelz was probably the most creative of them: in 1963 he was Fritz Leiber's Fafhrd, and in future years he was Jack Vance's "The Dragon Master," Poul Anderson's "Nicholas van Rijn," a one-legged fantasy figure, and one year he secretly shaved his beard off just before the masquerade and came out as "Gertrude the Bird Woman." His name wasn't announced until the end of the masquerade; it was the most surprised I've ever seen an audience.

Jon and Joni Stopa won a number of prizes throughout the 1960s and early 1970s. They were "Incubus and Succubus" at Discon I, some Leigh Brackett characters in 1969, and added daughter Debbie to their Phoenix costume of 1974.

Some of the others of that era who produced one memorable costume after another would be Drew and Kathy Sanders, Ann Layman Chancellor, Marjii Ellers, Astrid Anderson (Bear), Pat and Peggy Kennedy, and a little earlier you could count on Stu Hoffman to come up with a different B.E.M. every year.

Since the costumes were far less elaborate than by modern standards, a number of pros also participated. Perhaps the most famous was beloved old E. E. "Doc" Smith coming to the 1962 Chicon masquerade as C. L. Moore's "Northwest Smith." Fritz Leiber was his own "Mind Spider" at the same con.

Larry Niven came as "Implosion in a Time Machine" in 1966, and was back in costume with Bruce Pelz and both their wives at the 1972 LACon. One year David Gerrold did a striptease, revealing all 8 of his female breasts. Dick and Pat Lupoff were Captain and Mary Marvel back at Pittcon in 1960. At NYCon III in 1967 Isaac Asimov shoved a pipe in his mouth on the spur of the moment and walked across stage as "Harlan Ellison." Harlan retaliated a moment later by masquerading as "Isaac Asimov."

Many other pros competed over the years—Marion Zimmer Bradley, Chelsea Quinn Yarbro, Sandra Meisel. Carol and I competed 5 times in the 1970s, winning 4, and a photo of our 1974 Best in Show winner, Clark Ashton Smith's "The White Sybil and the Ice Demon," actually knocked Richard Nixon's image off Page 1 of the *Washington Post* during that month of Watergate's climax.

The general consensus of old-time costumers is that the greatest costume of the first 40 years of Worldcon masquerades was Karen and Astrid Anderson's "The Bat and the Bitten," which was Best in Show at the 1969 Worldcon.

The first nudity showed up in 1952. There was no more until 1971, but all throughout the 1970s and early 1980s there were half a dozen or so nude costumes every year—and a lot of them were prize winners. Probably the best of them was Kris Lundi (a/k/a Animal X) as a "Harpy" in 1974.

There were also a number of costumes that necessitated rule changes. In 1969 a space hero stood on a raised stage and fired his blaster at the audience—and a huge flame shot out maybe a foot above everyone's heads. From that day on, no more fire.

In 1972, a costumer came as his own underground cartoon character, "The Turd." He was covered by gallons of peanut butter, and he evidently never figured out what happens to peanut butter when it's exposed to hot stage lights and photo lamps for 4 hours. It turned rancid, destroyed every costume he rubbed against, and did serious damage to the carpeting and drapes. From that day on, no more peanut butter.

In 1974, the masquerade dragged on for 6 hours. One group from "The Wizard of Oz" sang the entire score of the movie. Three different belly dancers performed their entire routines. And so on. From that day on, one-minute time limits.

The Trekkies discovered Worldcon in 1967. 7 of them came as "Mr. Spock," each no doubt thinking no one else would ever come up with the idea.

As the masquerades got bigger, the dancing ended, the bands vanished, and by the early 1970s it was much as you see it today: strictly a costume competition, with the participants on a presidium stage and the audience in seats rather than at tables. By 1974 there were regularly more than 100 costumes per Worldcon, and while the masquerades always began at 8:00, I don't think the final judgment was ever rendered before midnight.

Worldcon masquerades got so cumbersome that in 1982 the competition was divided into the categories that still exist today: novice, journeyman, and master. Carol and I wore our last costumes in 1980, so you'll have to ask someone else about the past quarter-century. From what I've seen, most of the costumes that won prior to 1980 would barely merit honorable mentions today, which is as it should be.

Dragoncon 2007

DragonCon was an experience.

According to Kevin Anderson's blog, there were 61,000 attendees. Most blogs were more conservative, putting the number at 50,000. I'll swear all 50,000 were lined up for the elevators in my hotel every evening.

The committee couldn't have treated us better. Paid for our planefares. Hired a limo to drive us to and from the Atlanta airport. Gave us a suite in the Hyatt—and not just a bedroom and a little sitting room. We had a parlor that could have comfortably hosted a party for 20.

But we were on the 18th floor, and the elevators were even worse than the 1967 Worldcon in New York, my previous highwater (lowwater?) mark for them. They were bad enough so that 65-year-old Mike and 64-year-old Carol climbed the stairs to the 18th floor more than once.

Bad as the stairs were, the lobby was occasionally worse. On Saturday morning, I had a panel in something called Regency 5, an adjunct of the huge Regency ballroom in the Hyatt. The panel was at 11:30. I had nothing much to do at 10:30, so I thought I'd mosey down there and see where it was. I started in the lobby at 10:31. I got to Regency 5, two levels down, at 11:20. By the time I got there, the hotel staff *and* the police, realizing that the hotel had too many people and was in violation of the fire laws, decided that no one could go up from the level of the Regency rooms or down from the lobby, which didn't exactly get the numbers down to where they were legal, but jammed thousands of people together to the point where they literally could not turn around.

(What was the fuss? The main Regency ballroom, which held about 5000 people, had a bunch of Battlestar actors on stage. At 12:25, I whispered to the moderator that if he had a brain in his head he'd end the panel then and there so we could beat the hordes of Battlestar people out. He did.)

All of my panels, even my reading and my kind of free-form "Evening With Mike Resnick," were in large rooms, and all but one were SRO. This is not known as a readers' convention, and indeed there were only 3 bookdealers among the more than 800 tables in the various dealers rooms, but with 50,000 to 60,000 attendees, there were enough readers to fill all the panels, form endless autograph lines, and generally convince us that there are enough readers and potential readers to cultivate here that it's worth going back (provided it's not on Worldcon weekend—and with more and more Worldcons avoiding Labor Day, it won't be.) I'd say that 90% of the fans were under 30, and of course have grown up with computers, because the most enthusiastic responses I got on every panel were when I started talking about *Jim Baen's Universe*.

The costumes were magnificent. The masquerade competition only had 65 costumes, 6 or 7 outstanding ones, the rest so-so . . . but there had to be 2,500 hall costumes, hundreds of them superior to anything we've seen at a Worldcon in decades. (And, for the gentlemen attendees, a lot of the ladies' hall costumes—like a few hundred of them—showed a *lot* of flesh.)

Over the years I've probably met 95% of the sf writers, probably more . . . but there were two major ones I'd never met before, and I finally got to meet and visit with them at DragonCon—David Weber (with whom I'll be collaborating on a short story next year) and John Ringo. I had lunch with Kevin Anderson, dinner with List member and Escape Pod Emperor Steve Eley, sat at a banquet table with Jo Sherman and Bob Asprin, saw Terry Brooks for the first time in many years, spent a little time with Dave Drake, and had lunch with Bill Fawcett and Jody Lynn Nye. Harry Turtledove cancelled at the last second. Jack McDevitt showed up, but no one I knew saw him, including me, and most people assume he had cancelled too, which will give you a further idea of how big the con was. I saw Toni Weisskopf for only a few seconds, as she was staying at the Marriott.

I think one of the crowd-control problems was that they put the entire con on in the three hotels—Hyatt, Marriott, and Hilton—and never used a convention center.

I'm sure there were parties all the hell over, but the elevators were impossible, so we settled for walking down one floor and visiting with pros and fans in the Green Room, located on the 17th floor, where most of the writers hung out once they realized it could take them more than an hour to reach the lobby and at least another hour to get back up.

Every member of the committee treated us with the utmost courtesy, and seemed genuinely concerned that we have a good, trouble-free time. The fans were also about as polite as any we've encountered, which was mildly surprising given their numbers.

The biggest Worldcon I've ever been to could have fit in a small corner of DragonCon. It was a most unusual experience, very enjoyable except for the elevators and those particular periods in the lobby where if you were at all claustrophobic you would have wigged out. The restaurant prices were typical upscale big city downtown hotel—$5 for coffee, $15 for a hamburger, *real* money for a meal—but there was a mall attached to the Hyatt, filled with dozens of fast food kiosks for the fans. We ate one night at a Steak and Ale (with Steve), one night at the hotel (a banquet, with comped passes/tickets), and the last night we found a 24-hour restaurant that was attached not to the hotel but the mall, the Metro Diner, with the best (and most reasonably-priced) meal we had the whole convention. I can't remember the name of the place Kevin took me to lunch, but it was a micro brewery, which has always been Kevin's restaurant of choice. (I don't drink, but it was fascinating to tour the place and see all the different beers they were brewing.)

I got to meet Lou Ferrigno (the Hulk) and Lou Gossett, a fine actor, and a bunch of comic book people. Star Trek's Lt. Uhura, whose name eludes me, was there. The only artists whose work I knew in the art show were Don Maitz and Janny Wurtz, but there was some splendid stuff by artists I was unfamiliar with.

I'm glad I went. I know a lot of writers look down their noses and sneer at DragonCon, just the way they do at podcasting, and online publishing, and all the other innovations of the 21st Century—and they're just as wrong here as they are about all the others. Science fiction is for the young, and this is where they congregate. The writers and publishers who ignore it—and the opportunity to reach ten times the membership of a typical Worldcon—are just being ostriches. I may be a dinosaur myself, but at least I'm trying to evolve.

Denvention 3 Diary

Tuesday, August 5, 2008:

We decided to spend a couple of less days at Worldcon this year, simply because we had less time to spend. As a multiple-Hugo-winning writer, I get two or three Guest of Honor or Special Guest gigs a year… but as the co-editor of *Jim Baen's Universe*, with a decent budget and bi-monthly publication, I got *eleven* this year, and I still had all my writing commitments.

We flew from Dayton — the same distance from our house as the Cincinnati airport, and always *much* cheaper — and changed planes in Dallas, getting to Denver just after noon. We took the shuttle to our hotel, checked in, and found we were two rooms away from the CFG suite.

Maybe I should tell you about the hotel. When all the major hotels were sold out of their Worldcon blocks within two days, CFG — my home club, the venerable Cincinnati Fantasy Group — decided not to wait for them to have cancellations, or to go the outlying hotels…so Bill Cavin found us a Hilton that was kitty-corner from the convention center; only the Hyatt was closer. We blocked 40 rooms and a hospitality suite, and filled about 30 before the deadline. Our rooms had huge flat-screen TVs, refrigerators, and microwaves, and the elevators *always* worked. I also passed the word to some pro friends, so along with CFG and its fannish friends, the hotel was also home to Harry Turtledove, Kristine Kathryn Rusch, Dean Wesley Smith, Eric Flint, Kay Kenyon, Sharon Shinn, and Louise Marley.

Anyway, while Carol was packing I finally met Lesley Ainge, who will be my next collaborator. She'd arrived from Australia the night before, and since this was not just her first Worldcon but her first con of any kind, I escorted her over to the con center, where we both registered and picked up our various materials. Lesley was rooming with B.J. Galler-Smith, who showed up in late afternoon, and they, we, my cousin Bob Hamburg and his wife Glenda, and Tony and Suford Lewis, went out to the 16th Street Mall for dinner. The place I wanted to try — it was open 24 hours — had motorcycles and hookers in front of it, so we walked a little farther and wound up at the Rialto Café for a nice, serviceable, unmemorable meal.

We went back to the CFG suite for awhile. Carol, who had a serious case of altitude sickness in Colorado Springs when we were there for CoSine (the most enjoyable regional I've been to in a decade) in January, was being affected again, though not as badly, and she opted out of the 5-block walk, that night and every night, to the parties. After visiting a bit at the suite, B.J., Lesley, and I went off to the Sheraton — the party hotel — for the Australia-in-2010 party. We stayed for a couple of hours, but nothing else was going on, and finally we wandered back to CFG, and I turned in relatively early for a Worldcon — about 3:00 AM.

Wednesday, August 6:

Carol went to Denver's world-class art museum in the morning with B.J., Cokie Cavin and Debbie Oakes. I hung around the hotel for awhile, then met Lesley and went over to the con center, thoroughly explored the dealers room — which had a *lot* higher percentage of booksellers than usual — and stopped by the art show. There were a number of small and medium press publishers with their own tables, and though I hadn't come expecting to do any business — for a change I was happy with all my publishers — I did some anyway, a very pleasant surprise.

I met Bob Silverberg for our annual deli lunch. (We both grew up in Jewish neighborhoods and developed a taste for blintzes, chopped liver, and the like — and then moved to places that have absolutely no delis.) It was a pleasant visit, and we congratulated each other on being named science fiction's two greatest speakers in a long article in the then-current *File 770* (this year's Hugo-winning fanzine), a conclusion with which we are n total agreement.

Then it was back to the convention, and the dealers room.

One line of books was especially impressive: Planet Stories, a subsidiary of Paizo Publishing, is bringing out a line of classic pulp reprints — C. L. Moore, Henry Kuttner, Leigh Brackett, and more. Back in 1981 I put together all 13 of Moore's Northwest Smith stories (which I love) for Don Grant, when she was Guest of Honor at Denvention 2 — but she was in the early stages of Alzheimer's, didn't remember writing all of them, and would only agree to let Don print the ones she remembered. The Planet book reprints them *all* — and when I told them the story of 1981, they graciously asked me to write an Afterword to the next edition, as well as a forward to a new Leigh Brackett reprint.

I signed at the SFWA table for half an hour in the early afternoon, then did my official autographing at 4:00. Steve Feldberg, who had bought eight of my books for Audible.com during the past few months, stopped by to introduce himself, and we visited until dinnertime.

Kris and Dean treated Carol, Lesley and me to dinner at the Hilton, a very pleasant meal. Carol was really feeling kind of woozy, having walked to the museum (no one told her group that the free trolly stopped right in front of it), and again had an easy night of it. The SFWA suite officially opened, and there were a lot more parties, including the

Chicago-in-2012 bid party, so I took a group that included B.J., Lesley, Yvonne and Drew MacDonald, and Debbie Oakes to the party hotel and stuck with them long enough to make sure they all got their little stickers on their badges that would allow them to return to the SFWA suite the rest of the convention without needing a pro to get them in. Most of the parties were on the 22nd floor, and I have to say it was the most crowded, most physically uncomfortable, party venue in years. I got up there every night — Pyr and Baen, two of my publishers, were there — but for the most part I tried to stay in the Presidential Suites on the 6th and 8th floors, which, along with the basement and the 22nd, were the other party venues.

About one o'clock Lesley and I stopped by the Hyatt for some hot chocolate, I dropped her off at the Hilton, and I went back to the Sheraton to visit with old friends and do a little business. Got in about 5:00 AM, and I started feeling more like I was at a Worldcon.

Thursday, August 7:

Thursday was a busy day. I got up for breakfast with Carol, we went over to the con center and looked around and visited some. Then she went back to take a nap — the altitude was really bothering her — and I did a rather silly panel on galactic empires, a reading, and a really enjoyable panel on the old pulp magazines — and since BJ had just sold her first novel, I made sure to announce it at every panel and reading.

Carol showed up at the end of the pulp panel, and we met Bill Schafer, my editor/publisher at Subterranean, who has become a very good friend, and his incredibly efficient jack-of-all-trades assistant, Yanni Kuznia. We went back to the Rialto for dinner, discussed future projects — I already have a Subterranean book out this year, two more coming next year, and one the year after that, and as I write these words Subterranean's magazine is featuring its "special Mike Resnick issue". Hard not to like a publisher like that.

A few of us hit the Aussie party, but we were back early, because the committee had thoughtfully provided the Resnick Listserv with its own meeting room in the Hyatt at 10:00. I read some stories, Linda Donahue read one, Linda and Juli Mandala belly-danced between readings, Bob and Glenda Hamburg, Steve Dreksler, Guy and Rosy Lillian, and some other Listservers showed up (and some non-Listservers too) and a good time seemed to be had by all. (Eric Flint is still upset that he had a 10:00 PM panel and missed the belly-dancing.) It broke up about midnight, a few of us went back over to the Sheraton for the parties, came back for coffee and soft drinks around 2:30, and then I went back alone for maybe two more hours. Sold a reprint novella and accepted assignments to introduce a couple of collections, so it was a well-spent couple of hours.

Friday, August 8:

I dragged myself out of bed in time to show up to sign the *Asimov's 30ᵗʰ Annual Anthology* with Connie Willis and Jim Kelly — and Connie, for reasons that still elude me, wrote a few lines on a banana peel and inscribed it to me. Photos of the peel have since cropped up all the hell over the internet. After the signing, I stuck around awhile to visit with Tachyon's people; nice guys, and I hope we'll do some business one of these days.

Next was a panel with Tony Lewis and Tom Whitmore, about the appearance of Worldcon in works of fiction. Interesting, in a limited way. As the editor of *Alternate Worldcons* and *Again, Alternate Worldcons* I was the moderator.

Drew a full house for my kaffeeklatsch. Pyr and Ralph Roberts thoughtfully supplied jackets, cover flats, and ads sheets that I inscribed and gave away. I've still got maybe a hundred trading cards with a photo of me and a rhino from Chicon VI, and I suspect I'll keep giving away ten at every kaffeeklatsch until I run out.

Lou Anders had asked most of his writers to attend a promotional panel for Pyr Books, and since they've been publishing two or three books of mine every year since they started, I was happy to lend a little moral support. I can't remember everyone who was on the panel, but I know I sat next to Kay Kenyon, whose Pyr books are making a major splash.

Carol and I met Eleanor Wood, my agent of 25 years, for dinner at the Hyatt. Not a 5-star meal by any means, but the best meal we had during the convention. We discussed current and future business, and I reiterated my annual pronouncement that she is not allowed to retire or die before I do.

Then it was off to the Sheraton, where *Asimov's* and *Analog* were hosting their annual party in the SFWA Suite, and the Tor party was going strong two floors above it. And I had to do a duty dance at the Pyr party up on the 22ⁿᵈ floor. I helped newcomer Rebecca Hardy meet a couple of editors and agents she wanted to meet, and stuck around til maybe 1:30. Then I walked some of the ladies back to the Hilton, and returned to the Sheraton for a few more hours.

Saturday, August 9:

This was our last full day in Denver.

It started with an *Asimov's* signing — the magazine, not the anthology — after which Carol and I had lunch at the Hyatt with Lou Anders. Then came the panel that was supposed to be the highlight of the convention. Evidently they took a vote of the committee to choose the people best able to wing it on a panel and amuse the audience, and the winners (nominees?) were Connie Willis, Joe Haldeman, and me. There was no topic; it was simply listed as "The Best Panel Ever". They gave us a huge double room, and just about every seat was filled. They also gave us a last-minute panelist, David Zindell; no one knows why, and in truth he was overmatched from the outset. The original three seemed to amuse the audience enough that no one walked out disappointed.

Then I did my annual signing at Larry Smith and Sally Kobee's table, with my annual coterie of belly dancers. This year it was Linda and Juli and two other girls I'd never seen before. Didn't do as much business as usual. Part of it was because they'd already sold out all their copies of my new hardcover, *Stalking the Vampire*, and most of their copies of the new reprint of *Stalking the Unicorn*, and part of it was that the battery was running down on the dancers' boom box and people more than two aisles away didn't know there *was* any belly dancing going on, and hence didn't come by to be enticed into buying books.

We skipped dinner, since the Hugo reception began at 6:00, and they always lay out a spread at these shindigs. As usual each nominee was allowed two guests, but since I was also accepting for Barry Malzberg if he won, I was allowed four, two for me and two for Barry, so I brought four ladies: Carol, Eleanor Wood, Lesley and BJ. It was hot and crowded, but we found a backstage dressing room, invited Toni Weisskopf to join us, and relaxed in splendid isolation on comfortable leather couches until the ceremony started.

Wil McCarthy was a fine Toastmaster, and the ceremony went off without a hitch. (Well, one hitch: I lost another Hugo. So did Barry.)

I ran into Byron Tetrick and a number of his friends, and they joined BJ, Lesley, and a couple of CFGers and me at the Sheraton, where I got those who hadn't been into the SFWA suite and the rest into the Hugo Losers Party. Ace was holding a party, and so was Baen, up on the 22nd floor. As the co-editor of *Jim Baen's Universe* I had to make an appearance. I ran into my co-editor, Eric Flint, who looked as uncomfortable as I felt, and we decided to go over to the Hyatt's all-night coffee bar. Lesley and BJ came with us, and we spent a couple of hours talking. Then they all went back to the Hilton. I made one more trip to the Sheraton, where I talked a little business with Steve Saffel, and where my good friend, rival agent Joshua Bilmas, gave me some information I needed about a gaming offer, and I got back to our room about two hours before the alarm went off at 8:00.

We packed, went down to the lobby, ran into Louise Marley for the first time all weekend, said good-bye to BJ, Lesley, and Kay Kenyon, and took the shuttle to the airport. Going against the clock and changing planes in Dallas, we got home at about nine at night.

Overall memories: I was worried about Carol, who finally began adjusting to the altitude on Saturday. I was delighted to finally meet Lesley, who is a charming lady and a fine writer. I was almost as happy over BJ's first book sale as she was. It was fun to swap banter and barbs with the <shudder!> Female Person From Colorado. I really enjoyed visiting with Bill Schafer and Lou Anders and Toni Weisskopf, my three primary editors these days. And I always love to spend time with Eric Flint; three years ago we had never met, and now we co-edit *Jim Baen's Universe*, we have co-edited four anthologies, we've collaborated on a story that I think may be one of my two or three best-ever collaborations, and we've signed a contract to collaborate on the first book of a proposed trilogy.

It wasn't a big con. Only about 3,660 live bodies. I think part of it was the high airfares, part was surely four-dollar-a-gallon gas, and part of doubtless the number of hotels and poor location of most of them. Still, I enjoyed it, as I always do, and I'm already looking forward to Montreal.

From time to time a convention's program book will ask me to write an appreciation of one of their guests. Invariably, the guest is a good personal friend, and I always oblige. Here's a cross section of them.

Part II

Bios and Appreciations

Beating the Turtle

by Mike Resnick Runyon

So a bunch of us are sitting around, studying the morning line for the Hugos and wondering if Michael the Swan is going to run another two-or-three-horse entry in the sprint and if anyone can make The Female Person From Colorado work up a sweat in the feature race, and then someone says we should just make sure not to bet against Harry the Turtle at any distance, because the man can go short or long and it doesn't seem to make any difference, and that if there is any justice in the world they're going to make him start wearing weights on his typing fingers to bring him back to the field, and even Joey Forever, who is usually astride the favorite, says that you don't want to mess with the Turtle and especially not on Labor Day or Nebula weekend or come to think of it on any bestseller lists.

Now me, I don't know all that much about the Turtle, so I go off and do a little research, and I find that this guy has moves that no one has seen in years, and he has even sold books as Eric Iverson and parlayed that into a $93 million contract with the Philadelphia 76ers although the scribes keep getting his first name wrong and calling him Allen.

This is indeed an interesting guy, this Harry the Turtle, and to find out a little more about him I hunt up Gently Gently Norman, who as everyone knows has never had a bad word to say about anyone and who lives at the corner of Tact and Discretion, and Gently Gently Norman tells me that he thinks Harry the Turtle is a myth, that no one man could write so many outstanding books, and that probably del Rey and Tor have entire stables of Harry the Turtles, this one turning out sure-fire openings, that one coming up with brilliant plots, another one using his prodigious brain to come up with all the right details, and so on down the line, and that there are probably eleven of him but there could be up to fifteen because his books are getting thicker.

It makes sense to me, and the more I think about it the more a question occurs to me, so finally I ask Gently Gently Norman which one of these Harry the Turtles goes home to Laura Frankos at the end of the day, because it's a dead certainty that one of them does, as they have these three wildly talented daughters called Rachel and Rebecca and Alison but who I always think of as The One On The Left and The One On The Right and The One Without An R In Her Name, and Gently Gently Norman just stares at me and finally he says I hate it when people ask me questions like that.

I still need some background before I lay my bets, so I pick up a couple of tip sheets, one put out by Charlie the Beard and one by Andy the Other Beard. One has a definite bias for West Coast tracks, and the other has just as strong a bias for East Coast tracks, and the only thing they agree on is that it doesn't much matter where Harry the Turtle runs, because once he steps onto the track the competition just kind of fades away.

I figure I better check his past performances, so I look at his record, and as far back as it goes he's been a winner, and he's put together some mighty powerful winning streaks nicknamed the Legion and the Great War and the Worldwar, and he set a track record that still stands with *Guns of the South*, and he moved over from dirt to grass and did just as well with *The Case of the Toxic Spell Dump*, and people are still talking about the day he spread-eagled the field to win the gold cup (which looks strangely like a silver rocket ship) with "Down in the Bottomlands," and I figure that sometime somewhere he must have lost a race, had an off day, tripped over his prose or his pedigree, though probably not since the glaciers were still in California or Silver Bobby was a hyperthyroid 4-year-old, whichever came first.

Nobody can do everything well, so I figure maybe the place to beat him is not on the flat but over the jumps, which is a whole different kettle of fish, so I look to see how he's performed there, and wouldn't you know that he won half a dozen Anthology Cups while carrying Sprague the Lyon and Green Rollie on his back.

Long about this time I am figuring that the only serious difference between Harry the Turtle and Superman is that the Turtle isn't allergic to Kryptonite and has a better tailor, so I decide it is time to meet however many of him there are to better judge his quality, and much to my surprise there is only one of him (at least on the day I find him), and he is as friendly and pleasant and brilliant and tall and bearded as everyone says, and he quotes Thucydides and Socrates, who I figure must be his teammates when he is moonlighting on the 76ers, but he is at his most impressive when he quotes Harry the Turtle.

The word on the grapevine is that he is a walking advertisement for evolution in action, and that by the time the dust clears he will not only have a shelf full of Hugos and Nebulas and maybe a Pulitzer or two, but that at least two and maybe all three of his daughters are odds-on morning-line favorites to win the Campbell and write even better books than he does, and as the only other Hugo winner living or dead to sire a Campbell winner I tell him confidentially that his stud fee will triple when that happy event occurs, and far from thanking me he kind of backs away as if I am carrying a sociable disease, and I say to myself, okay, if that's the way you're going to be, I will not rest until I find someone to beat you.

I go through all the tip sheets and I check out all the competition, and after more than a year I am just about willing to concede defeat and admit there is no one around who can compete with Harry the Turtle even if he's giving weight to them (and except for Long John K back East he's been giving inches to all of them for decades), and then, suddenly, out of the blue, I find what I have been desperately looking for. I find a writer who's every bit as good as Harry, and I am ready to put my bankroll on him the next time they meet, and I have contacted Michael the Swan and Joey Forever and the rest of the gang and told them to do the same.

His name's H. N. Turteltaub, and boy, can this guy write!

Nancy Kress—A Class Act

If you work in the science fiction field, there are three certainties: death, taxes, and Nancy Kress.

If you're at all objective, you'd have to agree with me that Nancy is about 87 levels of magnitude preferable to the other two.

If Nancy has ever turned out a mediocre story, it must have been before my time, and since I'm older that she is, I feel confident in stating that it's never happened. What she *has* turned out is a set of books and stories that any writer alive would be proud to call his own. She's the author of one of the greatest novellas ever to grace the field, "Beggars in Spain," which won just about every honor science fiction has to give. To prove it wasn't a fluke, she followed it up with another classic novella, "The Flowers of Aulit Prison." And there are so many others that stick in the memory and refuse to leave: "The Mountain to Mohammed," "The Price of Oranges," "Dancing on Air," "Fault Lines," "Out of All Them Bright Stars," "Trinity"—each a Hugo or Nebula nominee or winner.

Then there are the once and future books: *Beggars in Spain*, *Beggars and Choosers* (also a Hugo nominee), *Probability Space*, *Probability Moon*, *Probability Sun*, *Crossfire*, *Crucible*, *Nothing Human*, and the list goes on.

I'll tell you something else. If you could learn how to write from just one expert, it's a simple and obvious choice: Nancy. I've edited 30-plus anthologies in the past decade, and have bought more first, second and third stories than any three magazine editors you can name, which is a roundabout way of saying that I work with a lot of beginners. The one conclusion I've reached is that if they are firmly grounded in the basics, if they know how to spin a plot, create a believable character, and push a noun up against a verb with some grace, then invariably they are graduates of one of Nancy's workshops. Two of her finest pupils are Nick DiChario and Mark Bourne, but the field is filled with others.

What else can I tell you about Nancy, aside from the fact that she's a brilliant writer and a thoroughly classy lady? She is a fascinating speaker, a charming companion, an elegant dresser, well-read and well-versed in a dozen fields, friendly, approachable, witty, charming, and a credit to her race (human). I'm a better pool player, but we'll save that story for another day.

She also has excellent taste in men, and while it's painful to bring this up so soon after his tragic passing, I would be remiss if I didn't point out that Nancy was married to the late Charles Sheffield, himself a Hugo winner and a wonderful man with a fabulous sense of humor. That she's here at all is more than ample proof of her devotion to the field that she honors by her mere presence. She has been my good friend for a quarter of a century, and if you'll take the time to meet her this weekend, I think she'll become yours as well.

The \<Shudder!\> Female Person from Colorado

You scare kids with stories of the boogeyman. You scare Democrats with talk about tax cuts. You scare Republicans with talk of abortion. You scare publishers with talk of royalty audits.

Stuff like that almost always works—on lesser mortals.

But only one thing in all the world scares me: the \<shudder!\> Female Person From Colorado.

Her name is Connie Willis—I avoid using it whenever possible—and I have lost 103 Hugos to her. (Okay, 87—but it *feels* like 103.)

So what is it (I hear you ask) that is so frightening about her? Why does she terrify me?

Let me count the ways.

1. *The Female Person is into humiliation.* I have 4 Hugos. That's a lifetime's worth, more than I ever dreamed of winning when I started out in this field. It should impress just about anyone. But not the Female Person From Colorado. She has 8, more than anyone in history.

I have a Nebula. Worked like hell to win it. Looked great on my trophy shelf—until I saw her collection of Nebulas. 6 of them. More than anyone in history.

Okay, so I can't out-trophy her. But I've won the *Asimov's* Readers Poll 4 times. That's something worth bragging about. Or it was until I found one that one person in history has won it more often. Guess who?

I have a Locus Award. She has 8. *sigh*

The list goes on and on. It really makes you stop and wonder: just how greedy can one woman get?

2. *She's a sadist, minus the whips and leather.* You think not? Ask any writer who has ever been nominated for a Hugo or Nebula when the wildly-popular Female Person From Colorado is the presenter. She not only gets the audience laughing hysterically with her endless presentations, but despite the tension, despite the importance to careers and to the accumulation of groupies, despite everything, she even gets the *nominees* laughing. Talk about cruelty.

(So why do we put up with it? I mean, besides the fact that she's so funny you'd *pay* to see her on a stage? The answer is simple: if you are a nominee and she is the presenter, the odds are 1-in-5 that she will present you with a major award. Whereas if you are both nominees, the odds are about 200-to-1 that she'll beat you without drawing a deep breath.)

3. *She made a fool out of Andy Warhol.* How does one do that? Easy. For decades we've all been quoting Warhol to the effect that everyone deserved 15 minutes of fame. Well, *Locus* just voted her the Best Author of the 1990s. Do you know how many 15 minuteses go into a decade? Pull out your calculator and do the math.

So much for Andy Warhol.

4. *She never repeats herself.* No 7-book trilogies for her. The only thing *Lincoln's Dreams, Doomsday Book,* and *To Say Nothing of the Dog* have in common is that the author's name is Connie Willis. (Uh . . . check that. They have one other thing in common: they all won major awards. Huge surprise, right?)

5. *She is impossible to imitate.* Not only is her felicity of expression totally unique, but so is her choice of subject matter and her approach to it. Who else could turn a screwball comedy about subatomic particles into a Nebula winner (see "At the Rialto")? Who but the Female Person From Colorado could turn a story about menstrual cycles into an hilarious Hugo and Nebula winner (see "Even the Queen," a story Gardner Dozois has dubbed her "period piece")?

6. *She's fickle.* All she ever wanted in life was Harrison Ford. Until he got divorced. Now she doesn't want him anymore. (I hear on the grapevine that she's transferred her affections to Cheech Spazio, who plays the fire hydrant in *Porky's XVII.*)

7. *She appropriates other people's religions.* She tells me that she is currently writing *All Clear,* a novel about the London Blintz. Hey, do *I* write novels about the Paris Pork Chops?

(Okay, so I'll buy it anyway. And probably nominate it. And vote for it. *sigh*)

And now we come to the really serious stuff:

8. *She is thinner than I am.*

9. *She has more hair than I do.*

10. *She's nicer than I am.*

11. *She's younger than I am.*

12. *She works harder than I do.*

And my fondest wish is that she wasn't so all-fired sweet and charming and friendly, and that I didn't like her so much, so I could hate her (just a little bit) on Labor Day weekends.

The Female Person in Verse

A Bibliographic History
by Mike Wadsworth Resnick

The Female Person is charming and sweet,
And it is a joy to be near her—
Until they open the envelope.
And then, to a man, we all fear her.

1982 (Nebula)
"She isn't serious enough!"
But it was a bum rap.
A Letter from the Clearys
Soon put her on the map.

1982 (Hugo, Nebula)
"What time is it?" I ask of her.
She stops and answers, with a grin:
"I'll check it on my Fire Watch."
(I hate the way she rubs it in.)

1988 (Hugo, Nebula)
The Last of the Winnebagos
Was not the last of her awards,
For she was writing Lincolns
While we were writing Fords.

1989 (Nebula)
At the Rialto—wasn't it fun?
Told in a way that hadn't been done:
Quantum mechanics, Hollywood plot—
And another award to sweeten the pot.

1992 (Hugo, Nebula)
Take a good look at Even the Queen—
The funniest prize winner you've ever seen.
Giggle and laugh, and smile without cease—
At The Female Person's period piece.

1992 (Hugo, Nebula)
The Doomsday Book spelled doomsday
To every hopeful pro.
It swept the boards of the awards
(I could have told you so.)

1994 (Hugo)
It really, truly raised my bile
When Connie wrote Death on the Nile.
My dreams of glory vanished when
I lost the Hugo to her again.

1997 (Hugo)
Her rivals got discouraged when
The Female Person won again:
The Soul Selects Her Own Society—
Told with grace and wit and piety.

1999 (Hugo)
To Say Nothing of the Dog,
Mighty fine and mighty funny—
Brought her fame and brought her prizes,
To say nothing of the money.

2000 (Hugo)
Another year, another prize—
This time The Winds of Marble Arch.
Her competition learns to walk
The literary Bataan March

2006 (Hugo)
We all were primed at LACon
An eager, upbeat, anxious mob.
The emcee never wins, of course—
'Til Connie pulled an Inside Job

I've lost two hundred Hugos
(And all but three to her)
The titles of her winners
Have fast become a blur
I really ought to hate her,
I ought to make her pay,
I really should . . . but what the hell—
I love her anyway.

Rosy and the Guy
She Lives With

I don't hate Guy Lillian because he lives in New Orleans and I don't.

I don't hate Guy Lillian because he's an (ugh) lawyer. Well, not entirely, anyway.

I don't even hate Guy Lillian because as a fan, a writer, an editor, and a human being he has talent and enthusiasm to burn and makes the rest of us feel unaccomplished and lazy by comparison.

No, I hate Guy Lillian because he convinced Rosy to marry him rather than become an Official Mike Resnick Auxiliary Wife.

Now, before he did that, he did a lot of Good Things, and he's done even more since then. He's been around since the glaciers were still in California, as a letterhack, then a fan, then (and still) a brilliant fan writer, and finally as the editor of *Challenger*, an annual Hugo nominee which has three less Hugos than I truly feel it deserves. Along the way he's been a member of FAPA, SAPS, NOSFA, SFPA and LASFAPA, none of which I can spell, and is the recipient of DeepSouthCon's coveted Rebel Award.

Guy claims that we have been friends for more than 30 years, which as everyone knows is quite impossible because I am only 23. I don't remember quite where I first met him—probably at a Worldcon, possibly in New Orleans—but we've been meeting ever since, and enjoying the hell out of it. I even offered him our guest room one night a couple of years ago when his flight from New York to New Orleans landed in Cincinnati to wait out a terrible storm (he *hates* flying, even in good weather) and helped him find a Greyhound bus to the French Quarter the next morning on the not-unreasonable assumption that the Quarter couldn't survive too long without him.

Whenever I'm the Toastmaster at a convention and doing my expected Toastmaster gig, I always try to pick out the biggest pro and the biggest fan in the audience and make them the butts of most of my jokes. The only time anyone ever objected was when a little old lady fan—(I think that should be one word: littleoldladyfan, kind of like femmefan only older)—came up to me at a DeepSouthCon to complain that I was picking on poor old Guy. I hadn't thought I'd been all that harsh on him, but I told her that if he agreed with her I would certainly apologize . . . but poor old Guy, who has that rare ability to laugh at himself, was laughing so hard that she couldn't get a cogent response out of him, let alone an injured protest.

When it came time to publish *Once A Fan . . .*, a collection of my fannish writings, there was only one person I considered asking to write the introduction. It was Guy Lillian, and it was probably the best thing in the book.

I want you to understand that all of the above is secondary to one special talent of Guy's. He's got a memory like an elephant—notice that I am too polite to suggest that he has a face to match—and he remembered meeting science fiction writer Joe Green's daughter Rosy at the 1977 DeepSouthCon. He remembered meeting her at the 1986 Worldcon, too. It wasn't too long before he was remembering meeting her in all of his dreams and most of his waking thoughts, and before he had a chance to forget, he got engaged to her at the 2000 Worldcon in Chicago and married her on June 20, 2001, not coincidentally the day she broke my heart. She is well on her way to a doctorate in Communications, but she has yet to communicate how she could possibly have chosen Guy over ***me***.

Her brilliance is unquestioned. So, after one glimpse at her, is her beauty. And more to the point, it should be noted that Rosy isn't merely an appendage to Guy, any more than she was to Joe. She's her own woman (which is a pity of cosmic proportions, since she could have been *my* own woman instead), and along with her academic achievements she is the winner of DeepSouthCon's Rubble Award (which is just like the Rebel Award, only different), and, with Guy, recently represented American fandom on a trip to Australia as this year's DUFF winners. It is also a fact that *Challenger* didn't start making the Hugo ballot until Rosy hooked up with Guy and taught him everything she knows (well, 6.37%, anyway) about science fiction and fandom.

What do I really think of the Lillians?

I think that Carol and I are incredibly lucky to count them among our friends. Spend a little time with them this weekend and I'm sure you'll come away feeling exactly the same.

An Appreciation of Tony Lewis

When I was asked to write this appreciation of Tony Lewis, my first thought was: "So they couldn't find a single person in NESFA or MITSFS to say anything nice about him."

My second thought was: "Hardly surprising."

My third thought was: "I have won four Hugos for my fiction. I am a professional liar of considerable skill. When all is said and done, who is better suited to say nice things about Tony Lewis?"

I didn't have any other thoughts until I reluctantly agreed to write this, and that thought was directed at God, and went something like: "Okay, Pal, I'm doing it, but You owe me big time."

So, where to begin?

I've known Tony for about a third of a century. Except for the fact that his beard's a little grayer, he hasn't really changed in all that time. Not even his socks, and I've been meaning to speak to him about it.

He chaired one of the very best Worldcons I've attended, and I've attended a *lot* of them. His legion of workers did everything he asked of them, and did it right. Some have suggested that this is because of his demonstrably brilliant leadership qualities. Me, I figure it's because they couldn't stand to be in his presence, and the best way to avoid endless meetings with him was to do everything right the first time.

He became addicted to working at conventions. I have a difficult time remembering any regional con or Worldcon where Tony wasn't on the staff. Some say it's because he's an altruistic fan with a heart as big as all outdoors. Me, I say it's because he's a greedy sonuvabitch who likes to collect ribbons, and I figure he does such a bang-up job because if he doesn't he won't get asked back and that'll be the end of his ribbon collection.

Somewhere along the way he gently suggested to me (my neck still bears the fingerprints) that he was a fine writer only nobody knew it yet. So I figured, what the hell, I'll buy a story from him for one of my anthologies, and he'll be so humiliated by the reaction to it that he'll never nag me again. (Well, I was half right: he's never nagged me again—but that's because his stories have been so well-received that *I* nag him these days. Look into those dull, lackluster eyes and you'd never imagine the wit and felicity of expression that lurks somewhere behind them.)

He's also an editor of note. And of books, too. He's compiled a number of annual magazine indices, he's edited a Worldcon program book, he's edited some of those wonderful NESFA books that seem to appear with amazing regularity, and he even co-edited *The Passage of the Light* with me. (I tell people that his primary contribution was stuffing and addressing the envelope, but actually he licked the stamps, too. And wrote a brilliant essay on Recursive Science Fiction, a term he gave birth to [Caesarian, as I recall] some years ago.)

And of course he publishes and edits his own fanzine, *Along Alpha Ralpha Boulevard*, and contributes to many others.

The man is a two-time Hugo nominee, which really rankles when you consider that neither H. G. Wells nor Mary Shelly were ever nominated for Hugos.

Always willing to humiliate himself in public, Tony has appeared in "The Decomposers" and "Rivets Redux," a pair of Boskone musicals. I have the videotapes, and use them to blackmail him whenever I'm short of rent money.

And then there's Suford. I'm told he married her when her hair was only 63 inches long, though personally I don't believe her hair was *ever* that short. I have to admit they make a nice pair, though I've explained to her over and over that she'd be much better off leaving him and applying for the position of Mike Resnick Auxiliary Wife.

Together, they produced their own first edition, yclept Alice. Tony had been regaling me with Alice stories for as long as there have been Alice stories to tell. Whenever he starts, I threaten to tell him Laura stories if he doesn't stop. He claims that he's happy to hear them all if I'll listen to all his Alice stories. Right about then I remark that I'm late for my plane home, and then I spend the next three days hiding at the airport until the con is over.

It's hard to believe that with all these accomplishments, he also has a Ph.D. That's right; he's actually Doctor Lewis. Of course, he doesn't call himself that any more, ever since the cops found him examining nubile young women without telling them exactly what kind of a doctor he was.

So there you have the life of Tony Lewis—fan, Worldcon chair, con worker, pro writer, pro editor, fanzine publisher, fan writer, Ph.D., husband, father, musical actor, Hugo nominee.

All that's on the one hand. On the other is that he never played third base for the Red Sox, he never ran for the U.S. Senate from Massachusetts, he never set foot on the Moon, and (worst of all) he never once asked for my autograph.

Balance the two, and what you get is a life that we in the trade call a fully-realized diminished expectation.

But I guess if he keeps paying me to be his friend, I'll let him stick around for another 30 or 40 years.

Eric Flint

Eric Flint just came down to Cincinnati for his very first Midwestcon. (It was Cincinnati's 58th, but who's counting?) While he was here, he stopped by my house. And while he was at my house, he smoked 1,421 cigarettes. (He claims he only had 1,418.) When he finally gives up the habit, three tobacco executives are going to slit their wrists.

Eric and I hit it off the moment we met. His very first words were, "You, sir, are unquestionably the finest writer alive." (Well, actually, what he said was: "Resnick . . . Resnick . . . didn't you used to play third base for the old St. Looie Browns?" But I knew what he meant.)

Eric, for those of you who have been living on some other planet, is just about the busiest writer and editor around. He broke into print late in life—he was busy overthrowing governments in his youth and middle age—but he made up for lost time. His first science fiction novel appeared in 1997, and now, a decade later, he's had his name on something like 50 science fiction books—novels, collaborations, anthologies— with more in press. And Eric believes in giving the reader his money's worth; ain't no thin 60,000-worders in that batch.

Now, you have to figure that 50 fat books, all laden with quality, is a couple of lifetimes' output, rather than a mere decade's. And with normal writer/editors you'd be right, but there's not much normal about my pal Eric (and I say that in an almost nice way). You see, along with all those books, he's the Editor-in-Chief of *Jim Baen's Universe*, the thickest and highest-paying magazine in the field. In his very first year he bought a Hugo nominee—modesty forbids me from telling you who wrote it—and if there is any justice in the world, he's going to start appearing regularly on the Best Editor ballot.

So when does he sleep?

Beats the hell out of me. Because in addition to all the above, he also publishes the *Grantville Gazette*. (You haven't heard of it? Then you don't know that it's paying professional rates. Out of Eric's own pocket. That alone was enough for me to edit three really neat insults out of this piece.)

And lest you think that Eric's a reincarnation of those pulp hacks who ground out a totally forgettable book every couple of weeks back in the 1930s and 1940s, pick up and read some of his novels. Start with *1632*. You'll have a lot of company; damned near a million other people have picked it up, and keep picking up the sequels. Far be it for me to say anything nice about him, but putting down an Eric Flint book before you finish it is, oh, I don't know, kind of like looking at Pamela

Anderson from the neck up. Not impossible, but difficult, foolhardy, and counter-productive.

Eric likes to collaborate. He's collaborated with all of what I call the Baeniacs—David Drake, John Ringo, Mercedes Lackey, David Weber, and that whole crowd. He'll be collaborating with me on a short story this summer, and on a novel later in the year, which will be a real trick: I'm right, he's left; I write short, he writes long; I like first person, he likes third person; I'm a chick magnet, he likes third person . . .

We've been working together as editors of *Jim Baen's Universe* for about 8 months now, and have yet to have a disagreement. I am constantly amazed that two people with such different backgrounds can see eye-to-eye on damned near everything concerning the magazine, and I suspect collaborating with him will be just as easy.

Because along with being left, writing long, and liking third person, Eric Flint is not only a fine writer and a fine editor, but is one of science fiction's very few Class Acts. I'm proud to call him my friend, and once you get to visit with him, I'm betting that you'll feel exactly the same.

One of the ways I thank fandom for all the love and support it has given me is to write, *gratis*, for some of the fanzines. It's fun, it keeps me in touch with my friends and my readers, and it's a way of paying my fannish dues. I appear in some fanzines regularly, some occasionally, some infrequently. One of the things I like about writing for the fanzines is that I'm usually given carte blanche to write about anything I want, as you'll see from the variety of articles in this section, ranging from my special interests (musical theatre, collie shows, etc.) to parody reviews of my own world to criticism of Hollywood to a remembrance of Third World bathrooms.

Part III

Articles

Why Carol Won't Sit
Next to Me at
Science Fiction Movies

Carol has a high threshold for embarrassment. You can't be married to me for 42 years and *not* have one. But recently she has announced that she will no longer sit next to me at science fiction movies, that indeed she will sit on the far side of the theater and do her very best to pretend that she doesn't know me.

She's right. I'm just not much fun to be around at science fiction movies. I don't know quite how this came about. I used to love them when I was growing up. I forgave them their lack of special effects and their B-movie casts and budgets. OK, so *Them* paid no attention to the square-cube law; except for that, it was as well-handled as one could possibly want. And maybe *The Thing* wasn't quite what John Campbell had in mind when he wrote "Who Goes There?", but it was treated like science fiction rather than horror (the same cannot be said for the big-budget remake), and the overall ambience was rational. As for *Forbidden Planet*, nothing I've seen in the last 50 years has stirred my sense of wonder quite as much as Walter Pidgeon's guided tour of the wonders of the Krell. A decade and a half later Stanley Kubrick made a trio of wildly differing but excellent science fiction movies—*Dr. Strangelove, 2001: A Space Odyssey*, and *A Clockwork Orange*—each of which treated the field with respect.

Then, just about the time I became a full-time science fiction writer, Hollywood started turning out one intellectually insulting science fiction movie after another. I mean, these things were almost dumber than network television shows. And I started muttering—louder and louder with each movie, Carol assures me—things like "No editor paying 3 cents a word for the most debased science fiction magazine in the world would let *me* get away with that!" Before long audiences would pay more attention to my rantings than to the movies.

I keep hearing that science fiction movies are getting better, that once George Lucas showed what could be done on the big screen we no longer have anything to be ashamed of when comparing ourselves to other genres.

That makes me mutter even louder.

So let me get it off my chest, which is a figure of speech, because actually the stupidity of science fiction movies is much more likely to eat a hole in my stomach lining.

And let me add a pair of stipulations:

First, I'm only interested in movies that aspired to be arch-bishop, which is to say, movies with major budgets and major talent that really and truly meant to be good movies. I will not consider such epics as *Space Sluts in the Slammer* (yes, it really exists), as it seems not unreasonable to assume it was never meant to be a contender for the year-end awards.

Second, when I speak of stupidities, I'm not talking about the nit-picking that goes on in outraged letter columns. If the math or science are wrong only in areas that scientists, mathematicians, or obsessive science fiction fans would find fault with, I'll ignore it. If George Lucas doesn't know what a parsec is, or Gene Roddenbury and his successors think you can hear a ship whiz by in space, I'm willing to forgive and forget.

So what's left?

Well, let's start with *Star Wars*. First, has no one except me noticed that it's not pro-democracy but pro-royalty? I mean, all this fighting to depose the Emperor isn't done to give the man on the street (or the planet) a vote; it's to put Princess Leia on the throne and let *her* rule the galaxy instead of him, which is an improvement only in matter of degree. And it drives me crazy that in 1991 we could put a smart bomb down a chimney, and that in 2002 we could hit a target at 450 miles, but that computerized handguns and other weaponry can't hit a Skywalker or a Solo at 25 paces.

Return of the Jedi? Doesn't it bother anyone else that Adolf Hitler— excuse me; Darth Vader—the slaughterer of a couple of hundred million innocent men and women, becomes a Good Guy solely because he's Luke's father?

And what could be sillier than that final scene, where Luke looks up and sees Yoda and the shades of Darth Vader and Obiwan Kenobi smiling at him. That was too much even for Carol, whose first comment on leaving the theater was, "Poor Luke! Wherever he goes from now on, he's a table for four."

Then along came *E.T.*, which, for a few years at least, was the highest-grossing film of all time, until replaced by an even dumber one.

You think it wasn't that intellectually insulting? Let's consider the plot of that billion-dollar grosser, shall we?

1. If E.T. can fly/teleport, why doesn't he do so at the beginning of the film, when he's about to be left behind? (Answer: because this is what James Blish used to call an idiot plot, which is to say if everyone doesn't act like an idiot you've got no story.)

2. What mother of teenaged children walks through a kitchen littered with empty beer cans and doesn't notice them? (Answer: in all the world, probably only this one.) This is the blunder that started me muttering loud enough to disturb other moviegoers for the first time.

3. While we're on the subject of the mother and the kitchen, what is a woman with an unexceptional day job doing living in an $900,000 house in one of the posher parts of the Los Angeles area? (Even I don't have an answer to that.)

4. Why does E.T. die? (Answer: so he can come back to life.)

5. Why does E.T. un-die? (Still awaiting an answer, even a silly one, for this.)

6. When E.T. finally calls home, the lights in the room don't even flicker. I'm no scientist, but I'd have figured the power required would have shorted out the whole city.

Cheap shots, Resnick (I hear you say); you're purposely avoiding the films that were aimed at an adult audience, films like *Blade Runner* and *Signs*, for example.

All right. Let's take *Blade Runner* (and someone please explain the title, since I never saw a blade or a runner in the whole damned movie). Great future Los Angeles; it really put you there. Nice enough acting jobs, even if Harrison Ford was a little wooden. Wonderful sets, costumes, effects.

But the premise is dumber than dirt. We are told up front that the androids are going to expire in two weeks—so why in the world is Harrison Ford risking his life to hunt them down when he could just go fishing for 14 days and then pick up their lifeless bodies?

But that premise looks positively brilliant compared to the critically-acclaimed Mel Gibson movie *Signs*, which grossed about half a billion dollars worldwide two short years ago.

Consider: would *you* travel 50 trillion miles or so for a little snack? That's what the aliens did. If they're here for any other reason except to eat people, the film never says so.

OK, let's leave aside how much they're paying in terms of time and energy to come all this way just to eat us for lunch. What is the one thing we know will kill them? Water (which also killed the Wicked Witch of the West, a comparison that was not lost on some perceptive viewers). And what are human beings composed of? More than 90% water.

So the aliens come all this way to poison themselves (and then forget to die until someone hits them with a baseball bat, which Hollywood thinks is almost as devastating a weapon against aliens of indeterminate physical abilities as a light-sabre.)

By now I didn't just mutter in the theater, I yelled at the screen-writers (who, being 3000 miles away, probably didn't hear me.) But I figured my vocalizing would soon come to an end. After all, we all knew that the sequel to *The Matrix* would show the world what real science fiction was like; it was the most awaited movie since Lucas' all-but-unwatchable sequels to the original Star Wars trilogy.

So along comes *The Matrix Retarded* . . . uh, sorry, make that *Reloaded.* You've got this hero, Neo, with godlike powers. He can fly as fast and far as Superman. He can stop a hail of bullets or even bombs, in mid-flight just by holding up his hand. He's really remarkable, even if he never changes expression.

So does he fly out of harm's way when a hundred Agent Smiths attack him? Of course not. Does he hold up his hand and freeze them in mid-charge? Of course not. Can Neo be hurt? No. Can Agent Smith be hurt? No. So why do they constantly indulge in all these easily avoid-able, redundant, and incredibly stoopid fights?

Later the creator of the Matrix explains that the first Matrix was perfect. It only had three or four flaws, which is why he built five more versions of it. Uh . . . excuse me, but that's not that way *my* dictionary defines "perfect."

You want more foolishness? The whole world runs on computers, which means the whole world is powered by electricity to a far greater extent than America is at this moment. So why is the underground city lit only by burning torches?

I hit J above high C explaining to the screen what the least compe-tent science fiction editor in the world would say to the writer who tried to pawn *The Matrix Reloaded* off on him.

Now, you'd figure Stephen Spielberg could make a good science fiction movie, wouldn't you? I mean, he's the most powerful director in Hollywood's history. Surely if he wanted to spend a few million dol-lars correcting flaws in the film before releasing it to the public, no one would dare say him nay.

So he makes *Minority Report*, and to insure the box office receipts he gets Tom Cruise to star in it and announces that it's based on a Philip K. Dick story. (Dick is currently Hollywood's favorite flavor of "sci-fi" writer, this in spite of the fact that nothing adapted from his work bears more than a passing resemblance to it.)

And what do we get for all this clout?

Well, for starters, we get a future less than half a century from now in which the Supreme Court has no objection to throwing people in jail for *planning* crimes.

We get a scene where Tom Cruise escapes from the authorities by climbing into a car that's coming off an assembly line and driving off in it. That one really got me muttering at a hundred-decibel level. Has *anyone* ever seen a car come off an assembly line with a full tank of gas?

We are told that the three seers/mutants/whatever-they-are can only foresee capital crimes. Even bank robberies slip beneath their psychic radar. But in a crucial scene, one of them foresees a necessary rainstorm. (I hit 120 decibels on that one.)

It's also explained that they have physical limits. If they're in Washington, D.C., they can't foresee a crime in, say, Wilmington, Delaware. But the villain of the piece, who knows their abilities and limitations better than anyone, plans to use them to control the entire nation, which the last time I looked at a map extends even beyond Delaware. (140 decibels that time.)

OK, I'm too serious. These are just entertainments. I should go see one made from a comic book—Hollywood's intellectual Source Material Of Choice these days—and just sit back and enjoy it.

Good advice. So we went to see *Hulk*. You all know the story; it's swiped from enough science fictional sources. I didn't mind the poor animation. I didn't mind the idiot plot that had Bruce Banner's father responsible for his affliction. I didn't mind this; I didn't mind that. Then we came to Thunderbolt Ross, the 5-star general—and suddenly I was muttering again.

I was willing suspend my disbelief for this idiocy, but alas, I couldn't suspend my common sense. Here's this top military commander, the film's equivalent of Norman Shwartzkopf or Tommy Franks. And here's the Hulk, who makes Superman look like a wimp. Now, you have to figure that even a moderately bright 6-year-old ought to be able to conclude that if attacking the Hulk and shooting him doesn't hurt him, but just makes him bigger and stronger and angrier and more destructive, the very last thing you want to do when he's busy being the Hulk rather than Bruce Banner is shoot or otherwise annoy him, rather than simply wait for him to change back into his relatively helpless human form. That, however, seems to be beyond both our general and our screenwriters.

Even the good science fiction movies assume that their audiences are so dumb that logic means nothing to them, as long as you dazzle them with action and zap guns and aliens and the like.

Take *The Road Warrior* (a/k/a *Mad Max 2*), which is truly a fine movie: well-acted, well-conceived, well-directed. And yet . . .

In *The Road Warrior's* post-nuclear-war future, the rarest and most valuable commodity in the world is refined oil (i.e., gasoline), because the distances in Australia, where it takes place, are immense, and you can't get around without a car or a motorcycle. The conflict takes place between the Good Guys, who have built a primitive fortress around a refining plant, and the Bad Guys, a bunch of futuristic bikers, who want to get their hands on that gasoline, which is so rare that it's probably worth more per drop than water in the desert.

So what do the bad guys who desperately need this petrol do? They power up their cars and bikes and race around the refinery for hours on end, day in and day out. If they would have the brains to conserve a little of that wasted energy, they wouldn't have to risk their lives trying to replace it. (And, while I'm thinking of it, where do they get the fuel to power their dozens of constantly-running vehicles?)

Then there were Spielberg's mega-grossing dinosaur movies, *Jurassic Park* and *The Lost World*. The former hypothesizes that if you stand perfectly still six inches from a hungry Tyrannosaurus Rex he won't be able to tell you're there. I would like to see the screenwriter try that stunt with any hungry carnivore—mammal or reptile—that has ever lived on this planet. The latter film shows you in graphic detail (and with questionable intelligence) that a T. Rex can outrun an elevated train, but cannot catch a bunch of panicky Japanese tourists who are running away, on foot, in a straight line.

Although these two films are the prime offenders, simply because Speilberg has the resources to know better, I am deathly tired of the superhuman (uh . . . make that supercarnosaur) feats with which Hollywood endows T. Rex, who seems to be the only terrifying dinosaur of which it was aware until someone told Spielberg about velociraptors. (Give them another decade or two and they might actually discover allosaurs and Utahraptors.)

T. Rex weighed about seven tons. By comparison, a large African bull elephant weighs about six tons, and could probably give old T. Rex one hell of a battle. But no one suggests that a six-ton elephant can throw trucks and trains around, break down concrete walls, or do any of the other patently ridiculous things T. Rex can do on screen.

And the list—and the intellectually offended muttering— goes on and on. In *Alien* they all go off by themselves to search for the creature; haven't they learned *anything* from five centuries of dumb horror movies? At the end of *Total Recall*, Governor Schwarzenegger is outside for maybe six minutes while Mars is being miraculously terraformed. Just how long do you think *you* could survive on the surface of Mars in 100-below-zero weather with absolutely no oxygen to breathe?

Some "major" films are simply beneath contempt. I persist in thinking that *Starship Troopers* was misnamed; it should have been *Ken and Barbie Go To War*. And if that wasn't a bad enough trick to pull on Robert A. Heinlein after he was dead, they also made *The Puppet Masters*, which was handled exactly like a 4th remake of *Invasion of the Body Snatchers*.

Then there's *Armageddon*, which seems to make the case that it's easier to teach hard-drinking functionally illiterate wildcatters how to be astronauts in a constricted time period than to teach highly intelligent physically fit astronauts how to drill for oil. And Ghod help us, it was Disney's highest-grossing live action film until *Pirates of the Caribbean* came along.

And when I was sure it couldn't get any worse, along came the stupidest big-budget film of all time—*The League of Extraordinary Gentlemen*.

Consider:

1. Alan Quatermain can hit a moving target at 900 yards in the year 1899 A.D. With a rifle of that era.

2. Bruce Banner—excuse me: Dr. Jeckyl—changes into the Hulk—oops: make that Mr. Hyde—and suddenly he's 15 feet tall and even his muscles have muscles. He's a bad guy—except when, at the end, the plot requires him to be a good guy and rescue all the other good guys at enormous personal cost, which he does for no rational reason that I could discern.

3. Mina Harker is a vampire. She's Jonathan Harker's wife, and Jonathan, as you'll remember, is the guy who visits Dracula and sells him an English estate. (I always felt Dracula shouldn't have stopped terrifying realtors with just one, but let it pass.) Well, Mina is a Good Guy, and certainly, given her physical features, a more Extraordinary Gentleman than any of the others. She can fly (Dracula couldn't), she can cross over water (movie vampires can't), and she can command a combat team (honest) of half a million bats. She also drinks blood, but only of Bad Guys.

4. The Invisible Man joins the team. Well, no one reads H. G. Wells any more, so they announced that the original Invisible Man was dead and this cockney guy has replaced him. He spends most of his time being invisible in sub-zero weather, occasionally mentioning that it's chilly without his clothes on, but he never gets dressed or goes inside.

5. Dorian Gray. Well, he's got this picture, see? Oh, and he can't be harmed. Cut him, shoot him, and two seconds later he's whole, un-harmed and unmarked. But if he should ever *see* his picture, he turns im-mediately and gruesomely and eternally to dust. Funniest action scene in the picture is a fight to the death (honest!) between Dorian Gray, who literally cannot be harmed or killed, and Mina Harker, who is *already* dead.

6. Captain Nemo is a bearded Indian who is a master of karate.

7. The only Victorian figure missing is Sherlock Holmes, so of course the youngish villain turns out to be Moriarty (who Sherlock killed when he was an aging professor a few years before 1899.)

8. And, oh yeah, there's an American secret agent named Tom Sawyer, who's about 22 years old—a really neat trick since he was a teenager before the Civil War.

I think it's nice that the screenwriter brought back all these Victorian and pre-Victorian characters. It would have been even nicer if he'd ever read a single book in which they appeared.

How do they travel? In a half-mile-long 20-foot-wide version of the Nautilus. (And as this 2500-foot-long ship is going through the canals of Venice, even Carol couldn't help wondering how it turned the corners.)

There is a convertible car. (After all, this is 1899. They hadn't invented hardtops yet.) Alan Quatermain and two other Extraordinary Gentlemen have to drive down the broad paved boulevards (broad paved boulevards???) of Venice. There are 200 Bad Guys on the roofs on both sides of the street, all armed with automatic weapons. They fire 18,342 shots at the car—and miss. Alan Quartermain and his ancient rifle don't miss a target for the entire and seemingly endless duration of the film.

What are the Extraordinary Gentlemen doing? They're stopping Moriarty from getting rich by selling weapons to rival European nations. And where is he getting these weapons? Easy. He has built a two-mile-square fortified brick city/fortress in the middle of an ice-covered Asian mountain range, and filled it with thousands of machines capable of creating really nasty weapons. I figure the cost of creating the city, shipping in the tons of iron he has to melt to make weapons, and building/importing the thousands of machines required to build the weapons, set him back about $17 trillion. But he's going to make $200 million or so selling weapons, so he's in profit. Isn't he???

Every single aspect of the film is on this level. Nairobi consisted of two—count them: two—tin-roofed shacks in 1899, but in the movie it's a city. And it's a city in clear sight of Kilimanjaro—which is passing strange, because every time I've been there it's a 2-hour drive just to see Kilimanjaro in the distance. Quatermain lives in a place which I suppose is meant to be the Norfolk Hotel, but looks exactly like an anti-Bellum Southern mansion, complete with liveried black servants who speak better English than Sean Connery (who plays Quatermain and will be decades living it down).

It's mentioned a few times that Alan Quatermain can't die, that a witch doctor has promised him eternal life. In the end he dies, and despite his having repeated this story about the witch doctor *ad nauseum,* the remaining Extraordinary Gentlefolk take his body—unembalmed, I presume—all the way from the Asian mountains to East Africa and bury him there, place his rifle on the grave, and walk away. Then the witch doctor shows up, does a little buck-and-wing and a little scat-singing, and the rifle starts shaking as if something's trying to get out of the grave. End of film. My only thought was: "It's the writer, and they didn't bury him deep enough."

OK, I've really got to calm down. I'm starting to hyperventilate as I write this.

(Pause. Take a deep breath. Think of flowers swaying in a gentle breeze. Pretend they are not about to be trampled by a 45-ton Tyrannosaur that has just eaten a *homo erectus* that looks exactly like Raquel Welch, make-up and wonder bra included. Return to keyboard.)

I prefer science fiction to fantasy both as a writer and a reader. I prefer the art of the possible to the impossible, the story that obeys the rules of the universe (as we currently know them, anyway) to the story that purposely breaks them all.

And yet . . . and yet, for some reason that eludes me, Hollywood, which seems unable to make a good science fiction movie to save its soul (always assuming it has one, an assumption based on absolutely no empirical evidence), has made a number of wonderful fantasy movies that are not intellectually offensive and do not cheat on their internal logic: *Field of Dreams, Harvey, The Wonderful Ice Cream Suit, The Devil and Daniel Webster, Portrait of Jennie*, even *The Wizard of Oz* and the Harry Potter films (well, the first one, anyway).

No, this is not blanket praise for all fantasy films. As I was walking out of *The Two Towers* I complained to Carol that I'd just wasted three hours watching what amounted to spring training for the *real* war in the next film. And about three hours into *The Return of the King*, as I was watching the 20th or 25th generic battle between faceless armies that I didn't care about, I had this almost-unbearable urge to find an usher and say, "Let my people go!"

But for the most part, I find that fantasy movies don't raise my bile the way science fiction movies do. How can big-budget science fiction films be so ambitious and so dumb at the same time, so filled with errors that no editor I've ever encountered (and that's a lot of editors, including some incredibly lax ones) would let me get away with?

Uh . . . Carol just stopped by. She said she heard me muttering and cursing and wondered what the problem was. I invited her to read a bit of this article over my shoulder.

Sigh Now she says she won't sit in the same room with me when I'm writing about science fiction movies.

Van Helsing Review

Just saw *Van Helsing*. I have to preface this by saying I thought Stephen Sommers' *The Mummy* was a better film than any of the Indiana Jones films, and that the sequel, though flawed, was at least enjoyable.

This one isn't quite as dumb or as bad as *The League of Extraordinary Gentlemen*, but it comes mighty close. An hour into it Carol, who never leaves a film or a play, turned to me and whispered that she was ready to walk out if I was. I couldn't believe it wouldn't get better, so we stayed. I was wrong. It got worse.

The culprit—well, there are a lot of culprits—but the major culprit is the ability of CGI to put anything on a screen that you can imagine—and lately, movies have been substituting it for character development and rational plots. Just stick a werewolf on the screen battling a vampire and no one will care that it's dumber than dirt, right? (For example, the hero was left on the doorstep of an Italian church when still a baby, presumably centuries ago—so why is he Van Helsing instead of Luciano? And for that matter, why is he still alive and why, at age 400+, does he look like Hugh Jackman?)

The CGI effects in this film are remarkable—but they are overused beyond belief. One vampire might, under the right circumstances, be interesting; 8,000 of them are not. A hero fighting one supernatural being might, under the right circumstances, be interesting. A hero who has something like 25 encounters with them, each more grotesque than the last, in a little over 2 hours, is not.

If you saw *The Mummy*, which is not, I freely admit, *Lawrence of Arabia* or even *The Maltese Falcon*, you know more about the hero, the heroine, the heroine's brother, the mummy, the smarmy little bad guy, and the 3 Americans than you know about *any* character in *Van Helsing*, including Van Helsing himself.

And the film swipes from *everywhere*. These are not so much homages as a total lack of creativity. From Universal, we get Dracula, the Wolf Man, and Frankenstein's monster (which is, of course, called "Frankenstein" throughout the film except for the first 5 minutes); from *The Stepford Wives*, we get three lady vampires—a blonde, a redhead, and a brunette; from *The Good, the Bad, and the Ugly*, we get Tuco's great line—rather bolluxed here—about "If you have to shoot, shoot—don't talk"; from *The League of Extraordinary Gentlemen* we get a Mr. Hyde who looks like The Hulk but without the green skin (and does anyone currently working in Hollywood remember that Spencer Tracy played him with no makeup?); and cetera.

If there is one thing I never thought Sommers could do with a $135 million budget, it was produce a boring movie. But he proved what every beginning author is taught: if the reader/audience doesn't care about your characters to begin with, then they won't care about what happens to them or who wins and loses.

The two happiest people in the afterlife right now must be Mary Shelly and Bram Stoker. Reason: neither received any mention in the film's credits.

French Safari Diary

Part 1

Friday, May 5, 2000: Went to airport. Got on plane. Slept. Not a wildly exciting day.

Saturday, May 6: We landed at de Gaulle Airport at 8:50 AM. The Etonnants Voyageurs festival had thoughtfully booked a charter train on the other side of Paris that was scheduled to leave at 9:15. The odds of our landing on time, getting our luggage, clearing customs, and reaching the other side of town in anything less than two hours were astronomical. So it was Pierre-Paul Duristanti, my erstwhile translator, to the rescue. He met us at the airport, took us to the train, led us through a transfer that took us under half the city to a large station, and then we boarded our third train of the morning, the Bullet Train to Rennes.

(One comment about the Parisian subways. They're safe and efficient, like those of London. But Carol had bought us a new, huge piece of luggage, kind of a closet on wheels, so that everything we took for a week could fit in it. The Paris subways exist on half a dozen different levels—and they are connected by stairs, not escalators. I thought I was going to die lugging that damned suitcase up and down.)

I'd always wanted to take a bullet train, to skim through the countryside at 200 miles per hour . . . and we actually did a little of that, for maybe ten minutes. Mostly we raced across France at a stately 30 miles per hour, sometimes a little slower.

When we hit Rennes we transferred to a fourth train—by now we realized that getting to Saint Malo was so complicated that were it not for Pierre-Paul we'd probably be pulling into a station in Brussels—and finally made it the lovely seaside resort of Saint Malo.

The festival committee had booked us into the Hotel Atlantis Bleu Marine, a very charming 3-star hotel backing up to the sea. We were on the top floor. As we were walking down the corridor to our room, Norman Spinrad burst out of his room, cursing a blue streak. He hated the place, and wasn't going to stay there one minute longer (which did not make an overwhelmingly favorable first impression on us.) But once we opened the door of our room and found that it had a beautiful balcony overlooking the sea, we were a little happier. (The source of at least some of Norman's displeasure was that the charter train we had missed managed to misplace everyone's luggage. I may have been the last writer to arrive, but I was the only one in possession of his luggage.

The other reason is that we were a couple of miles from the festivities, and he wanted a closer hotel.)

We went downstairs, found a little coffee shop a few doors away, and stopped in for some lunch, where we ran into Connie Willis and her brother, Lee Trimmer, and also Brian Aldiss, who was getting ready to pick up his well-deserved Nebula Grandmaster Award the following week.

As mentioned, the hotel could have been better located in terms of the festival. It was a two-mile walk each way. The first time I did it with Pierre-Paul (while Carol unpacked), I was exhausted; by the 7th time I walked it a couple of days later, I didn't even work up a sweat—demonstrating, I suppose, that if you're dumb enough you can get used to *anything*.

We'd had a 9-hour flight and 5 hours' worth of train rides, and although we had arrived too late for opening ceremonies (which, I am told, consisted of a few speeches and a lot of champagne and oysters), we decided we were tired enough to skip the evening's festivities as well. So while everyone tramped off for dinner and a cocktail party aboard a boat, we found a French pizza shop and were tucked away in bed at 10:00, having been up and on the go for about 35 hours.

Sunday, May 7: Ran into Connie and Lee for breakfast. Connie is a truly sweet woman who would never dream of saying No to anyone, and she seemed mildly surprised that God hadn't struck us dead for not attending the shipboard dinner the night before.

Turns out that, because no one in authority had seen me yet, they decided I must be feeling ignored, so to make amends for it, I was invited to lunch with Richard Matheson, Orson Scott Card, and the mayor of Saint Malo. Nine course meal. Unfortunately, 5 of the courses were fish, which I don't eat—but three of them were dessert, which I definitely do eat.

The festival wasn't quite as thoroughly organized as the ABA here, or even some of the better-run conventions. You hunted up your publisher when you thought of it and autographed at his table when you felt like it. Since I have a number of French publishers—Flammarion, Denoel, and Gallimard (a new one)—and I write for a number of the magazines—*BiFrost, Galaxies*—I just made the rounds of the exhibits each day, and every time I came to one of my book or magazine publishers I sat down and did half an hour's worth of autographs. Pierre-Paul left in the afternoon, but promised to meet our train the next night and show us to our hotel. Among the American contingent I saw Jim Morrow, and I'm told Jonathan Lethem was there but I never ran into him.

There was another cocktail and fish party in the early evening, followed by another huge dinner. Some of the English-speaking sf writers exercised a little independence and decided not to go. Instead, Carol and I, Connie and Lee, Scott and Kristine Card, and British sf writer Paul McCauly snuck off to a wonderful little restaurant that Scott had found the night before. We had a delightful dinner and chat that lasted maybe three hours, and then made the long trek back to our hotel. (When I was Guest of Honor at a convention in Nancy a couple of years ago, that committee did the same thing as this one: it put all the English-speaking writers in the same hotel. It's thoughtful, since it gives us old friends to visit with, but it does hinder our ability to meet the local fans.)

Monday, May 8: Breakfasted with Connie, Lee, Paul McCauly, and Brian Aldiss, who was quite under the weather, having posed for photos all the previous afternoon in a driving rainstorm. Connie and I both noted that we had half a dozen or more official photo sessions with pro photographers, which we almost never have in the States. The French are evidently much more interested in Capturing The Moment.

I made the autograph rounds for the third day, stopped long enough to attend my one panel, which seemed to be about Africa—it certainly wasn't about science fiction—and consisted of myself, a British writer who wrote a novel about three Jamaican homnosexuals in a men's room, and a French doctor who wrote about tropical diseases and African magic. Fortunately my pal Stephane Nicot from *Galaxies* was one of the moderators, since the other one had never read a word any of us had written.

About 5:30 we were all herded into a building across street of the festival, and then shepherded onto five buses, one for each cluster of hotels. We took the buses all the way to Rennes, where, much to our surprise, we found our luggage waiting for us. Since Pierre-Paul and I had tried the bar car on the way in and found that they didn't have much in the way of food, Carol suggested we all buy huge ham and cheese sandwiches on French bread to take along, and while everyone else starved until the train arrived in Paris at 10:30, the Resnicks, Willises and Cards pigged out on enormous sandwiches.

Pierre-Paul was there waiting for us, and took us to the hotel we had chosen after an exhaustive Internet survey—and let me tell you, we chose the right one. It was the Hotel Brighton, a 3-star hotel directly across the rue de Rivoli from the Tuileries, which are the mile-long public gardens behind the Louvre. The Brighton has 5 floors, and our room—#515, remember it if you ever get to Paris—had a bedroom, a small sitting room, a bathroom, and two balconies overlooking the Tuileries. In fact, when you stood on the balcony, you could see the Eiffel Tower, the Arc de Triomphe, the huge Ferris wheel, the National Assembly, the Orsay Museum, and the glass pyramid at the Louvre, all lit up like Christmas trees. They were so bright that you could almost take a book out onto the balcony at midnight and read by their light. Almost.

The hotel had two elevators: a service elevator that went to the fourth floor, which worked; and a regular elevator that went to the fifth, and which was out of order. So once again I got to carry that enormous, million-pound suitcase up some stairs. (Well, actually, Pierre-Paul carried it. But he's 20 years younger than I am, and was just showing off.)

Carol wasn't hungry, so Pierre-Paul and I went down to a little coffee shop on the corner, bought him a beer, and had some typical Parisian dessert—creme caramel, creme brulee, whatever. And when we said good-night and I went back up to the room, I found Carol taping her ankle. There was a slight step, maybe 4 inches, between the bedroom and the sitting room, and she'd forgotten it and tripped over it.

Tuesday, May 9: We love walking through cities, and Carol decided her ankle was up to it, so after having breakfast in our room, we went out the front door, turned right, and began window shopping our way to the end of the rue de Rivoli. We turned at the Place de la Concorde, walked a block or two to the Champs Ellysees, walked through about a mile and a half of public park, and then came to rows and rows of stores again as we neared the Arc de Triomphe. The street didn't really have much to appeal to us, but we started walking down some side streets, and that's where we found all the internationally-famed designers and exquisite and exclusive little boutiques. After a couple of hours we turned around and walked back to the hotel.

We stopped at the room, each picked up the book we were reading, then went back out. We bought a couple of sandwiches and a couple of bottles of water, walked over to the Tuileries (where hundreds of people meet, visit, eat lunch, drink wine, and feed birds), pulled a couple of chairs into the shade, and ate and read our books and watched the birds and the gardens for a few hours.

I had a photo appointment at Flammarion at 3:30—evidently my five photo sessions at Saint Malo weren't enough—so Carol went upstairs to take a nap and rest her foot and I took a cab to Flammarion. Less than a minute after I got there all the power went out, trapping some people in the elevator. The photographer explained that while his studio was in the building, he couldn't photograph me there since there was no power, so we went outside, found some famous buildings, and took the pictures there. Before we had finished a couple of hundred people had stopped to watch and wonder which American movie star I was. I finally explained that I was Harrison Ford, this was what I really looked like, and the artists would touch up the photos before the public got to see them.

We'd made arrangements to meet Connie and Lee for dinner. Pierre-Paul took us all to his favorite restaurant, a wonderful little place across the Sienne called Bar de l'X. (Say it fast: it's Bar Deluxe.) It was a tiny restaurant, capable of serving maybe 12 people at once, half of us sitting out on the sidewalk—but oh, did they have great food. They are said to have the best meat in town, and the proprietor, who seems, Ghod knows why, to have a crush on Pierre-Paul, explained to us that she drives 50 miles outside of Paris to get the cuts of meat she wants.

(I promised Connie that I wouldn't tell everyone how she got drunk on three or four different flavors of wine and danced naked on the table, so I won't.)

Though we took a cab to get there, we decided to walk back, dropping Connie and Lee at their hotel along the way. It was maybe a three or four mile walk, taking us through wildly popular sections (you can tell, because every third building in Paris is some kind of eatery, and in the popular sections you can go blocks without seeing an empty chair), and then through an exclusive, expensive area of clothes designers, art importers and the like. Lovely walk.

Wednesday, May 10: Breakfast in the room, as usual. Carol did her gift shopping in the morning—we always get something for Laura, and something for Darien, the girl who cleans our house and takes care of it and the cat whenever we're gone—and then we bought lunch and went back to the Tuileries with our sandwiches and our books.

In the afternoon I had an interview with Aurelia Jakmakejian, a journalist who works for *Livres Hebdo*, the French equivalent of *Publisher's Weekly*. I didn't really want to go out searching for any more addresses, so I talked the hotel into letting her come there and interview me in the breakfast room. (Most 3-star hotels serve breakfast, but no other meals, and the breakfast room sits, pristine and empty, the rest of the day.) It took a couple of hours, at the end of which she said she'd be joining us for dinner.

It seems that I'd been teasing Pierre-Paul on my Listserv and on the Delphi network for more than a year that I would only come to the festival and Paris if he would take us to Maxim's and to the Crazy Horse Saloon, one of the more expensive and notorious nightclubs in Paris. Well, no one was about to spend $200 a head on what has come to be considered rather mediocre food at Maxim's, but Pierre-Paul actually convinced Gilles Dumay, my editor at Denoel, that I wouldn't come if he didn't take Carol and me to the Crazy Horse. And Aurelia not only enjoys the Crazy Horse, but decided that Carol might feel a little awkward being the only woman at the table while all the men were hooting and whistling at all the naked ladies on stage. (Wouldn't have bothered Carol at all, but I decided not to mention it since Aurelia obviously wanted to see the show.)

So we meet Gilles in the evening, and he takes us to one of his favorite bars, and then it's on to La Table du Perigord, a restaurant specializing in duck. (Pierre-Paul also told him I love duck, which happens to be the truth.) Aurelia joins us, and we have a wonderful meal. I have a duck appetizer in some exotic sauce, and then a huge leg of duck for the main course. And as I'm eating my duck leg it starts thundering, and as I'm finishing off my Grand Marinier souffle the heavens open and it pours.

This is when we find out that we are a few blocks from the subway, and once it lets us out we are a few blocks from the Crazy Horse, and no one has thought to bring an umbrella. So we decided to skip the Crazy Horse this year, and try again in the fall of 2001, when I've been invited back again as the Guest of Honor at the International SF Festival of Nantes. I'm sure the same girls will be a year older and wiser and more mature, which is all for the good, since I've never had much to say to naked 18-year-old girls (at least, not since I was 19.)

Thursday, May 11: Breakfast in the room again, which Carol loves. I'm less thrilled with it, because the maid tends not to come by until about 2:00 PM, and that means the table where we eat is totally unusable until then.

We walked across the Tuileries and the river and went to the Orsay Museum in the morning. This is where they store all the French impressionists: Monet, Renoir, van Gogh, Gaughin, Seurat, Rodin, Degas, that whole crowd. Big building. It used to be a train station; now it holds thousands of paintings and sculptures on its three levels . . . though it's still tiny compared to the Louvre, which is over a mile long and has five levels and is far and away the most impressive building I've ever seen.

I prefer the artwork at the Orsay. Lots of naked women, hardly any crucifixions. (You have no idea how hard it is to appreciate the Louvre's four thousand crucifixions when you are a color-blind Jewish atheist.)

We were going to eat in the Tuileries again, but it started pouring, so we walked up and down the rue de Rivoli, which is protected by an overhang, and used our favorite method of choosing a French restaurant. All of them, classy and non, are wide-open affairs, flowing out onto the sidewalks. We would simply start walking past them until we came to one that was crowded and where everyone seemed to be happy; then we'd grab a table and order a meal. We've done it maybe a dozen times in Paris, and have yet to be disappointed.

For a change I wasn't scheduled for any photo sessions or interviews, and since it was too wet to consider going anywhere, we went up to the room and read and napped the afternoon away. Then 8:00 rolled around (no one in that city ever seems to eat early), and we went down to the lobby to meet Jacques Chambon, my long-time editor at Denoel who had moved over to Flammarion a couple of years ago and taken me with him. Pierre-Paul joined us, and we drove off in Jacques' very roomy car to one of his favorite restaurants, La Cigale. I had ravioli in a fabulous cream sauce for an appetizer, a mouth-watering filet in luscious gravy for the main course, and a chocolate soufflé (with chocolate fondue sauce) for dessert. I don't remember what Carol had, but I think all three of her courses were soufflés, even the one with all the vegetables.

We spent a few hours talking business and non-business. Jacques wants to start a matching set of my books, almost a Resnick line, to which of course I have no objection. The Denoel books start reverting soon. Jacques tells me that Gallimard, which just bought Denoel, will want to keep (i.e., buy) them, and that they'll get better circulation there, but Jacques is the guy who made me a star in France, and I tend to be loyal to people who are loyal to me, so if he wants any of the Denoel titles, I'll make sure he gets them. (Jacques gave me the nicest compliment I think I've ever had on the Galactic Comedy trilogy, to the effect that he knew nothing about Africa and African history before he read *Paradise, Purgatory* and *Inferno*, and when he was through with them he felt like an expert.)

He drove us back to the hotel at about 11:30. Carol went up to pack, and Pierre-Paul and I went to the corner coffee shop for some coffee and dessert—and who should come by a few minutes later than Jacques, who found a parking place just a couple of blocks away and decided he was enjoying the conversation so much he didn't want to go home.

We broke up about 12:30—the subways stop running at 1:00, and Pierre-Paul didn't want to walk home, since he lives halfway across the city—and that was how I spent my last evening in Paris. (On our previous trip we'd stayed at the Grand Hotel du Champagne, about a mile away. Not as nice a hotel, but surrounded by all-night brasseries, so we could always sneak out at three in the morning for a cup of coffee.)

Friday, May 12: Up at dawn. Off to the airport. Got to watch *Anna and the King*—produced by Ed Elbert, who's also producing *Santiago*—for the second time in a week, and came home to some awards (2 HOmer wins and a Seiun nomination), some movie option money, some GalaxyOnline.com money, and my 32nd check (royalties, reprints, foreign sales) for "The Trials and Tribulations of Myron

Blumberg, Dragon", known in the Resnick household as The Piece Of Insignificant Fluff That Refuses To Die.

Part 2

Well, I *thought* I was all through telling you about Paris for awhile.

We got home, spent five days catching up on mail and bills and laundry, then went down to Jekyll Island for DeepSouthCon, stayed in Florida for a week, and wound up at Oasis, the Orlando science fiction convention. We flew home on May 29, having spent most of the month on the road, and I, for one, was looking forward to not leaving home again for a couple of months.

There was a fax waiting for me. It was from Jacques Chambon, my editor at Flammarion.

My novel, *The Dark Lady*, which appeared here in 1987 but had just been translated and published in France in 1999, had just won the prestigious Tour Eiffel Award, and could I please fly to Paris and accept it on June 8?

How prestigious can it be, I faxed back. I've never heard of the damned thing.

That's because no American has ever won it before, answered Jacques. You should be deeply honored.

Okay, I'm deeply honored, I said. Can't they just mail me the trophy or plaque or whatever it is?

They can, but they'd rather you came and got it yourself, said Jacques. There will be a lot of people at the ceremony.

That's a long way to come for a goddamned trophy, I complained.

Well, in addition to the trophy, they're also going to present you with a check for 100,000 francs, said Jacques.

Which put a whole new light on things. I checked the exchange rates and found that 100,000 French francs translated into $14,237.

So OK, I'll come, I said begrudgingly.

Then I went to Delta, which owns 108 of the Cincinnati airport's 120 gates, and has never offered a cut-rate fare to a Cincinnatian in the recorded history of Man.

How much for a pair of economy-class tickets to Paris, leaving June 6, coming home June 9, I ask.

$2,005 apiece, they answer.

Could you speak more distinctly, I say; I know it's ridiculous, but it sounded like you just quoted a fare of more than $2000.

I did, answers the clerk.

But I just took the same goddamned plane to the same goddamned location for $491 a ticket not four weeks ago, I scream.

But you ordered those tickets three months in advance, and you're ordering these tickets a week in advance, she explains sweetly.

Keep 'em, I say. I fax Jacques and tell him that I'm staying home, that the price for tickets is ridiculous.

We'll pay for your hotel, offers Jacques.

Big fucking deal, says Mike; I'm staying home.

I get three quick faxes about how this award is more important than I think and I really should come. In the last fax, he says Flammarion will pay half my ticket.

Carol decides to stay home, and suddenly I find myself in the position of either agreeing to go, or of telling Jacques and the award committee that I am so cheap that I'm unwilling to spend $1,000 to pick up my $14,000 check. So I go back to Delta and buy the ticket.

I got a lot of comments about this when I mentioned it online. The most typical came from Tony Lewis:

"You mean they're paying you money to fly to Paris so they can pay you more money? How can I get in on something like this?"

So I pack my bag—much smaller and lighter than the closet on wheels Carol had me drag in early May—and off I go.

Tuesday, June 6: No one at the Delta office would give me a seat assignment when I forked over two grand for the ticket. I'm a big man, and I like to sit on the aisle, where I can at least stretch my feet out a little, so I get to the airport at 1:30 PM for a 6:50 PM flight, just to make sure I get an aisle seat. I walk up to the check-in counter, show the lady in charge my ticket and passport—and *again* they won't give me a seat. She tells me I can get a seat assignment 90 minutes before takeoff. I ask why, since I've paid for my ticket, no one is willing to give me a seat? She gives me a look that I have seen on exceptionally retarded cattle and nowhere else outside of Delta employees, and I just sigh and go out for lunch with Carol.

I show up at the gate at 2:45 and ask for a seat assignment. I should have known better. The guy there—much brighter than the lady at check-in; he has the look of a steer with an IQ of at least 50—tells me that I can get it from him 90 minutes before flight time, or I can walk down the hall to the Delta Information Booth and they'll be happy to assign me a seat.

So I go there, and find myself about 15th in line. Seems New York is socked in with thunderstorms, and a few dozen Delta passengers who were making foreign connections through New York are being forced to find new routes. There are four clerks working the booth, and even so it is 4:55, more than two hours later, when it is finally my turn. I walk up and ask for an aisle seat. They give me a window.

Comes 5:20, I walk up to the guy at the gate and ask to change seats. No problem, he says, giving me an aisle with even more leg room than I had anticipated, since it's the exit row. Gee, he says, I wonder why they didn't give this to you when you purchased the ticket.

I look around for Delta employees to kill, but all I find are people trying to get to Europe without touching New York.

The plane takes off only 20 minutes late—excellent for Delta—and the flight is uneventful. I find myself sitting next to a very pretty, very earnest young girl who is reading *Flowers for Algernon*, which gives us a basis for conversation, and after we talk a bit I find we have something else in common: Africa. She and some exceptionally devout Christian friends are flying to Togo to spend the next three months working in a leper colony. I figure if leprosy is the worst thing she catches in West Africa, she'll be ahead of the game.

Wednesday, June 7: We land at 8:50 AM, and I find that Madame Nebout, who runs the Tour Eiffel Society, has sent her uniformed chauffer to pick me up. I know this because he is holding up a card with my name on it. I say "Hello." He says "Bonjour." I say, "Where are we going?" He says "Jabber jabber jabber" in a language that sounds like French. It seems that Madame Nebout has sent a driver who speaks no English to pick up a writer who speaks no French.

I follow him to the car which turns out to be the first stretch Lexus limo I've ever seen. I try to get into the front seat. He has a conniption fit. I get into the back seat.

We start driving. He says "Jabber jabber jabber Tour Eiffel jabber." I say, "I don't want to see the Eiffel Tower. Take me to my hotel." He says "Jabber jabber Tour Eiffel jabber." I make it simple and say just one word: "Hotel". He nods, smiles, and says "Tour Eiffel," and I get the definite notion that what we have here is a failure to communicate.

After half an hour of aimless driving, we emerge from a tunnel and he points to a world-famous restaurant: "Maxim's." I say "Hotel." Five minutes later he points again: "Place de la Concorde." I say "Hotel." Then it's "Louvre." I say "Hotel or I will cut out your French heart and eat it for dinner." He smiles; obviously I like the Louvre.

I can sense that he is about to take me to the Eiffel Tower, if only because he mentions it four or five times, and I pull out the address of the hotel, thrust it in front of his nose, and say, once again, "Hotel."

"Ah, oui!" he says, and my blood pressure drops half of the 100 points it has risen.

We go to the Hotel Delavigne, which is about a block from Flammarion, 2 blocks from Rivages, and 3 blocks from Denoel—all of them major science fiction publishers. In fact, there are upward of 20 publishers within a half-mile radius. I get out and walk in to register, and he jabbers at me again, and I hear him mention Jacques Chambon, and I grab him by the arm and drag him to the front desk and ask the clerk to translate. It seems that he has congratulated me maybe 20 times for winning the Tour Eiffel Award, and is under the impression that "Hotel" means "Thanks." Also, Jacques will phone me at noon. I shake his hand, tell him "Hotel," and he smiles and leaves.

Problem is, it's 10:00 in the morning and they won't have my room ready until noon. I leave my bag at the desk and decide to walk around, since I've been sitting at the airport, on the plane, and in the limo for the better part of 12 hours.

The hotel is very near the Odeon, which is kind of like a hub with eight or nine streets going off in different directions. I walk down each for a block, no more, because I don't want to lose track of where the hotel is. I pass a couple of interesting bookstores, and I walk a little further, and suddenly I look ahead and walking toward me is Pierre-Paul Durastanti. He figured that neither Flammarion nor the Tour Eiffel committee would make any arrangements for me until the ceremony the next day, so he decided to hunt me up and spend the day being my guide and translator. I can't remember the last time I was so happy to see anyone (well, at least anyone of his gender).

We grabbed a quick breakfast, checked out some bookstores, and went back to the hotel at 11:45, only to find out that Jacques had already called and would call back at 12:30. My room was ready, so we went up to it.

Remember that I did potential tourists a huge favor by telling them to reserve room 515 at the Hotel Brighton? I'm about to do you another one: *never* stay in room 51 at the Hotel Delavigne. My bathroom at home is, quite literally, larger than room 51. It is newer and cleaner. It has more shelf and closet space. It is air-conditioned—and believe me, room 51 *needed* air-conditioning. Paris was hot as hell, and when I opened my window—it opened inward, thereby preventing me from laying on the bed, which was parked just under it—far from getting a breeze, what I got was a look at the wall of another centuries-old building. (On its behalf, I will say that the staff was remarkably friendly, and breakfast was served in a charming brick cellar with sloping walls and an arched ceiling.)

Jacques called to tell me (surprise!) that he couldn't possibly see me today, but he'd pick me up at 10:00 in the morning for the ceremony.

That left the whole day free, as Pierre-Paul had known it would. Having had breakfast a whole hour ago, we decided it was time for lunch, and we stopped by Rivages, where I met Doug Headline, the science fiction editor, and Nicolas Cluzeau, a freelance editor who bought one of my stories for an anthology while we were there. We visited a bit, then Nicolas left and Doug took us out to a fine local restaurant, Le Temps Perdu (which means "The Lost Time," and indeed one could observe entire editorial staffs losing all kinds of time while they sipped their espresso.)

After lunch Doug went back to his office and Pierre-Paul and I took a bus to the Museum of Natural History. Very impressive, with a nice display of African animals. We were considering going to the dinosaur exhibit, but it was in an adjoining building, and they wanted us to pay another fee, so we walked around the extensive gardens instead. Then we came to a sign pointing to a zoo and we followed it. Somewhere in Paris there is a major zoo, the equivalent of the Bronx Zoo or Brookfield Zoo. This wasn't it. The most exciting thing we saw was a sleeping kangaroo, and after about half an hour we left and took another bus a few miles to a store that has Paris' best selection of out-of-print English-language science fiction.

We stopped by Denoel, which has published about 15 of my books, visited for a few minutes with my current editor, Giles Dumay, and a local sf writer who was pitching some book or other, and then the four of us went out for a drink. (They had wine and beer, I had water.)

Finally, at about 9:00, Pierre-Paul and I wandered over to the Bar de l'X for dinner. The couple who run the place remembered me from three weeks ago, tried their best to get me to drink some wine (I stuck to water), and cooked up a mouth-watering filet and a desert made of something moist and chocolate in a vanilla sauce that was every bit as good as it had been the last time.

I get to the room at about 11 at night. I haven't slept since Monday night, and I'm pretty tired. I figure I'll sit by the window (as I said, you can't lay on the bed when it's open), get a bit of cool air for a few minutes, then shave and shower and go to sleep. I sit down and turn on CNN. I blink. I open my eyes. It is 8:00 in the morning. I am still clothed and still sitting.

Thursday, June 8: I grab breakfast in the cellar, then get into a jacket and tie and wait for Jacques to pick me up. Pierre-Paul has decided he hates ceremonies and isn't coming, which is a shame, since I am enough of a realist to know that *he* is the one responsible for the book winning the award.

We stop by Flammarion to pick up the publisher, a charming young woman who can't be 30 yet, then drive to the Tower. We flash our engraved invitations and get into a special line to the elevator, which takes us up a few hundred feet and lets us off at a broad platform.

We're ushered into a huge room that holds a couple of hundred people. There are bottles of Dom Perignon everywhere, and maybe twenty pounds of Beluga caviar, and I begin to get the impression that this is not quite like a Hugo ceremony. The impression is confirmed when I am introduced to the Mayor of Paris.

At 11:00 sharp we sit down, me in the front row, and Madame Nebout gets up and starts talking in French. Every few minutes I hear my name mentioned. Then I hear some other familiar names, and Aurelia, the reporter who interviewed me last month and is sitting directly behind me, leans forward, does a little quick translating, and explains that *The Dark Lady* beat out the last two Hugo winners, Joe Haldeman's *The Forever Peace* and Connie Willis' *To Say Nothing of the Dog*, for the award.

Then the Mayor climbs onstage and starts speaking, and Aurelia and two other girls I know start whispering in my ear, and this time it's not a translation, its a catalog of the crimes the Mayor will soon be standing trial for, including the old Chicago specialty of having the populations of entire cemeteries vote for him and his party.

Suddenly Aurelia pokes me in the ribs and I jump to my feet and turn to see what the problem is, and she gestures me to go up on stage, that I have been Summoned. So I climb up on the stage, while everyone watches and waits, and then I stand there like an idiot for ten minutes while the Mayor continues reading his speech, part of which includes the fact that we are old friends and he loves my books.

Then comes the highlight. He presents me with a three-foot-long one-foot-high replica of my 100,000-franc check. We hold it up together, and 30 or 40 press photographers come up and blind us with flashbulbs for the next ten minutes while the TV cameras capture us trying not to stagger sightlessly off the stage and into the audience.

Then Madame Nebout hands me the *real* check, and a gold medallion with the Eiffel Tower on it, and I somehow intuit that it's time for me to give a speech.

So I walk over to the microphone and decide to see if anyone can understand English. I explain that Pierre-Paul Durastanti, my translator, deserves half the fame and honor and glory, and I freely give it to him, but I think I'll keep all the money. Ninety percent of the audience laughs, and I realize with some gratitude that I don't have to speak in monosyllables. So I talk for five or ten minutes, and then we pose for more photos, and I meet a bunch of well-dressed men and women from the American embassy, most of whom feel compelled to pose for still more photos with me. Then I give seven or eight brief interviews for radio and TV.

Finally we walk across the platform to the other side of the Tower, and there is a fabulous display of science fiction artwork which I get to see while I am still being interviewed by a couple of daily newspapers.

Then we adjourn to one of the most elegant dining rooms in all Paris, a few hundred feet above the ground. (If you watched the movie *Company Business* with Gene Hackman and Mikhail Baryshnikov, this is the restaurant where they were trapped by the Russians.) I get to sit next to the window, with an absolutely fabulous view, and Madame Nebout sits opposite me. Jacques Sadoul, who is the John Campbell of French science fiction and whom I had met at a number of Worldcons, sits next to her, Jean-Pierre Marliac, a member of the jury, sits next to me, and between the two of them, they manage to translate just about everything Madame Nebout and I say to each other for the next three hours.

The meal was as good as it was supposed to be. The first course was shrimp in a cream sauce. Then tomatoes stuffed with crabmeat. Then a salad. Then something that looked like lox (I don't eat any fish except shrimp and lobster, so I can't tell for sure what it was.) The main course was a 12-ounce filet that was so tender you literally didn't need a knife to cut it. Then a soft, cold cheese that looked like (and almost tasted like) ice cream. Then real ice cream in a bed of fresh strawberries. And finally espresso. I didn't drink any wine, but the liveried waiters kept bringing a steady flow of it, in all colors, to the table.

Madame Nebout's chauffeur, old Tour Eiffel himself, was waiting to take me home, but this time I had Jacques Sadoul with me—he was going to Flammarion, a block away from the hotel—so we managed to travel a direct route.

Jacques Chambon was picking Pierre-Paul and me up for dinner at eight, and having nothing better to do, I lay down at 4:00 and took a three-hour nap. Pierre showed up with Cathy Martin-Legat, who owns the biggest science fiction bookstore in France and whom I had met at the ceremony. Her store is in Toulouse, which, Pierre tells me, is one of the reasons he spent so many years living in Toulouse before moving to Paris last year.

Jacques came by in his car and picked us all up, and suggested that we go to the Bar de l'X, since he'd heard such wonderful things about it. We didn't have the heart to tell him we'd been there the night before (especially since he was paying), so we went again. This time I had duck, and it was every bit as good as their filets . . . and since I don't change winners in midstream, I had the same dessert again. Cathy left us at about ten, and Jacques, Pierre-Paul and I stayed there until after midnight, basically laying the groundwork for future sales. (Jacques still wants to start a Resnick line.)

Then Jacques dropped us off at the hotel, Pierre-Paul walked to the subway station, and I went to sleep.

Friday, June 9: I heard the alarm ringing so I reached out and turned it off. Then, bleary-eyed, I trudged to the bathroom, shaved and showered, and started getting dressed.

And looked out the window.

And realized that it was dark.

I checked the clock. It was 5:00 AM.

Turns out I had heard the alarm in the next room ring. The guy had an 8:00 flight to the States, and I turned off my alarm at precisely the same time he turned his off, so I never knew it wasn't my clock that was ringing.

So, fully dressed and totally packed, I sat down, opened the window, turned on the television, and watched CNN for the next four hours. Then I grabbed some coffee, came upstairs, and watched CNN again until 11:30. Finally I turned it off and checked out, and met Pierre-Paul in the lobby at noon. He had thoughtfully volunteered to be my guide to de Gaulle airport via subway, which cost about five dollars, rather than the thirty-plus dollars a cab would cost.

We got there, I popped for lunch, and we said good-bye. Then, pulling my suitcase on wheels and carrying my oversized facsimile 100,000-franc check—talk about an attention-getter!—I boarded the plane, slept for seven of the eight hours, and came home to the news that what had become my favorite novel, *The Outpost*, was sold to Tor, and that one of the Miramax execs who loved Carol's and my screenplays had become an independent producer and wanted a new Resnick Project.

It's been a nice few days. I think I may keep writing science fiction for a profession.

Tales of the Prozines

There is a lot more to the science fiction magazines than the stories they run. More than the cover art, more than the articles. They have an almost secret history of their own. I'd like to share some of the more interesting incidents with you before there's no one left to remember them.

The Shaver Mystery

In 1938, Ray Palmer, an undersized hunchback with a pretty thorough understanding of his readership, took over the editorship of *Amazing Stories*. At the time, John Campbell's *Astounding Science Fiction*, featuring the best of Heinlein, Asimov, Sturgeon, Hubbard, van Vogt, de Camp, Simak, and Kuttner, ruled supreme among the magazines— but then Palmer came up with a gimmick the changed everything: the Shaver Mystery.

He ran a novel—rather generic, rather poorly written— called *I Remember Lemuria!* It was all about these creatures called Deros that lived hidden away from humanity, but were preparing to do dire things to us. Nothing special in any way—

—except that Palmer swore to his readers, who consisted mostly of impressionable teen-aged boys, that the story was *true*, and that Richard Shaver was forced by the Powers That Be to present it as fiction or no one—including Ziff-Davis, Palmer's bosses—would dare risk publishing it.

Sounds silly, doesn't it?

Well, the *really* silly part came next: while Palmer was running another dozen or so "Shaver Mystery novels"—each worse than the last—from 1945 to 1948, his circulation skyrocketed. *Amazing* passed *Astounding*, spread-eagled the field, and became the top-selling science fiction magazine, not only of that era, but of *any* era.

I'll tell you a little story about the Shaver Mystery. Back when I was editing men's magazines in Chicago in the late 1960s, I used, among others, a very talented artist, slightly older than myself, named Bill Dichtl. One day we got to talking, and found out we were both science fiction fans, and Bill told me about *his* adventures with the Shaver Mystery.

He was a 14-year-old subscriber to *Amazing* in the late 1940s, living in Chicago (where *Amazing* was published), and one day he got a mysterious phone call, asking if he would like to help in the secret war against the Deros. Of course he said he would. He was given an address to go to that Friday night, and was warned to tell no one about this assignation.

So on Friday night, Bill sneaked out of his house and dutifully went to the address, which happened to be the building that housed the Ziff-Davis publishing empire. He took the elevator up to the appointed floor, found himself in a darkened corridor, saw a single light coming out from beneath a door at the far end of it, walked to the door, saw it was the room number he had been given, and entered. There was a long table, and maybe a dozen other earnest teen-aged boys were sitting at it.

Bill took a seat, and they all waited in silence. About ten minutes later a little hunchbacked man entered the room. It was Ray Palmer, of course. He explained that the Deros would soon be making their move against an unsuspecting humanity, and it was the duty of the boys in that room to spend the rest of the night warning as many people as possible of the coming struggle so they wouldn't be caught unaware.

He had lists of thousands of addresses, which the boys dutifully copied onto blank envelopes. He had thousands of folded and stapled "warnings" that they stuffed into the envelopes. He had thousands of stamps that they licked and stuck onto the envelopes. They finished at sunrise, and Palmer swore them all to secrecy and thanked them for helping to save humanity.

Bill had stuffed a copy of the warning into his pocket to give to his parents, just in case they had somehow been omitted from the mailing list. On the subway home, he opened it and read it—and found out that Palmer had duped the boys into mailing out thousands of subscription renewal notices.

By 1949 Palmer was gone. He started *Other Worlds*, hired a gorgeous Cincinnati fan, Bea Mahaffey, to edit it for him, and even brought Shaver along. (To this day, some people think Palmer *was* Shaver. They were wrong; he was actually seen with Palmer by some fans and pros. Someone purporting to be Shaver wrote some letters to Richard Geis' Hugo-winning fanzine, *Science Fiction Review*, in the 1970s, but no one ever saw him or followed up on it.)

Palmer's gimmick at *Other Worlds* was to get readers to pressure Edgar Rice Burroughs, Inc. to hire his discovery, "John Bloodstone," as the legal successor to Burroughs. ("Bloodstone" was actually Palmer's pal, hack writer Stuart J. Byrne, who had written a copyright-infringing novel, *Tarzan On Mars*, that Palmer wanted to publish.) ERB Inc. refused, and that was the end of that, and pretty much the end of *Other Worlds* (though you can still find illegally-photocopied copies of *Tarzan On Mars* for sale here and there).

Palmer's final stop was at *Fate Magazine*, begun in 1949, where he got rich one last time off a gullible reading public.

As for Shaver, not a single word of the million-plus that he wrote remains in print.

The Prediction Issue

The November, 1948 issue of *Astounding* was typical of its era. It was not the best issue that John Campbell edited that year, nor was it the worst, and like all other issues of *Astounding* prior to 1950, it was far superior to its competitors.

Astounding's letter column was (and still is) "Brass Tacks," and in that particular issue there was a cute letter by a Richard A. Hoen who, like most fanboys, went over the most recent issue story by story, explaining in goshwowboyoboy fashion what he liked and disliked and why. Robert A. Heinlein's "Gulf" was pretty good, though not quite up to *Beyond This Horizon*, opined Mr. Hoen. He ranked it second best in the issue, just ahead of A. E. van Vogt's "Final Command," with Lester del Rey's "Over the Top" coming in fourth. He wasn't much impressed with L. Sprague de Camp's "Finished," which was fifth, and he absolutely hated Theodore Sturgeon's "What Dead Men Tell," ranking it last. Mr. Hoen also words of praise for the cover painting by Hubert Rogers.

Only one problem: he was ranking the stories in the November, *1949* issue, and of course none of them existed. It was a cute conceit, everyone got a chuckle out of it, and everyone immediately forgot it.

Except Campbell, who went out of his way to make it come true.

The November, 1949 issue of *Astounding* featured the first part of Heinlein's serial, "Gulf"; Sturgeon's "What Dead Men Tell"; de Camp's "Finished"; van Vogt's "Final Command"; and del Rey's "Over the Top." And of course it had a cover by Rogers.

There was only one place the prediction fell short. Mr. Hoen had ranked a story called "We Hail," by Don A. Stuart, first. Don A. Stuart was Campbell's pseudonym when he was writing works of ambition (such as "Twilight") rather than space opera, and was taken from his first wife's maiden name, Dona Stuart. Well, Campbell didn't write a story for the issue—but in its place he ran the first part of "And Now You Don't," the three-part serial that formed the climax of Isaac Asimov's Foundation Trilogy. I don't imagine anyone had any serious objections to the substitution.

So when you hear writers like me say that science fiction isn't really in the predicting business, just remind us of the November, 1948 *Astounding*.

The Prozines are Officially Noticed

Science fiction tends to cry and carry on because no one pays any attention to it, that it's a ghetto beneath the notice of the New York Literary Establishment and most of the Powers That Be in academia.

And yet science fiction has been officially Noticed (and more than once) by the United States Government, and that was long before that government started naming weapons and defense systems after rather silly science fiction movies.

Back in the Good Old Days of the pulps, more often than not the cover art showed a partially-clad (or, if you prefer, a mostly-unclad) girl, usually at the mercy of aliens who seemed more interested in ripping off the rest of her clothes than doing anything practical, like killing or communicating with her.

The thing is (and I refer you to the two introductory articles in my anthology, *Girls For the Slime God*), only one magazine actually delivered the salacious stories that went hand-in-glove with those cover illos, and that magazine was *Marvel Science Stories*. The first issue, back in August of 1938, featured Henry Kuttner's "The Avengers of Space," a rather pedestrian novella to which I suspect he added all the sex scenes to after it had been turned down by the major markets. Then out came issue number two, and there was Kuttner with another novella of the same ilk: "The Time Trap."

What was the result?

Well, there were two results. The first was that Kuttner was labeled a debased and perverted hack, and had to create Lewis Padgett and Lawrence O'Donnell, his two most famous pseudonyms (but far from his only ones) in order to make a living, since it would be a few years before the top editors wanted to buy from Henry Kuttner again.

The second was that the United States government, through its postal branch, gave science fiction its very first official recognition. They explained to the publisher that if the third issue of *Marvel* was as sexy as the first two, they were shutting him down and sending him to jail.

And with that, *Marvel Science Stories* became the most sedate and— let's be honest—*dull* science fiction magazine on the market. It died not too long thereafter, the first prozine to be slain by the government.

But the government wasn't quite through Noticing the prozines. Move the clock ahead five years, to March, 1944, which was when *Astounding*, under the editorship of John Campbell, published a forgettable little story called "Deadline," by Cleve Cartmill.

It became one of the most famous stories in the history of the prozines—not because of its quality, which was minimal, but because it brought the prozines to the official notice of the government for the second time.

We were embroiled in World War II, and in early 1944 the Manhattan Project—the project that resulted in the atomic bomb—was still our most carefully-guarded secret.

And Cartmill's story, which used knowledge and facts that were available to anyone, concerned the construction of an atomic bomb that used U-235.

Cartmill was visited by the FBI and other select governmental agencies the week the story came out, each demanding to know how he had managed to steal the secrets of the bomb. He pointed out that his "secrets" were a matter of public record. He was nonetheless warned never to breach national security again, upon pain of truly dire consequences.

The government representatives then went to Campbell's office, where he explained to them, as only Campbell could, that if they were not uneducated, subliterate dolts they would know exactly where Cartmill got his information, and that *Astounding* had been running stories about atomic power for years. They tried to threaten him into promising not to run any more stories of atomic power until the war was over. Campbell didn't take kindly to threats, and allowed them to leave only after giving them a thorough tongue-lashing and an absolute refusal to censor his writers.

So the next time you hear a writer or editor bemoaning the fact that science fiction doesn't get any notice, point out to him that there were actually a couple of occasions in the past when we got a little more official notice than we wanted.

Vietnam and the Prozines

Nothing since the War Between the States aroused more passions on both sides than did the Vietnam War. In 1968 Judith Merril and Kate Wilhelm decided to do something about it: they enlisted a large number of writers—the final total was 82— and took out ads against the war in the March issue of *F&SF* and the June issues of *Galaxy* and *If.* Included in their number were most of the younger New Wave writers such as

Harlan Ellison, Barry Malzberg, Norman Spinrad, Robert Silverberg, Philip K. Dick, Terry Carr, and Ursula K. Le Guin, as well as a smattering of old masters like Isaac Asimov, Ray Bradbury, and Fritz Leiber.

Word got out—the rumor is that it was leaked by Fred Pohl, Merril's ex-husband—and the pro-war faction also ran ads in all three magazines. (Pohl had them on facing pages in his two magazines.) Included in the ads were Robert A. Heinlein, Poul Anderson, John W. Campbell Jr. (the only then-current editor to appear on either list), Fredric Brown, Hal Clement, Larry Niven, Jack Vance, and Jack Williamson. The pro-war ads contained only 72 names, leading the anti-war faction to claim that they had "won."

Pohl was editing both *Galaxy* and *If*, and he offered to donate the ad revenues to the person who came up with the best "solution" to the Vietnam War. It was won by Mack Reynolds, but Pohl never published his "solution"; runners-up were Hubert Humphrey, Lyndon Johnson, and Richard Nixon.

The Man Who Saved the Lensman

E. E. "Doc" Smith was clearly the most famous and most popular writer of the late 1920s and most of the 1930s as well. He broke new ground with the Skylark series, but it was the four Lensman books upon which his fame and adoration rests. (Yes, four; the first two in the six-book series were afterthoughts, *Triplanetary* being expanded and rewritten to become the chronological first in the series, *First Lensman* written last of all to fill a gap between *Triplanetary* and the four Kimball Kinnison books.)

Doc introduced Kimball Kinnison, the Gray Lensman, to the world in 1937, with *Galactic Patrol*, which ran in *Astounding* from September, 1937 to February, 1938—just about the time a young John Campbell was beginning his lifelong tenure as editor and preparing to reshape the field. This was followed in a few years by *The Gray Lensman* and then *Second Stage Lensman*.

But while Doc was slowly completing the saga of the Kinnison clan, Campbell was bringing Robert A. Heinlein, Isaac Asimov, Theodore Sturgeon, and A. E. van Vogt into the field, and finding room for Fritz Leiber, Clifford D. Simak, and L. Sprague de Camp.

Doc was many things as a writer, but graceful wasn't one of them, and subtle wasn't another. It didn't matter when he was competing against the likes of Nat Schachner and Ray Cummings and Stanton A.

Coblentz—but against Campbell's stable he seemed like a dinosaur, thousands of evolutionary eons behind where Campbell had pushed, pulled and dragged the field.

So when he delivered the climactic volume of the Lensman saga, *Children of the Lens*, Campbell didn't want to run it. It just didn't belong in a magazine that had published "Nightfall" and "Sixth Column" and "Slan" years earlier.

One fan had the courage to seek Campbell out and disagree. He's the one who told me this story, and Campbell later kind of sort of grudgingly agreed that it was pretty much the truth. Ed Wood, who'd been active in fandom for a few years, and would be active for another 50, cornered Campbell and explained that he owed it to Doc, who had given him the original Lensman story when *Astounding* badly needed it, to buy *Children of the Lens*. Moreover, he owed it to the field, for we were not then a book field, and if Doc's novel didn't run in *Astounding*, there was an excellent chance that it would never see the light of day. Campbell finally agreed. The novel appeared without the customary fanfare accorded to a new Doc Smith book, and was the only Lensman novel to receive a single cover, though it ran for six issues beginning in November of 1947.

So for those of you who are Lensman fans—and tens of thousands of people still are, more than half a century later— you owe two debts of gratitude, one to Doc for writing it, and another to a motivated fan, Ed Wood, for making sure you got to find out how it all ended for Kimball Kinnison and his offspring.

The Writers Revolt

Horace Gold was known for his inability to keep his hands off stories. As one author said, he could turn a good story into a very good one—but he could also turn a great story into a very good one.

Theodore Sturgeon used to cross out his favorite words and phrases, then pencil them in again above the scratchmarks. One day Gold complained that Sturgeon left him no room in which to change those particular words and phrases. "I know," replied Sturgeon. "That's why I do it."

Science fiction writers didn't have anything like SFWA in those days, but they did have the equivalent of the *SFWA Forum*. It was called PITFCS, an acronym for *The Proceedings of the Institute for Twenty-First Century Studies*, and it was the brainchild of Theodore R.

Cogswell, who edited and published it. It went to almost every active science fiction writer and editor, and once they discovered they were all having the same problem with Gold (who of course also received the magazine) they began debating what to do about him, while he adamantly insisted that as editor he had every right to edit any story he bought. Eventually the writers threatened a boycott of *Galaxy*, and at last Gold caved in to their demands: from that day forth he would buy or reject only, but would not change a word. Any changes had to be made by the writers themselves.

It's a policy that's still in effect throughout most of the field more than 40 years later.

How *Unknown* Was Born

Ask 20 experts (or fans; there's not much difference) which was the greatest science fiction magazine of all time, and you'll get some votes for the 1940s *Astounding*, the 1950s *Galaxy*, the 1960s *New Worlds*, the 1970s *F&SF*, and the 1990's *Asimov's*.

Now ask that same group to name the greatest fantasy magazine, and the odds are that at least 19 will answer *Unknown*. It was that good, that unique, and remains that dominant in the minds of the readers.

How did it begin?

There are two versions.

The first is that John Campbell wanted to start a fantasy magazine, he convinced Street & Smith to publish it, he called it *Unknown*, and it ran 43 issues until the wartime paper shortage killed it off.

The other version, which has been repeated in dozens of venues, is that Campbell was sitting at his desk at *Astounding*, reading submissions, and he came to a novel, *Sinister Barrier*, by Eric Frank Russell. It was too good to turn down, but it didn't fit into the format he had created for *Astounding*, and hence there was nothing to do but create a brand-new magazine, *Unknown*, which could run stories like *Sinister Barrier* and Fritz Leiber's Gray Mouser stories, and Theodore Sturgeon's "Yesterday Was Monday" and Robert A. Heinlein's *Magic, Inc.*, and *that's* how *Unknown* came into being. A number of histories of the field have reported that *this* was the start of *Unknown*.

Which version is true?

The first one, of course—but the second one is so fascinating and evocative that I suspect it'll never die, and if we all keep repeating it enough, why, in another 60 years or so, it'll be History. (See my novel *The Outpost* to discover how these things work.)

Walter Who?

It all began with a radio show hosted by a mysterious male character known only as the Shadow. The show was owned by Street & Smith, the huge magazine publisher, and when it became increasingly obvious that the Shadow was far more popular than the show, they decided they'd better do something to copyright and trademark him before it was too late—so they decided to publish a one-shot pulp magazine about a crimefighter known as the Shadow.

To write the story, they hired magician and sometime pulp author Walter Gibson, and, for whatever initial reason, they decided to have him write it as "Maxwell Grant."

The rest is history. That first issue of *The Shadow* sold out in record time. Street & Smith immediately ordered more novels from Gibson— who was getting $500.00 a novel, not bad pay in the depths of the depression—and in mere months *The Shadow* was selling more than a million copies an issue.

So Street & Smith decided the next step was to go semi-monthly. They called Gibson into their offices and asked if he was capable of turning out a Shadow novel every 15 days. Gibson said he could do it, but since it was no secret that *The Shadow* had, almost overnight, become the best-selling pulp magazine in America, he wanted a piece of this bonanza. He wasn't going to be greedy or hold them up for some phenomenal sum. He'd write two novels a month, never miss a deadline, and keep the quality as high as it had been—but in exchange, he wanted a raise to $750.00 a novel.

His loving, doting publishers immediately metamorphosed into businessmen and said No.

Gibson thought he had them over a barrel. You give me $750.00 a novel, he said, or I'll leave and take my audience with me.

Leave if you want, said Street & Smith, but next week there will be a new Maxwell Grant writing *The Shadow* for us, and who will know the difference?

It took Gibson ten seconds to realize that far from having Street & Smith over a barrel, they had him *inside* the barrel. He went back home and continued to write Shadow novels for $500.00 a shot.

This ploy worked so well that when Street & Smith began publishing *Doc Savage*, which was primarily written by Lester Dent, all the novels were credited to "Kenneth Robeson."

Rivals saw the beauty in this—Street & Smith didn't exactly have a monopoly on publishing's notion of fair play and morality—and thus *The Spider* novels, written mostly by Norvell Page, bore the pseudonym of "Grant Stockbridge."

"Kenneth Robeson," Doc Savage's author, was so popular that "he" also became the author of *The Avenger* pulp series.

And so on. Soon all the other "hero pulps"—pulps with a continuing hero and cast of characters, such as the above-mentioned—were written under house names, so that no author could either hold up the publishers for a living wage or leave and force the magazine to close down.

There was only one exception.

Edmond Hamilton wrote most of the 22 *Captain Future* novels under his own name.

The reason?

He was the only established science fiction writer working for Better Publications, Cap's publisher, and his employers freely admitted that no one else in the house knew the first damned thing about writing that crazy Buck Rogers stuff.

Who is Edson McCann?

One day Horace Gold, the editor/publisher of *Galaxy*, got the notion of having a contest for the best novel by an unknown writer. He offered a prize of $7,000—more than the average American made in a year back then—and was immediately whelmed over by hundreds of booklength manuscripts, 99% of them dreadful and the other one percent even worse. (Ask anyone who has ever read a slush pile. This was nothing unusual or unexpected—at least, not by anyone except Horace.)

Horace had already bought *Gravy Planet* (later to become *The Space Merchants*, which eventually outsold, worldwide, just about every other science fiction novel ever written except perhaps for *Dune*.) When he couldn't find an even mildly acceptable novel among the entries, he approached Fred Pohl and Cyril Kornbluth and said he'd like *Gravy Planet* to be the winner. The stipulation, though, was that it had to appear under a pseudonym, since the contest had to be won by an unknown.

Pohl and Kornbluth talked it over, decided they could get $7,000 from normal serial and book rights, and opted to keep their names on it, which disqualified it from the contest.

Now Gold was getting desperate. The deadline was almost upon him, and he still hadn't found a single publishable novel among all the entries. So he turned to Pohl again.

Pohl and his Milford neighbor, Lester del Rey (a whole passel of science fiction writers lived in Milford, Pennsylvania back in the 1950s) had decided to collaborate on a novel about the future of the insurance industry, called *Preferred Risk*. Gold begged them to use a pseudonym and let it be the contest winner. Lester was less concerned with receiving credit for his work than Kornbluth was—or perhaps he was more concerned with a quick profit. At any rate, he agreed, and Pohl went along with him.

They divided up the pen name. Pohl chose "Edson" for a first name, and del Rey came up with "McCann". They invented a whole life for him (for the magazine's bio of the contest winner), in which he was a nuclear physicist working on such a top secret hush-hush project that *Galaxy* couldn't divulge any of the details of his life.

And so it was that *Preferred Risk*, commissioned from two top professionals by Horace Gold, won the $7,000 prize for the Best Novel By An Unknown.

And why did they choose "Edson McCann"?

Well, if you break it down to its initials, it's "E. McC"— or E equals MC squared.

The No-Budget Prozines

Hugo Gernsback is considered the Father of Science Fiction. That title is more than a little at odds with the facts, since Mary Shelley, Jules Verne and H. G. Wells were writing it long before Hugo came along—but Hugo named the field and was the first publisher to bring out a magazine devoted entirely to "scientifiction" (*Amazing Stories* in 1926).

Parenthetically, he also guaranteed that we would be inundated with bad science fiction for years to come . . . because by creating a market for science fiction, he gave it a place where it no longer had to compete with the best of the other categories. Science fiction writers no longer had to fight for spots in a magazine against Dashiell Hammett and James T. Cain and Frank Gruber and Max Brand; now they competed with Ray Cummings and Nat Schachner and Ross Rocklynne. The first—and for years only— science fiction magazine in the world was edited by Hugo

Gernsback, an immigrant whose knowledge of the English language was minimal, and whose knowledge of story construction was nil. He felt science fiction's sole purpose was to interest adolescent boys in becoming scientists, and that was pretty much the way he edited.

The way he published was even worse. He liked to buy stories, but he hated to pay for them. Finally Donald A. Wollheim took him to court for the $10.00 he was owed. Neither Gernsback nor Wollheim ever forgot it.

Now move the clock ahead a few years, to about 1940. Wollheim had helped form the Futurians, that incredibly talented group of youngsters that would someday dominate the field. Among its members were Cyril Kornbluth, Damon Knight, Judith Merril, Frederik Pohl, Isaac Asimov, Robert A. W. Lowndes, James Blish, and Wollheim himself (and indeed, in a year or two they'd be editing just about every magazine in the field except for John Campbell's *Astounding*.)

Anyway, while Pohl edited *Astonishing* and *Super Science* on a pitifully small budget, Wollheim picked up two of his own to edit: *Cosmic* and *Stirring Science*. Their pages abounded in stories by Futurians Kornbluth, Pohl, Lowndes, and Knight, with illos by the finest Futurian artist, Hannes Bok. Those magazines put many of the Futurians on the map.

And do you know *why* Wollheim used Futurians almost exclusively?

Because his budget was Zero—not small, not minimal, but zero—and only his fellow Futurians would work for free for the man who once sued Hugo Gernsback for $10 that was owed on a story.

Horace Gold Goes Out to Play

Horace Gold returned home from World War II a disabled veteran . . . but his disability took a most peculiar form: agoraphobia. He was literally afraid to leave the comfort and security of his New York apartment.

It didn't stop him from selling investors on the idea of *Galaxy* magazine. And it didn't stop him from editing it, and turning it into (in my opinion) the only serious rival the *Astounding* of the late 1930s and early 1940s had for the title of Best Science Fiction Magazine of All Time.

He turned part of his apartment into an office. He worked at home, he ate at home, he slept at home, he wrote at home, he edited at home. Any writer who wanted a face-to-face with Horace visited him at home. He hosted a regular Friday night poker game that included his stable of writers: Bob Sheckley, Phil Klass (William Tenn), Fred Pohl, and Algis

Budrys. Lester del Rey occasionally sat in, as did rival editor (of *F&SF*) Tony Boucher.

And because they were his friends, and they thought they were doing him a favor, this coterie of card-players and writers was constantly urging Horace to go outside, to breathe in the fresh air (well, Manhattan's approximation of it, anyway), to just take a walk around the neighborhood so that he would know there were no secret dangers lurking beyond the doors of his apartment. They urged, and they cajoled, and they implored, and finally the big day came.

Horace Gold left his apartment for the first time in years—

—and was promptly hit by a taxi.

(There is a second version of this story, in which he actually spent a few evenings wandering around Manhattan, and then got into a crash while riding home in a taxi. Either way, the result was the same. He stopped eating, stopped editing, and was eventually institutionalized.)

F&SF Loses An Editor

Cyril Kornbluth was one of the original Futurians, living in New York with Frederik Pohl, Donald A. Wollheim, Robert A. W. Lowndes, John Michel, and that whole crowd. He was the youngest of them, and at short story length he was the best of them. He came out of World War II with a bad case of hypertension, and he certainly didn't help it any by his constant smoking and drinking. But his writing got better and better, as he turned out "The Marching Morons," "The Little Black Bag," and a number of other brilliant stories. He also collaborated with Pohl on the classic *The Space Merchants*, and a number of near-classics as well. But along with his infirmities, he had a wife and kids, one of them in constant need of special care, and he needed more money than he could make writing science fiction in the 1950s. For a few years he ran a small news bureau in Chicago. When he got back to New York, an editorial position had opened up at *The Magazine of Fantasy and Science Fiction*. He arranged an interview to apply for it, but it was a foregone conclusion that the interview was just a formality and the job was his if he wanted it.

It snowed on the day of the interview, so Kornbluth, still suffering from hypertension, ignored his doctor's orders and spent half an hour shoveling his driveway, drove to the train station—and while he was waiting for the train that would take him to the perfect job for a man of his gifts and needs, he collapsed and died of a heart attack. Science fiction lost one of its finest writers, and *F&SF* lost what just might have been the best editor it ever had.

ERB: The Man Who
Held the Hero's Horse

There have been a lot of theories advanced as to why Edgar Rice Burroughs remains a popular author more than 90 years after he first broke into print, when dozens of Pulitzer and Nobel winners (and a few Hugo winners as well) can't be found this side of Bookfinder.com.

A lot of people credit his imagination, and yes, it certainly worked overtime, coming up with Tarzan, Barsoom, Amtor, Pellucidar, Caspak, Poloda, and the rest.

Others point to his break-neck pacing. You follow Tarzan until he's unarmed and facing a ferocious man-eater at chapter's end, then cut to Jane until she's one grope away from a Fate Worse Than Death at the end of the next chapter, then back to Tarzan, and so forth. Works pretty well.

A few point to his remarkable facility at creating languages. And truly, what *would* you call an elephant except Tantor? What could a snake possibly be other than Hista? What better name for an ape-king that half-barks and half-growls his language than Kerchak? Yes, he was damned good at languages.

But there's another aspect to Burroughs that lends enormous verisimilitude, especially to his younger readers, and it's an aspect that has been addressed only once before, by the late Burroughs scholar (and Royal Canadian Mountie) John F. Roy—and that is the interesting fact that ERB wrote himself into almost all his greatest adventures.

When I first discovered *A Princess of Mars* at age 8, I *knew* the story was true. I mean, hell, Burroughs was writing about his own uncle, the man who had entrusted him with the manuscript of his adventures on that distant and wondrous planet. Wasn't that proof enough that Barsoom existed?

Well, if you were young and impressionable, it *was* proof enough— but even if you weren't, it was a very effective and informal way of getting you into the story.

And while ERB was not a trained writer, at a gut level he knew it worked. He might not have known what "distancing mechanism" or "stream of consciousness" meant, but he sure as hell knew how to lasso a reader and pull him along, and his favorite and most effective gimmick was to tell you how he himself had been thrust into the company of this book's hero.

So here he was, the nephew of John Carter, gentleman of Virginia and Warlord of Mars, explaining how he had come upon this remarkable manuscript, how he had watched his uncle standing outside at night reaching out his arms to Mars, how he had followed instructions and buried him in a well-ventilated coffin that could only be opened from the inside, and only now understood the meaning of it all.

And it didn't stop with the one book. He meets John Carter again and is given the manuscripts to *The Gods of Mars* and *The Warlord of Mars*. Some years later he meets Ulysses Paxton (a/k/a Vad Varo) by proxy when John Carter delivers Paxton's long letter (i.e., *The Master Mind of Mars*) to him, and he is visited by John Carter at least twice more. It is made clear that ERB is now an old man (as indeed he was), while the Warlord remains the thirtyish fighting man he has always been.

But ERB's interaction with his characters wasn't limited to Barsoom.

For example, he knows the man who knows the man who knows Tarzan—or some permutation of that. The very first line in his most famous book, *Tarzan of the Apes*, is: "I had this story from one who had no business to tell it to me, or to any other." A Burroughs scholar would probably conclude that the "one" was Paul d'Arnot, but it makes no difference. The point is that here is ERB, inserting himself in the beginning of the story again to lend some degree of authenticity.

Did he ever meet Tarzan? He never says so explicitly, but he *did* meet Barney Custer, hero of *The Eternal Lover*, and his sister, and based on the internal evidence of the book, the only place ERB could possibly have met them was on Lord Greystoke's vast African estate.

It was while vacationing in Greenland that ERB came across the manuscript that became *The Land That Time Forgot*. (Yes, he was pretty sharp at finding saleable manuscripts.)

Burroughs gets around. *At the Earth's Core* finds him in the Sahara, where he stumbles upon David Innes, who in turn had stumbled upon the hidden world of Pellucidar and felt compelled to spend the night telling ERB his story. A reader in Algiers summons him back a few years later, where he is reintroduced to David Innes, who once again pours out his story, which was published as *Pellucidar*.

After moving to California, who should ERB's next-door neighbor turn out to be but the brilliant young scientist Jason Gridley, creator of the remarkable Gridley Wave, by means of which Burroughs received still more tales of that mysterious world at the center of the hollow Earth. (And Gridley himself later went to Pellucidar, which means that ERB rubbed shoulders with still another hero.)

Burroughs even wrote his company's secretary, Ralph Rothmond (who was later fired, more than a decade after ERB's death, for carelessly allowing a number of copyrights to lapse) into one of the books. Rothmond introduces ERB to young, handsome, blond, heroic Carson Napier, the Wrong-Way Corrigan of space, who takes off for Mars and somehow winds up on Venus. Napier remains in telepathic contact with Burroughs long enough to dictate *Pirates of Venus* and three-plus sequels.

There was just something about ERB that made heroes seek him out and tell him their strange stories, always on the condition that he not publish the tale until they were dead, or if he couldn't wait that long, to at least change their names. The last to find him and unload on him was Julian V, who narrated the tale of *The Moon Maid*.

ERB never met the author of *Beyond the Farthest Star*—after all, that would have been quite a voyage—but of all the people in the universe, the author was, perhaps unsurprisingly by this time, drawn to Burroughs, and mystically compelled ERB's typewriter to produce the story one night in Hawaii while ERB watched in awe.

The interesting thing is that though he associated with Tarzan and John Carter and David Innes and Carson Napier and many others, ERB never once performed an exciting or heroic deed in any of the books, and *that* lends a little verisimilitude too. These are extraordinary men, these heroes, and neither ERB nor you nor I can begin to match their skills or heroism, so it makes much more sense for him to tell us about it and for us to read and appreciate it. Fighting lions or green men or allosaurs is for heroes; reading about it is for the rest of us mortals.

And maybe that's why we loved and identified with Edgar Rice Burroughs. He didn't lop off heads with his longsword, or bellow the victory cry of the bull ape over the corpse of an enemy, or make his way to the center of the Earth. But he seemed to know the remarkable men who *did* do those things, and, by golly, he got to hold the hero's horse.

Most of us would have traded places with him in a New York—or Barsoomian—minute.

Review of *Adventures*, *Exploits* and *Encounters*, the first three volumes in *The Chronicles of Lucifer Jones*

Mike Resnick must lead a hopeless, unhappy life. Nothing else explains *The Chronicles of Lucifer Jones*.

Here is a protagonist, a man of deep religious convictions who communes with God on a daily basis, who wants nothing more than to build a tabernacle, and yet Resnick arranges for events to conspire against him time after time. Every time he is on the brink of achieving his life's ambition (and a modest ambition it is, creating a place where the poor and the downtrodden can come to seek spiritual comfort), his moment of triumph is snatched away from him.

Lucifer's travails and tribulations extend to every facet of his life. He falls in love with an Oriental businesswoman, only to be cast aside at the last minute. He achieves some degree of political power in a small municipality, only to watch it slip away. He is quick to make friends, but is eventually betrayed by every last one of them. Clearly a man without a prejudiced bone in his body, he enters into partnerships with men and women of all races and all walks of life, but just as we find ourselves hoping that the poor man has finally found some small measure of happiness in his blameless life, Resnick pulls the rug out from under him again.

This modern-day Job has done nothing to deserve his Fate. A simple man, he is unable to use the language without mangling it almost beyond recognition. A lonely man, he is unable to establish a lasting relationship with a woman, despite his willingness to try again and again. A man who wants nothing but stability in his life, he seems doomed to wander the world, expelled by one otherwise charitable country after another.

Why would Resnick write such a book? What personal demons is he trying to exorcise? How can he visit *any* character with so many unrealized hopes and dreams? What kind of twisted nihilist would create a man of God, a man who constantly believes the Lord will come to his aid, that tomorrow will be a new beginning, and then do to him what Resnick continually does to Lucifer Jones?

Recommended only for those twisted minds that find fulfillment in the throes of terminal depression.

The Sport of Kings

I am a horse-racing fanatic. I don't bet, but I've been known to fly halfway across the country to watch Seattle Slew hook up with Affirmed, or Dr. Fager take on Damascus.

I've written for *The Blood-Horse, American Turf, Horseman's Journal*, and half a dozen other racing publications, and I wrote a weekly column on racing for more than a decade.

So it stood to reason that sooner or later Guy Lillian was going to ask me to Explain It All To You.

Terms

To understand horse-racing, you really should learn some of the lingo. So let's start with it.

Furlong. A furlong is an eighth of a mile, 220 yards. The term originated because that was approximately the length of a farmer's furrow. Almost all horse race distances are described in furlongs. A 6-furlong race is 3/4 of a mile; an 8 1/2 furlong race is a mile and a sixteenth; a 12-furlong race is a mile and a half.

Turf. Turf means grass. Most American races—80% or more—are run on the dirt. The rest, and almost all races in Europe, South America, Australia and Asia, are run on the turf.

Track conditions are fast, good, slow, muddy, and sloppy. Strangely enough, you get your second-fastest times not on good tracks, but on sloppy ones, because if there's standing water on the track, it means that it hasn't soaked in and the track is reasonably hard beneath the water. Good and slow tracks are tiring, and this affects front-runners the most. Muddy tracks are a class by themselves: some great horses, such as Swaps, could barely stand up in the mud, let along run in it; others, such as Bold Ruler, were far better in the mud than on fast tracks. Most horses are relatively unaffected by it.

Weight. It's impossible to stagger a start the way you can do with human runners, so when the track handicapper tries to give every horse an even chance, he does it by assigning different weights to them. The usual rule of thumb is that 2 pounds equals a length, and scale weight is usually 126 pounds—so if I think that horse A is 4 lengths better than horse B, and that horse A is probably a length and a half poorer than the average good horse of his age and class, I would assign horse A 123 pounds and horse B 115 pounds. Most jockeys weigh between 95 and

112 pounds, and any extra weight the horse must carry is made up by putting lead weights in the saddle pads. Over the past century, only truly exceptional horses have been asked to carry 130 pounds or more, and only one in the past 50 years has won with 140 pounds.

How to Watch a Race

Horses don't just run hell for leather from flagfall to finish. They can't. The very best horses can sustain an all-out drive for about half a mile. There are no races that short for Thoroughbreds anywhere in America.

Competition saps a horse's energy. A horse running three lengths ahead of the field after a half-mile in 47 seconds uses much less adrenaline than the same horse, running neck-and-neck for the lead with a rival, uses after a half mile in that same time of 47 seconds.

The purpose of the jockey is twofold: to keep his horse free of trouble (and by trouble, I mean traffic jams), and to conserve his horse's energy and get him to relax, whether he is running in front or coming from behind.

How do you know if your horse is doing well?

Easy. Watch the jockey. If his rump is way up in the air, well above the saddle, if his toes are up and his heels are down, he's restraining the horse. (Remember: he weighs 110 pounds. The horse weighs about 1,100 pounds. He *has* to practically stand up and lean back to restrain the horse.)

How do you know when your jockey is asking for speed? His rump will come down to the saddle, he'll lean forward, and he'll drop his hands (thus releasing his restraint on the reins).

How do you know when your horse isn't responding? Every major jockey since the now-retired Bill Hartack is right-handed, so each of them uses his crop (it's called a "popper," because it makes a startling sound but doesn't hurt or leave welts) in his right hand. If, in the homestretch, you see your jockey has shifted the crop to his left hand, it means he wasn't getting any response from his mount and is trying to startle it by whipping it on a side that never gets whipped.

How do you know if your jockey has confidence in your come-from-behind horse? It's generally considered that for every horse you pass on a turn, you're giving up a length. So if your jockey goes five wide on the far turn, he's saying, in essence: "My horse is so strong today, so full of run, that I'm willing to spot the leader 5 lengths in the homestretch, just to make sure I'm outside of all the traffic and have a clear lane to the wire." (Tired horses, like tired humans, tend not to run in a straight line. The easiest way to avoid them is to go wide and come down the middle of the track—*if* you feel your horse is good enough to go wide.)

And, of course, if the jock tries to sneak through on the rail, or pick his way through horses like a broken-field runner in football, he's not as confident and he's saving every bit of ground he can.

Off-tracks: if you like front-runners, the best time to bet them is on muddy tracks. Why? First, they won't get mud thrown up in their faces like the horses behind them (and enough mud in the eye or up a nostril can discourage *any* horse), and second, the horses directly behind the front runner could pick up 10 to 20 pounds of mud on their necks, chests, and shoulders. (Remember the handicapper's rule of thumb, that two pounds equals a length? That means if you pick up 16 pounds of mud, you're spotting the front-runner an extra 8 lengths.)

Time

You can also get a notion of how the race will turn out by looking at the fractions, which are posted every quarter-mile on the infield tote board.

A good, usually victorious, time for 6 furlongs is 1:10; for a mile, 1:35; for a mile and a quarter, 2:01; for a mile and a half, 2:29. As you can see, the average quarter-mile takes a bit longer as the distance increases (and for those of you who care, it's estimated that a Thoroughbred can run 5 lengths in a second, which makes it very easy for a sport that divides times by fifths of a second.)

The world records are, of course, a good bit faster: 1:06 1/5 for 6 furlongs, 1:32 for a mile, 1:57 3/5 for a mile and a quarter, 2:24 for a mile and a half.

Anyway, once you know what a good time should be, and how long a horse can sustain his top speed, it doesn't take much to look at the time and figure out what's likely to happen.

For example, you're watching the Kentucky Derby. It's a mile and a quarter. Five horses are bunched near the lead. The time for the first half-mile is :45 3/5 seconds. What conclusion can you draw? That none of those five will be around at the end. They've used themselves up too early, and there's more than half the race to go.

Okay, now we're watching a 6-furlong sprint. Same scenario: five horses bunched up front in :45 3/5 seconds. What conclusions can you draw from that? That one of them will probably win the race—after all, a final quarter of 24 seconds, much slower than they've been running, will still get him home in 1:09 3/5, usually a winning time. Which horse is the likeliest? Check those jockeys: whose rump is highest in the air? Who's already whipping his horse before the others do? Is the one on the outside riding confidently, or asking for an all-out effort already?

How do you beat a top front-runner, a Seattle Slew or a Dr. Fager? By making him use himself early. You get him to run that first half-mile in 44 seconds, and he won't be around at the end. You let him get away to an opening half-mile in 48 seconds, and the race is as good as over. If he's a front-runner, he very likely will not relax and let another horse take the lead without putting up a struggle. A front-runner's only weak spot is his stamina, and if you don't force him to expend his energy early, you've lost before the race is half done.

How do you beat a top come-from-behinder, a Forego or a Damascus? By setting the slowest possible pace. That come-from-behind horse wins by catching tired horses with a final burst of speed. Run that first half mile in 45 seconds and you're properly softened up for him; sneak away in 48 seconds, and your horse will be a lot fresher, and harder to catch, in the homestretch.

Did the favorite draw an inside post position? Good. Run alongside him, right behind the leader, and never give him room to move ahead. If he wants the lead, his jockey will have to slow him down until he's behind you and has enough room to maneuver to the outside.

You're in front, your horse is tiring a bit, and you know that the come-from-behind favorite has yet to make his run? Don't hug the rail. Move out as far as you dare toward the middle of the track, and make that favorite go even wider. His jockey will have just a fraction of a second to decide if you're purposely going wide (and hence he can cut inside of you) or if your horse is getting leg-weary (and hence might bear to his left any instant and close the inviting hole he just made). Usually the jockey will play it safe and go wide—and you might have made him go just wide enough so you can hang on and win.

It's all strategy, and it's fascinating when you understand what you're seeing.

16,307

There are, to date, 16,307 ways to lose a horse race. There is only one way to win: get home first.

Bill Shoemaker is widely considered to be one of the two or three greatest jockeys in history. He was the winningest rider of all time, both in numbers of wins and in money won, when he retired. (Both totals have been surpassed.)

And yet Shoemaker was capable of some of the most bone-headed blunders in major races that anyone ever saw.

Take the 1957 Kentucky Derby. Please.

A racetrack places poles every sixteenth of a mile, so the jockeys can look at the pole as they pass it and know how far they are from the finish. The sixteenth pole is a sixteenth of a mile from the finish wire, the eighth pole an eighth of a mile, and so forth.

Shoemaker was riding Gallant Man. He was a "plodder," a come-from-behind horse who lacked early speed but got better and stronger as the races got longer. He'd been running 7th for most of the way, but then Shoemaker put him to a drive, and he began catching tiring horses. At the head of the stretch he caught the tiring favorite, Bold Ruler. At the eighth pole he caught Round Table. At the sixteenth pole he was within inches of catching the leader, Iron Liege—and then Shoemaker, who'd ridden in half a dozen Derbies and already won one, mistook the sixteenth pole for the finish wire and stood up in the stirrups, easing his horse. He realized his mistake in less than a second and sat back down and started whipping Gallant Man again . . . but at the finish wire it was Iron Liege by a nose, and there is no question that Shoemaker standing up for that second cost Gallant Man more than the four inches he lost by.

It came less than a year after an equally glaring blunder. In horse racing, 2-year-olds and 3-year-olds usually run at equal weights—but after two years on the track, there's usually very little doubt as to which is the best horse, and racetracks couldn't draw competitive fields if they didn't start handicapping the outstanding horses by making them carry more weight.

Now, if you're riding horse A, and carrying 125 pounds, and you beat horse B, who is carrying 119 pounds, by 2 lengths, in all likelihood the handicapper is going to increase the weight spread from 6 pounds to 10 pounds the next time the two horses meet . . . so, from the point of view of the trainer and jockey, you want to win a handicap race not by the biggest possible margin, but by the smallest safe margin. Why win by 5 lengths and pick up 10 pounds in your next start when you can win by one length and only pick up two pounds?

Shoemaker was riding the brilliant Swaps in the 1956 Californian Stakes. Swaps had just set a world record in Florida; he would proceed to set world records in 4 of his next 5 starts, something that neither Man o' War nor any other thoroughbred ever did. And since all those upcoming races were handicaps, Shoemaker knew that he didn't want to win by a dozen lengths (though Swaps was clearly good enough to do so). The race began, Swaps lay back in 3rd place, moved up to the lead on the far turn, and entered the homestretch four lengths in front—and Shoemaker decided he'd better cut that victory margin down so that Swaps didn't pick up too much weight in his next race.

And of course, as he was slowing Swaps down, Porterhouse, a nice but not outstanding horse, ran the race of his life and caught him two jumps short of the wire. By the time Shoemaker realized what was happening, it was too late to get Swaps going again, and he lost by a head.

There are 16,305 more ways, but you don't really need to learn them all today.

They Don't Lose on Purpose

Eddie Arcaro, considered the greatest jockey of his time, was riding a mediocre horse in a very unimportant race at Belmont Park. It came in 9th in a 10-horse field.

Upon returning to the unsaddling enclosure, Arcaro was confronted by an irate trainer.

"Why didn't you listen to instructions?" demanded the trainer in a loud, piercing voice. "I told you to lay fourth to the far turn, move up to third at the head of the stretch, and then come on to win!"

"What did you want me to do?" responded Arcaro. "Leave the horse?"

Names

There are names that conjure up equine greatness: Man 'o War, Citation, Equipoise, Secretariat, Ruffian.

There are names that don't, but they usually have more interesting origins.

For example:

Seattle Slew, the 1977 Triple Crown winner, was named because one set of his owners had a logging camp just outside Seattle, and the other set lived next to a Florida swamp.

Swaps, the 1955 Kentucky Derby winner, was named because Rex Ellsworth, his breeder, and Mish Tenney, his trainer, spent all of one night suggesting and rejecting monickers, and finally got tired of "swapping names."

The great British stallion, Ballydam, sired a colt who had colic as an infant. Named Bally Ache, he went on to win the 1961 Preakness.

Alfred Gwynn Vanderbilt was considered a master at naming his horses. The great Native Dancer, winner of 21 of his 22 races, was by Polynesian out of Geisha. Find was sired by Discovery. But it was the Dancer's and Find's stakes-winning stablemate who gets my vote as the best-named: by Shut Out out of Pansy, he became Social Outcast.

Alydar, who ran 10 memorable races against Affirmed, was named for Aly Khan, whom his owner knew as Aly Darling.

Tom Fool's greatest son was Buckpasser, but his best-named one was Dunce.

Trainer John Nerud had successful brain surgery, so he named a horse after the surgeon to thank him. The horse turned out to be Dr. Fager, the 1968 Horse of the Year.

Ponder, winner of the 1944 Kentucky Derby, sired Pensive, winner of the 1949 Kentucky Derby.

Sometime the names are so obvious you would never guess their origin. The winner of 30 stakes races, Swoon's Son was by The Doge out of (surprise!) Swoon.

The Most Important Races

To the man on the street, the most important race to win is the Kentucky Derby. Sports writers who don't know which end of the horse has teeth all become experts on the first Saturday in May, just as they become gymnastics experts every 4th year during the Olympics.

To the racing professional, there are more important races. One is the Belmont Stakes, because the 12-furlong distance is a quarter-mile longer than the Derby and requires that much more stamina (which is always a prime selling point in a stallion). Also, far more Belmont winners than Derby winners become divisional champions.

Another more important race is the Breeders Cup Classic, because it brings together the best horses in America, not just 3-year-olds but older handicap horses as well, at the Derby distance . . . and it's a rare 3-year-old than can beat a top-notch older horse.

In France, the Prix de l'arc de Triomphe, run at 12 furlongs on the grass about 3 weeks before the Breeders Cup, is considered by Europeans to be the most important race in the world.

Greatness

The mark of a great horse is to carry weight over distance. That's been the criterion for as long as there have been horses and races.

Put in simple terms, a horse cannot be considered great until he has won—hopefully repeatedly—at the classic distance of a mile and a quarter. Or more.

And he cannot be considered great until he has carried more than scale weight, in practical terms 130 pounds or more, and given away chunks of weight to good competition.

By this criterion, Secretariat was not a great horse—or, rather, let us say that he was never given the opportunity to prove he was a great horse, because he retired as a 3-year-old, and hence never had to carry enormous weights and give weight away. Another horse from his crop, 3-time Horse of the Year, Forego, was demonstrably a great horse, winning more than a dozen times at 10 furlongs or more, successfully carrying 137 pounds to victory, and always giving away weight to his rivals.

Could Forego have beaten Secretariat? Possibly not. The one time they met was in the Kentucky Derby, when Forego was still a year away from his best efforts. But there is no question of Forego's greatness; there will always be some doubt as to whether Secretariat could have carried, say, 135 pounds, and given 15 and 20 pounds to good horses as Forego did so many times.

My own criteria would include not only the ability to carry weight over distance, but also the ability to win a huge percentage of one's races. Man 'o War won 20 of 21; Native Dancer 21 of 22; Personal Ensign 13 of 13; Seattle Slew 14 of 17; Dr. Fager 19 of 22; Ruffian 10 of 11. Allowances can be made for Kelso and Forego, because, as geldings, they raced at the mercy of handicappers for many years, whereas most complete horses give the handicapper a single year to slow them down and then retire with their reputations mostly intact. (Which is to say, they retire at 4, or in some cases, such as Secretariat, at 3; whereas Kelso was Horse of the Year at 3, 4, 5, 6, and 7, and was still running at 9; Forego was Horse of the Year at 4, 5, and 6, and handicap champion at 7; and old Find, a stablemate of Native Dancer and Social Outcast, was still winning stakes at 9 and placing in them at 11.) Thus, I'm less impressed with Secretariat, who lost 5 times to very ordinary horses in 21 starts, than I am with Seattle Slew, who lost two photo-finishes to year-end champions, and lost only one other race when he clearly wasn't fit.

I can also make allowances for injury. Citation won 32 of his 45 starts, hardly a percentage for one of the 3 or 4 greatest American race horses—but he won 27 of his 29 starts at ages 2 and 3, missed his entire 4-year-old season due to injury, and was hardly the same horse when he came back at 5 and 6.

Rivalries

The Yankees and Dodgers. The Lakers and Celtics. The Cowboys and Steelers. Great rivalries are essential to any sport, and horse-racing has had its share of them.

The most famous rivals, of course, were Affirmed and Alydar. They met 10 times in 15 months. Affirmed won 7 of them, 5 in photo finishes, and was second 3 times. Alydar won 3, and was second 6 times. At the end of 10 races and almost 11 miles, they were something less than 2 lengths apart.

But they weren't the only ones.

Back in the late 1950s, there was a trio of outstanding horses, all of whom had been born in 1954—Bold Ruler, Gallant Man, and Round Table. When the dust had cleared, Bold Ruler and Gallant Man had met 8 times, splitting 4 apiece. Bold Ruler and Round Table had met twice, splitting one apiece. Gallant Man met Round Table three times and won all three.

Probably the two greatest horses to engage in a top-drawer rivalry in the past half-century were Dr. Fager and Damascus. They met twice in 1967, each winning once; and twice in 1968, splitting again. In 1968, neither ever carried less than 131 pounds.

Money

There's a lot of money in racing and breeding, far more than there used to be. I can remember when a Hyperion colt named Rise 'n Shine set the all-time yearling auction record by selling for a then-unheard-of $87,500. These days yearlings sold at the Keeneland Summer Auction *average* more than half a million dollars apiece. The record, for a half-brother to Seattle Slew—remember, this was a yearling who'd never even had a saddle put on him—was for more than $13 million.

And never won a stakes race.

In fact, of the first 100 yearlings to sell for more than a million dollars, only 4 earned back their purchase price, and only one—A. P. Indy, a son of Seattle Slew—became a champion.

Stud fees have also skyrocketed. These days the leading sire in the country is Storm Cat, and a date with him costs $500,000—*if* you can get to him. He's usually booked years in advance.

(Cheer up. If he's busy, maybe you can get a date with Danzig. He's only $350,000 per service.)

You can also run up a tidy profit if you pick right. People talk about Seabiscuit and Stymie, former claiming horses (horses that were for sale for a set price on the day of the race) who were bought for peanuts and went on to win hundreds of thousands of dollars. John Henry sold for $25,000 in 1979 and went on to win more than $6 million.

But for a *real* success story, look no further than Seattle Slew. His "call name" around the barn as a yearling was Baby Huey, because he was so clumsy. He was rejected for the Keeneland Summer Sales, because neither his pedigree nor conformation were perfect enough, and the team of Mickey and Karen Taylor, and Jim and Sally Hill, bought him in the fall for $17,500.

When did they get for their investment?

Well, to begin with, they got the only undefeated Triple Crown winner in history, who went on to win over a million dollars on the track.

Then they syndicated him for $12 million, keeping 20 shares ($6 million worth at the time) for themselves and selling 20 shares.

By 1986, 8 years after his initial syndication, he had been so phenomenally successful at stud that a share in Seattle Slew sold at auction for $4 million, making the horse's value $160 million—more than any skyscraper in downtown Cincinnati, to put it in some perspective.

But that wasn't all. The Taylors and Hills entered into a foal-sharing arrangement with major breeders like Claiborne Farm and others of that ilk. It worked like this: Claiborne, to take a concrete example, got two free seasons to Seattle Slew. They would flip a coin, and Claiborne got one foal and the Taylors and Hills got one. In this particular case, Claiborne got Derby and Belmont winner Swale, who died tragically only eight days after winning the Belmont; and the Taylors and Hills got champion Slew o' Gold, who not only won close to $4 million but in turn was syndicated for $15 million (and again, they kept half the shares and sold half the shares.)

Between his owners, and his syndicate members, and the breeders who sold his yearlings, and the people who raced his offspring, it's estimated that this one $17,500 yearling created more than 100 millionaires. Hard to do if you're not franchising MacDonald's.

Colors

Probably because binoculars are a relatively recent invention, horse-racing is an incredibly colorful sport. Not only do the horses come in a number of colors, but every owner has his own silks, and some of the designs are truly eye-catching (as they were meant to be, since they originated to help an owner spot his horse as a cluster of them raced down the backstretch half a mile away).

The most famous colors?

Probably Calumet's devil's red and blue—a red jersey, with two blue bars on each sleeve.

Then there's Claiborne's pure orange, and Odgen Phipps' pure black.

The Vanderbilt silks are cerise and white diamonds, with red sleeves. (When I was 10, and already a fanatic, I wrote a number of owners and stables, asking for their silks. Only two—Brookmeade Stable [white with blue cross sashes] and Vanderbilt—sent them to me. One of the most mournful days of my life came two years later when I realized I had outgrown them forever.

There are currently more than 5,000 colorful designs registered with the Jockey Club. Makes baseball uniforms seem even duller than they are.

Equipment

The most common equipment for a racehorse is a set of blinkers. It keeps his attention straight ahead, and stops him from getting distracted by movements in the stands or the infield.

Then there's the shadow roll, about two inches thick and cylindrical, which goes over his nose, and prevents him from seeing (and jumping) shadows.

From time to time you'll see a horse with a tongue-tie; this stops him from trying to swallow his tongue in the heat of the race (or not trying and doing it anyway).

Some horses will wear protective bandages on front or rear legs.

On off tracks, some horses will wear mud caulks, the equivalent of spiked shoes, which gives them better purchase.

None of these things should give you any concern; none imply that a particular horse is at anything less that his best or fittest.

On the other hand, a bar shoe—the program book will tell you if he's wearing one—is a protective device for horses with quarter cracks (cracks on their hooves). The track vet won't let the horse run if he's lame, or in any way unfit, but a bar shoe is an indication that he's had problems in the past and may again.

Medication

Almost every horse runs on Lasix these days. When a horse makes an extreme effort, he may occasionally bleed—which is to say, capillaries burst in his lungs, the blood comes up through his nostrils, and he can't breathe easily. Lasix used to be outlawed in New York, but now it's legal everywhere in the country, and used as a preventative far more than a cure. (If a horse *does* bleed, he is forbidden to race again until the track veterinarian is convinced the problem has been solved.)

Many horses run on Bute—short for Butazolidin, a brand name for phenylbutazone. (I used it once myself, when I tore some tendons in my foot and my doctor prescribed it.) Bute doesn't cure anything, but if a horse is sore—and sooner or later, most athletes get sore if they stay in training—the Bute will mask his pain. Again, it used to be outlawed at about half the tracks—the one disqualification in the history of the Kentucky Derby came in 1968 when it was discovered that Dancer's Image had used Bute—but today it's legal everywhere.

Again, if you find a horse is running on Bute and/or Lasix, it's absolutely standard. He probably doesn't even need it, but as long as it doesn't hurt and might help, trainers will use it.

So Take a Look

Okay, that's your primer. It can't begin to tell you what it's like to watch Affirmed and Alydar locked in head-and-head battle all the way around the track, or seeing Forego starting to pick up lagging horses as he straightens out to begin his stretch run, or old Kelso wiping out yet another generation of pretenders to his throne, or Ruffian turning into the stretch 10 lengths in front when her jockey hasn't asked her for speed yet.

But maybe when you see it next time, you'll have a little better idea of what you're looking at.

PART II

Now that you know a little something about it, let's examine a few races and see not only how they played out, but *why*.

The 1985 Kentucky Derby

The lukewarm favorite was Chief's Crown, but five or six horses were considered to have a good chance to win. One of them was a front-runner, Spend A Buck, ridden by Angel Cordero. There was another speed horse in the race, owned by the Yankees' George Steinbrenner.

The gate opened, Cordero sent Spend A Buck to the front as expected, and Steinbrenner's horse stumbled, just as War Emblem stumbled at the start of the 2002 Belmont—and suddenly, only a furlong into the 10-furlong race, Spend A Buck was 5 lengths in front. Each of the other jockeys had to decide whether to engage Cordero's horse in a speed duel to soften him up for the homestretch (which would soften their own mounts up as well) or wait for someone else to do it. Every jockey elected to wait. Spend A Buck entered the backstretch with an uncontested 6-length lead, and the race was over. Turning into the stretch he was every bit as fresh as the horses who were trying to catch him, and he won by 5 lengths without drawing a deep breath.

The 1955 Kentucky Derby

The heavy favorite was Nashua, with Eddie Arcaro riding him. Nashua had had a pair of all-out wars with Summer Tan, ridden by Eric Guerin, and Arcaro felt that was the horse to beat.

An unknown California horse, Swaps—who would not remain unknown for long—got a comfortable 2-length lead going around the far turn. Nashua was laying third, a length ahead of Summer Tan, and Arcaro didn't want to use his horse up and soften him for Summer Tan's stretch run, so he kept him under light restraint. And he kept him, and he kept him—and by the time he realized that Summer Tan was never going to pass him, and Swaps was running far too easily at the front end, it was too late and he never could catch the California colt.

The 1968 Suburban and Brooklyn Handicaps

Two of the great ones hooked up. Damascus, the 1967 Horse of the Year, winner of 13 of his last 15 starts, possessor of the most powerful stretch run in racing, carried 133 pounds—far above scale—in the Suburban Handicap. His lifelong rival, Dr. Fager, winner at the time of 15 of 17 lifetime starts, and perhaps the fastest front-runner in history, carried 132 pounds.

There were only five horses in the race. Every horse was good, though the other three weren't quite in a class with the top two—but they didn't have to be, since this was a handicap, and they were in receipt of 15 to 20 pounds each. But the point is, none of them was willing to sacrifice himself on the altar of pacemaking to soften Dr. Fager up for Damascus. As a result, Dr. Fager broke on top, and when he had run half a mile in 47 seconds, the race was as good as over. Damascus made a run at him in the homestretch, but never seriously threatened him and came in second.

They met two weeks later in the Brooklyn Handicap. This time Dr. Fager carried 135 pounds to 131 on Damascus—but this time, Damascus had help. His trainer also entered his stablemate Hedevar, the previous year's champion sprinter. Hedevar wasn't there to win; his trainer didn't even care if the jockey pulled him up once his job was done. And his job was to force the headstrong Dr. Fager into such rapid early fractions that Damascus would have a chance to catch a tiring horse in the stretch.

The gate opened, Dr. Fager broke on top, as usual, and Hedevar broke almost as fast. He got within a neck of Dr. Fager, who absolutely wouldn't be passed. They ran the first quarter mile in a phenomenal 21 3/5 seconds, the half in 44 seconds flat—and even though Hedevar tossed in the towel and Dr. Fager found himself 3 lengths in front, the race was as good as over. Damascus moved up on the far turn, got the leg-weary Dr. Fager in his sights, ran him down in the homestretch, and beat him to the wire by 2 lengths.

The 1977 Belmont Stakes

In the Kentucky Derby, For the Moment had pressed front-running Seattle Slew. They'd run the first 6 furlongs in 1:10, and Slew went on to win rather handily while For the Moment finished 5th.

In the Preakness, it was Cormorant's turn. He was heads apart with Seattle Slew after 6 furlongs in 1:09 3/5. Slew won by a daylight margin, while Cormorant faded to 4th.

In the Belmont, having seen what happened to For the Moment and Cormorant, no one was willing to press the pace, and as a result Seattle Slew had a comfortable lead after running the first 6 furlongs in 1:14 1/5. A horse runs a length in a fifth of a second. All any fan had to do was look at the time, realize that Seattle Slew had just been allowed to run the first 6 furlongs 21 lengths slower than the Derby and 23 lengths slower than the Preakness, and you knew that no one was going to catch him on this particular day. (He won, eased up, by 4 lengths.)

The 1979 Belmont Stakes

Affirmed was our last Triple Crown winner, back in 1978. But we should have had one in 1979. He was good enough, and fit enough, and no one in the field was within five lengths of him in quality. He was Spectacular Bid, coming into the race off 12 wins in a row, including the Derby and Preakness.

He had just one problem. He was ridden by a 19-year-old kid named Ronnie Franklin, a totally-inexperienced jockey who didn't have all that much talent. But when you've got a team that's won twelve in a row, even if a few of them were closer than they should have been, you don't break it up and hire a new jockey, especially for the most important race in your horse's life.

So Ronnie Franklin was aboard Spectacular Bid when the gates opened and ten horses began the grueling, 12-furlong contest. A 30-to-1 longshot who'd never won a stakes race in his life raced off to a long lead. Franklin had Spectacular Bid in second place, running easily along the rail. This in itself was unusual, because usually the Bid came from the back of the pack with a powerful late run.

There was another unusual thing. General Assembly, the horse with the most early speed in the field, the horse who had set the pace in the Derby and Preakness, was three lengths behind Spectacular Bid. His jockey, the experienced Angel Cordero, realized that the leader was setting a suicidal pace and wanted no part of it.

When they'd run almost half a mile, the leader was still 6 lengths in front, and Franklin panicked. Fearful that the longshot would get an insurmountable lead, and unaware that they'd just run the half mile in 46 seconds, a murderous pace for the shorter Derby let alone the Belmont,

Franklin sent Spectacular Bid after the frontrunner. He caught him in less than a quarter mile, and the longshot threw in the towel without a fight. Suddenly Franklin found himself four lengths in front with half a mile to go, and all the sportswriters who knew nothing about racing felt the race was as good as over.

It was—but not the way they thought. The Bid was four lengths in front, true—but he'd used up too much energy catching that meaningless frontrunner, and his time for the first mile was much too fast. He turned into the stretch with a diminishing two-length lead . . . and then Coastal, whom he'd never met before, and General Assembly, whom he'd beaten like a drum all year long, caught and passed him. So much for the Triple Crown.

Franklin was fired the next morning—one day too late—and Bill Shoemaker was hired. Shoemaker rode Spectacular Bid for the rest of the Bid's career, losing only one more race in the next two years. But thanks to a kid who couldn't judge pace, he lost the race he had to win.

The 2002 Belmont Stakes

Every now and then strategy goes right out the window. You plot and you plan for weeks, and two seconds into the race everything's changed.

It happened in the 2002 Belmont Stakes. Everyone knew War Emblem was the horse to beat. He'd been a surprise winner of the Kentucky Derby (which, in retrospect, after examining his pedigree and his last couple of races, wasn't so surprising after all), and had won the Preakness just as easily. He was a front-running horse possessed of remarkable speed, and enough stamina to win the 10-furlong Derby by a large margin. Every trainer and jockey had to decide what to do: run with War Emblem and perhaps use their own horse up in the process, or let him go and hope he couldn't last for a mile and a half.

It became meaningless in less than a second. The hard ground broke under War Emblem's feet as the gate opened, and he fell to his knees. He was up and running a second later, but for all practical purposes his Belmont was over.

Not all the other jockeys saw what had happened, but they all saw that War Emblem wasn't on or close to the lead. What to do now?

If only one jock had decided to go for the lead, he could probably have set a sane, reasonable pace—but four of them went for it, and they began running too fast for such a long, grueling race. And then War Emblem sealed their fates. Left at the post, he moved up along the rail.

His jockey, knowing how much ground he had lost and how much energy he had expended already, wasn't asking him for speed, but he had a champion's competitive heart, and damned if he didn't forge to the front half a mile from home.

It had taken everything he had left to get there, and he would soon fade to 8th place—but the other jockeys didn't know that. They just knew that today the horse they had to beat had come from behind and suddenly he was in the lead, and they pushed their horses even harder—and by the head of the homestretch, after a mile and a quarter, every horse that was on or within 6 lengths of the lead was cooked. The two trailers, longshot Sarava and second-choice Medaglia d'Oro, ridden by two jockeys who had kept their wits about them, passed all the others as if they were standing still, ran neck-and-neck to the wire, and Sarava became the longest-priced winner in Belmont history.

The 1984 Breeders Cup Classic

When John Henry, one of the two contenders for Horse of the Year honors, scratched, the other contender, Slew o' Gold, was made the heavy favorite for the 10-furlong Breeders Cup Classic. He hadn't lost all year, hadn't even worked up much of a sweat. This was to be the final race of his career, at his favorite distance, and he was carrying 126 pounds, a burden he'd been winning with for two years.

But he had a physical problem: a quarter crack on his hoof. They flew his very own blacksmith out and gave him a bar shoe that would protect the tender area, but his jockey, Angel Cordero, was very aware that the horse wasn't quite 100%.

The race began, Slew o' Gold lay 5th, about 10 lengths off the pace, and then made his move turning into the stretch. By mid-stretch, with an eighth of a mile to go, he was only a length behind the two leaders, Wild Again and Gate Dancer, and gaining ground, though not as rapidly as Cordero had expected. And, because he was aware of that foot, and of the fact that Slew o' Gold, while he was running a winning race, wasn't running a devastating one, Cordero chose to save ground and go *between* Gate Dancer and Wild Again, rather than lose ground while angling to the outside in order to get a clear run to the wire . . .

. . . and as Slew o' Gold began moving up, Gate Dancer moved to his left and the hole closed. It was too late for Cordero to slow his horse down, take him outside, and put him to a drive again, so he stayed where he was, hoping Wild Again would bear in or Gate Dancer would bear out sometime in the final 70 yards so his mount could forge to the front.

It never happened, and Slew o' Gold, demonstrably the best horse in the race, lost for the only time all year—and, it turned out, simultaneously lost Horse of the Year honors to John Henry, the horse who stayed in the barn.

The 1976 Marlboro Cup

And sometimes strategy—either right strategy or wrong strategy—means nothing.

The great gelding Forego, seeking his third successive Horse of the Year title, was entered in the Marlboro Cup.

He was assigned 137 pounds, more weight than any horse had won with since Dr. Fager, and more weight that any horse had won with at more than a mile in close to half a century. By rights, he should have scratched rather than accept that burden, but he didn't.

It rained all morning and most of the afternoon, and the track was officially labeled muddy. Forego hated the mud. He had chronically sore ankles, and a misstep in the mud could end his career. Even if he didn't take that misstep, he was probably 5 lengths better on a fast track.

He was giving 20 pounds—10 lengths—to millionaire Honest Pleasure, and even more weight to other top-caliber stakes winners.

He was running without mud caulks.

Once he'd possessed some tactical early speed, but as he grew older it deserted him, and these days he came from well behind. On a muddy track, that meant he'd probably pick up 15 pounds of mud on his chest and neck—a gift of 7 1/2 lengths to his rivals.

He drew an outside post position, and never got close to the rail. Going around the far turn, Shoemaker had to go six horses wide—another 6-length gift to the front runners.

They straightened away in the stretch, with a quarter mile to go. Honest Pleasure had just taken the lead. Forego was eleventh, floundering in the mud, 17 lengths behind.

So much for strategy. So much for luck. This was Forego, and from somewhere deep within himself he found a way to ignore the mud striking his face, to ignore the footing, to ignore the 137-pound impost, and just run hell-for-leather down the stretch. He was 9 lengths back at the furlong pole, 4 lengths back at the sixteenth pole, 2 lengths back with 50 yards to go, and just when everyone knew that valiant effort would fall short, he found yet another gear and caught Honest Pleasure 10 yards from the wire and won by a nose.

It's performances like that, when a equine athlete is so good and so determined to win that everything you know about analyzing a race becomes meaningless, that it truly is the Sport of Kings.

The Unsinkable Teddy Roosevelt

His daughter, Alice, said it best:

> "He wanted to be the bride at every wedding and
> the corpse at every funeral."

Of course, he had a little something to say about his daughter, too. When various staff members complained that she was running wild throughout the White House, his response was: "Gentlemen, I can either run the country, or I can control Alice. I cannot do both."

He was Theodore Roosevelt, of course: statesman, politician, adventurer, naturalist, ornithologist, taxidermist, cowboy, police commissioner, explorer, writer, diplomat, boxer, and President of the United States.

John Fitzgerald Kennedy was widely quoted after inviting a dozen writers, artists, musicians and scientists to lunch at the White House when he announced that "This is the greatest assemblage of talent to eat here since Thomas Jefferson dined alone." It's a witty statement, but JFK must have thought Roosevelt ate all his meals out.

Roosevelt didn't begin life all that auspiciously. "Teedee" was a sickly child, his body weakened by asthma. It was his father who decided that he was not going to raise an invalid. Roosevelt was encouraged to swim, to take long hikes, to do everything he could to build up his body.

He was picked on by bullies, who took advantage of his weakened condition, so he asked his father to get him boxing lessons. They worked pretty well. By the time he entered Harvard he had the body and reactions of a trained athlete, and before long he was a member of the boxing team.

It was while fighting for the lightweight championship when an incident occurred that gave everyone an insight into Roosevelt's character. He was carrying the fight to his opponent, C. S. Hanks, the defending champion, when he slipped and fell to his knee. Hanks had launched a blow that he couldn't pull back, and he opened Roosevelt's nose, which began gushing blood. The crowd got ugly and started booing the champion, but Roosevelt held up his hand for silence, announced that it was an honest mistake, and shook hands with Hanks before the fight resumed.

* * * *

It was his strength of character that led to his developing an equally strong body. His doctor, W. Thompson, once told a friend: "Look out for Theodore. He's not strong, but he's all grit. He'll kill himself before he'll ever say he's tired."

In 59 years of a vigorous, strenuous life, he never once admitted to being tired.

Roosevelt was always fascinated by Nature, and in fact had seriously considered becoming a biologist or a naturalist before discovering politics. The young men sharing his lodgings at Harvard were probably less than thrilled with his interest. He kept a number of animals in his room. Not cute, cuddly one, but rather snakes, lobsters, and a tortoise that was always escaping and scaring the life out of his landlady. Before long most of the young men in his building refused to go anywhere near his room.

Roosevelt "discovered" politics shortly after graduating Harvard (*phi beta kappa* and *summa cum laude*, of course). So he attacked the field with the same vigor he attacked everything else. The result? At 24 he became the youngest Assemblyman in the New York State House, and the next year he became the youngest-ever Minority Leader.

He might have remained in New York politics for years, but something happened that changed his life. He had met and fallen in love with Alice Hathaway Lee while in college, and married her very soon thereafter. His widowed mother lived with them.

And then, on February 14, 1884, Alice and his mother both died (Alice in childbirth, his mother of other causes) twelve hours apart in the same house.

The blow was devastating to Roosevelt. He never mentioned Alice again and refused to allow her to be mentioned in his presence. He put his former life behind him and decided to lose himself in what was left of the Wild West.

He bought a ranch in the Dakota Bad Lands…and then, because he was Theodore Roosevelt and couldn't do anything in a small way, he bought a second ranch as well. He spent a lot more time hunting than ranching, and more time writing and reading than hunting. (During his lifetime he wrote more than 150,000 letters, as well as close to 30 books.)

He'd outfitted himself with the best "Western" outfit money could buy back in New York, and of course he appeared to the locals to be a wealthy New York dandy. By now he was wearing glasses, and he took a lot of teasing over them; the sobriquet "Four Eyes" seemed to stick.

Until the night he found himself far from his Elkhorn Ranch and decided to rent a room at Nolan's Hotel in Mingusville, on the west bank of the Beaver River. After dinner he went down to the bar — it was the only gathering point in the entire town — and right after Roosevelt arrived, a huge drunk entered, causing a ruckus, shooting off his six-gun, and making himself generally obnoxious. When he saw Roosevelt, he announced that "Four Eyes" would buy drinks for everyone in the bar — or else. Roosevelt, who wasn't looking for a fight, tried to mollify him, but the drunk was having none of it. He insisted that the effete dandy put up his dukes and defend himself.

"Well, if I've got to, I've got to," muttered Roosevelt, getting up from his chair.

The bully took one swing. The boxer from Harvard ducked and bent the drunk in half with a one-two combination to the belly, then caught him flush on the jaw. He kept pummeling the drunk until the man was out cold, and then, with a little help from the appreciative onlookers, he carried the unconscious man to an outhouse behind the hotel and deposited him there for the night.

He was never "Four Eyes" again.

The dude from New York didn't limit himself to human bullies. No horse could scare him either.

During the roundup of 1884 he and his companions encountered a horse known only as "The Devil". He'd earned his name throwing one cowboy after another, and was generally considered to be the meanest horse in the Bad Lands. Finally Roosevelt decided to match his will and skills against the stallion, and all the other cowboys gathered around the corral to watch the New Yorker get his comeuppance — and indeed, The Devil soon bucked him off.

Roosevelt got on again. And got bucked off again.

According to one observer, "With almost every other jump, we would see about twelve acres of bottom land between Roosevelt and the saddle." The Devil sent him flying a third and then a fourth time.

But Roosevelt wasn't about to quit. The Devil couldn't throw him a fifth time, and before long Roosevelt had him behaving "as meek as a rabbit", according to the same observer.

The next year there was an even wilder horse. The local cowboys knew him simply as "The Killer", but Roosevelt decided he was going to tame him, and a tame horse needed a better name than that, so he dubbed him "Ben Baxter". The cowboys, even those who had seen him break The Devil, urged him to keep away from The Killer, to have the horse destroyed. Roosevelt paid them no attention,

He tossed a blanket over Ben Baxter's head to keep him calm while putting on the saddle, an operation that was usually life-threatening in itself. Then he tightened the cinch, climbed onto the horse, and removed the blanket. And two seconds later Roosevelt was sprawling in the dirt of the corral.

And a minute later, he was back in the saddle.

And five seconds later he was flying through the air again, to land with a bond-jarring *thud!*

They kept it up most of the afternoon, Roosevelt climbing back on every time he was thrown, and finally the fight was all gone from Ben Baxter. Roosevelt had broken his shoulder during one of his spills, but it hadn't kept him from mastering the horse. He kept Ben Baxter, and from that day forward "The Killer" became the gentlest horse on his ranch.

Is it any wonder that he never backed down from a political battle?

Having done everything else one could do in the Bad Lands, Roosevelt became a Deputy Sheriff. And in March of 1886, he found out that it meant a little more than rounding up the town drunks on a Saturday night. It seems that a wild man named Mike Finnegan, who had a reputation for breaking laws and heads that stretched from one end of the Bad Lands to the other, had gotten drunk and shot up the town of Medora, escaping — not that anyone dared to stop him — on a small flatboat with two confederates.

Anyone who's ever been in Dakota in March knows that it's still quite a few weeks away from the first signs of spring. Roosevelt, accompanied by Bill Sewell and Wilmot Dow, was ordered to bring Finnegan in, and took off after him on a raft a couple of days later. They negotiated the ice-filled river, and finally came to the spot where the gang had made camp.

Roosevelt, the experienced hunter, managed to approach silently and unseen until the moment he stood up, rifle in hands, and announced that they were his prisoners. Not a shot had to be fired.

But capturing Finnegan and his friends was the easy part. They had to be transported overland more than 100 miles to the town of Dickenson, where they would stand trial. Within a couple of days the party of three lawmen and three outlaws was out of food. Finally Roosevelt set out on foot for a ranch — *any* ranch — and came back a day later with a small wagon filled with enough food to keep them alive on the long trek. The wagon had a single horse, and given the weather and conditions of the crude trails the horse couldn't be expected pull all six men, so Sewell and Dow rode in the wagon while Roosevelt and the three captives walked behind it on an almost non-existent trail, knee-deep in snow, in below-freezing weather. And the closer they got to Dickenson, the more likely it was that Finnegan would attempt to escape, so Roosevelt didn't sleep the last two days and nights of the forced march.

But he delivered the outlaws, safe and reasonably sound. He would be a lawman again in another nine years, but his turf would be as different from the Bad Lands as night is from day.

He became the Police Commissioner of New York City.

New York was already a pretty crime-ridden city, even before the turn of the 20th Century. Roosevelt, who had already been a successful politician, lawman, lecturer and author, was hired to change that — and change it he did.

He hired the best people he could find. That included the first woman on the New York police force — and the next few dozen as well. (Before long every station had police matrons around the clock, thus assuring that any female prisoner would be booked by a member of her own sex.)

Then came another innovation: when Roosevelt decided that most of the cops couldn't hit the broad side of a barn with their sidearms, target practice was not merely encouraged but made mandatory for the first time in the force's history.

When the rise of the automobile meant that police on foot could no longer catch some escaping lawbreakers, Roosevelt created a unit of bicycle police (who, in the 1890s, had no problem keeping up with the cars of that era which were traversing streets that had not been created with automobiles in mind.)

He hired Democrats as well as Republicans, men who disliked him as well as men who worshipped him. All he cared about was that they were able to get the job done.

He was intolerant only of intolerance. When the famed anti-Semitic preacher from Berlin, Rector Ahlwardt, came to America, New York's Jewish population didn't want to allow him in the city. Roosevelt couldn't bar him, but he came up with the perfect solution: Ahlwardt's police bodyguards were composed entirely of very large, very unhappy Jewish cops whose presence convinced the bigot to forego his anti-Semitic harangues while he was in the city.

Roosevelt announced that all promotions would be strictly on merit and not political pull, then spent the next two years proving he meant what he said. He also invited the press into his office whenever he was there, and if a visiting politician tried to whisper a question so that the reporters couldn't hear it, Roosevelt would repeat and answer it in a loud, clear voice.

As Police Commissioner, Roosevelt felt the best way to make sure his police force was performing its duty was to go out in the field and see for himself. He didn't bother to do so during the day; the press and the public were more than happy to report on the doings of his policemen.

No, what he did was go out into the most dangerous neighborhoods, unannounced, between midnight and sunrise, usually with a reporter or two in tow, just in case things got out of hand. (Not that he thought they would help him physically, but he expected them to accurately report what happened if a misbehaving or loafing cop turned on him.)

The press dubbed these his "midnight rambles", and after awhile the publicity alone caused almost all the police to stay at their posts and do their duty, because they never knew when the Commissioner might show up in their territory, and either fire them on the spot or let the reporters who accompanied him expose them to public ridicule and condemnation.

Roosevelt began writing early and never stopped. You'd expect a man who was Governor of New York and President of the United States to write about politics, and of course he did. But Roosevelt didn't like intellectual restrictions any more than he liked physical restrictions, and he wrote books — not just articles, mind you, but *books* — about anything that interested him.

While still in college he wrote *The Naval War of 1812*, which was considered at the time to be the definitive treatise on naval warfare.

Here's a partial list of the non-political books that followed, just to give you an indication of the breadth of Roosevelt's interests:

Hunting Trips of a Ranchman
The Wilderness Hunter
A Book-Lovers Holidays in the Open
The Winning of the West, Volumes 1-4
The Rough Riders
Literary Treats
Papers on Natural History
African Game Trails
Hero Tales From American History

Through the Brazilian Wilderness
The Strenuous Life
Ranch Life and the Hunting Trail

I've got to think he'd be a pretty interesting guy to talk to. On any subject.

In fact, it'd be hard to find one he hadn't written up.

A character as interesting and multi-faceted as Roosevelt's had to be portrayed in film sooner or later, but surprisingly, the first truly memorable characterization was by John Alexander, who delivered a classic and hilarious portrayal of a harmless madman who *thinks* he's Teddy Roosevelt and constantly screams "Charge!" as he runs up the stairs, his version of San Juan Hill, in *Arsenic and Old Lace*.

Eventually there were more serious portrayals: Brian Keith, Tom Berenger, even Robin Williams…and word has it that, possibly by the time you read this, you'll be able to add Leonardo Di Caprio to the list.

Roosevelt believed in the active life, not just for himself but for his four sons — Kermit, Archie, Quentin, and Theodore Junior, and two daughters, Alice and Edith. He built Sagamore Hill, his rambling house on equally rambling acreage, and he often took the children — and any visiting dignitaries — on what he called "scrambles", cross-country hikes that were more obstacle course than anything else.

His motto: "Above or below, but never around." If you couldn't walk through it, you climbed over it or crawled under it, but you never ever circled it. This included not only hills, boulders, and thorn bushes, but rivers, and frequently he, the children, and the occasional visitor who didn't know what he was getting into, would come home soaking wet from swimming a river or stream with their clothes on, or covered with mud, or with their clothes torn to shreds from thorns.

Those wet, muddy and torn clothes were their badges of honor. It meant that they hadn't walked around any obstacle.

"If I am to be any use in politics," Roosevelt wrote to a friend, "it is because I am supposed to be a man who does not preach what he fears to practice. For the year I have preached war with Spain…"

So it was inevitable that he should leave his job as Undersecretary of the Navy and enlist in the military. He instantly became Lieutenant Colonel Roosevelt, and began putting together a very special elite unit, one that perhaps only he could have assembled.

The Rough Riders consisted, among others, of cowboys, Indians, tennis stars, college athletes, the marshal of Dodge City, the master of the Chevy Chase hounds, and the man who was reputed to be the best quarterback ever to play for Harvard.

They were quite a crew, Colonel Roosevelt's Rough Riders. They captured the imagination of the public as had no other military unit in United States History. They also captured San Juan Hill in the face of some serious machine gun fire, and Roosevelt, who led the charge, returned home an even bigger hero than when he'd left.

While on a bear hunt in Mississippi, Colonel Roosevelt, as he liked to be called after San Juan Hill and Cuba, was told that a bear had been spotted a few miles away. When Roosevelt and his entourage — which always included the press — arrived, he found a small, undernourished, terrified bear tied to a tree. He refused to shoot it, and turned away in disgust, ordering a member of the party to put the poor creature out of its misery. His unwillingness to kill a helpless animal was captured by *Washington Post* cartoonist Clifford Berryman. It made him more popular than ever, and before long toy companies were turning out replicas of cute little bears that the great Theodore Roosevelt would certainly never kill, rather than ferocious game animals.

Just in case you ever wondered about the origin of the Teddy Bear.

Some 30 years ago, writer/director John Milius gave the public one of the truly great adventure films, *The Wind and the Lion*, in which the Raisuli (Sean Connery), known as "the Last of the Barbary Pirates", kidnapped an American woman, Eden Perdicaris (Candice Bergan) and her two children, and held them for ransom at his stronghold in Morocco. At which point President Theodore Roosevelt (Brian Keith, in probably the best representation of Roosevelt ever put on film) declared that America wanted "Perdicaris alive or Raisuli dead!" and sent the fleet to Morocco.

Wonderful film, beautifully photographed, well-written, well-acted, with a gorgeous musical score.

Would you like to know what *really* happened?

First of all, it wasn't *Eden* Perdicaris; it was *Ion* Perdicaris, a 64-year-old man. And he wasn't kidnapped with two small children, but with a grown stepson. And far from wanting to be rescued, he and the Raisuli became great friends.

Roosevelt felt the President of the United States had to protect Americans abroad, so he sent a telegram to the Sultan of Morocco, the country in which the kidnapping took place, to the effect that America wanted Perdicaris alive or Raisuli dead. He also dispatched seven warships to Morocco.

So why wasn't there a war with Morocco?

Two reasons.

First, during the summer of 1904, shortly after the kidnapping and Roosevelt's telegram, the government learned something that was kept secret until after all the principles in the little drama — Roosevelt, Perdicaris, and the Raisuli — had been dead for years...and that was that Ion Perdicaris was *not* an American citizen. He had been born one, but he later renounced his citizenship and moved to Greece, years before the kidnapping.

The other reason? Perdicaris's dear friend, the Raisuli, set him free. Secretary of State John Hay knew full well that Perdicaris had been freed before the Republican convention convened, but he whipped the assembled delegates up with the "America wants Perdicaris alive or Raisuli dead!" slogan anyway, and Roosevelt was elected in a landslide.

Roosevelt was as vigorous and active as President as he'd been in every previous position. Consider:

Even though the country was relatively empty, he could see land being gobbled up in great quantities by settlers and others, and he created the national park system.

He arranged for the overthrow of the hostile Panamanian government and created the Panama Canal, which a century later is *still* vital to international shipping.

He took on J. P. Morgan and his cohorts, and became the greatest "trust buster" in our history, then created the Department of Commerce and the Department of Labor to make sure weaker Presidents in the future didn't give up the ground he'd taken.

We were a regional power when he took office. Then he sent the Navy's "Great White Fleet" around the world on a "goodwill tour". By the time it returned home, we were, for the first time, a world power.

Because he never backed down from a fight, a lot of people thought of him as a warmonger — but he became the only American President ever to win the Nobel Peace Price while still in office, when he mediated a dispute between Japan and Russia before it became a full-fledged shooting war.

He created and signed the Pure Drug and Food Act.

He became the first President to leave the United States while in office when he visited Panama to inspect the Canal.

* * * *

Roosevelt remained physically active throughout his life. He may or may not have been the only President to be blind in one eye, but he was the only who to ever go blind in one eye from injuries received in a boxing match *while serving as President.*

He also took years of *jujitsu* lessons while in office, and became quite proficient at it.

And, in keeping with daughter Alice's appraisal of him, he was the first President to fly in an airplane, and the first to be filmed.

Roosevelt's last day in office was February 22, 1909.

He'd already been a cowboy, a rancher, a soldier, a marshal, a police commissioner, a governor, and a President. So did he finally slow down?

Just long enough to pack. Accompanied by his son, Kermit, and the always-present journalists, on March 23 he boarded a ship that would take him to East Africa for the first organized safari on record. It was sponsored by the American and Smithsonian museums, which to this day display some of the trophies he shot and brought back. His two guides were the immortal F. C. Selous, widely considered to be the greatest hunter in African history, and Philip Percival, who was already a legend among Kenya's hunting fraternity.

What did Roosevelt manage to bag for the museums?

9 lions.
9 elephants.
5 hyenas.
8 black rhinos.
5 white rhinos.
7 hippos.
8 wart hogs.
6 Cape buffalo.
3 pythons.

And literally hundreds of antelope, gazelle, and other herbivores.

Is it any wonder that he needed 500 uniformed porters? And since he paid as much attention to the mind as to the body, one of those porters carried 60 pounds of Roosevelt's favorite books on his back, and Roosevelt made sure he got in his reading every day, no matter what.

While hunting in Uganda, he ran into the noted rapscallion John Boyes and others who were poaching elephants in the Lado Enclave. According to Boyes's memoir, *The Company of Adventurers*, the poachers offered to put a force of 50 hunters and poachers at Roosevelt's disposal if he would like to take a shot at bringing American democracy, capitalism and know-how to the Belgian Congo (not that they had any right to it, but from their point of view, neither did King Leopold of Belgium). Roosevelt admitted to being tempted, but he had decided that his chosen successor, William Howard Taft, was doing a lousy job as President and he'd made up his mind to run again.

But first, he wrote what remains one of the true classics of hunting literature, *African Game Trails*, which has remained in print for just short of a century as these words are written. (And half a dozen of the journalists wrote *their* versions of the safari to the book publishers, whose readers simply couldn't get enough of Roosevelt.)

William Howard Taft, the sitting President (and Roosevelt's hand-picked successor), of course wanted to run for re-election. Roosevelt was the clear choice among the Republican rank and file, but the President controls the party's machinery, and due to a number of procedural moves Taft got the nomination.

Roosevelt, outraged at the backstage manipulations, decided to form a third party. Officially it was the Progressive Party, but after he mentioned that he felt "as fit as bull moose", the public dubbed it the Bull Moose Party.

Not everyone was thrilled to see him run for a third term. (Actually, it would have been only his second election to the Presidency; he became President in 1901 just months after McKinley's election and assassination, so though he'd only been elected once, he had served in the White House for seven years.) One such unhappy citizen was John F. Schrank.

On October 14, 1912, Roosevelt came out of Milwaukee's Hotel Gillespie to give a speech at a nearby auditorium. He climbed into a open car and waved to the crowd — and found himself face-to-face with Schrank, who raised his pistol and shot Roosevelt in the chest.

The crowd would have torn Schrank to pieces, but Roosevelt shouted: "Stand back! Don't touch that man!"

He had Schrank brought before him, stared at the man until the potential killer could no longer meet his gaze, then refused all immediate medical help. He wasn't coughing up blood, which convinced him that the wound wasn't fatal, and he insisted on giving his speech before going to the hospital.

He was a brave man...but he was also a politician and a showman, and he knew what the effect on the crowd would be when they saw the indestructible Roosevelt standing before them in a blood-soaked shirt, ignoring his wound to give them his vision of what he could do for America. "I shall ask you to be as quiet as possible," he began. "I don't know whether you fully understand that I have just been shot." He gave them the famous Roosevelt grin. "But it takes more than that to kill a Bull Moose!"

It brought the house down.

He lost the election to Woodrow Wilson — even Roosevelt couldn't win as a third-party candidate — but William Howard Taft, the President of the United States, came in a distant third, capturing only eight electoral votes.

That was enough for one vigorous lifetime, right?

Not hardly.

Did you ever hear of the River of Doubt?

You can be excused if your answer is negative. It no longer exists on any map.

On February 27, 1914, at the request of the Brazilian government, Roosevelt and his party set off to map the River of Doubt. It turned out to be not quite the triumph that the African safari had been.

Early on they began running short of supplies. Then Roosevelt developed a severe infection in his leg. It got so bad that at one point he urged the party to leave him behind. Of course they didn't, and gradually his leg and his health improved to the point where he was finally able to continue the expedition.

Eventually they mapped all 900 miles of the river, and Roosevelt, upon returning home, wrote another bestseller, *Through the Brazilian Wilderness*. And shortly thereafter, the *Rio da Duvida* (River of Doubt) officially became the river you can now find on the maps, the *Rio Teodoro* (River Theodore).

He was a man in his mid-fifties, back when the average man's life expectancy was only 55. He was just recovering from being shot in the chest (and was still walking around with the bullet inside his body). Unlike East Africa, where he would be hunting the same territory that Selous had hunted before and Percival knew like the back of his hand, no one had ever mapped the River of Doubt. It was uncharted jungle, with no support network for hundreds of miles.

So why did he agree to map it?

His answer is so typically Rooseveltian that it will serve as the end to this chapter:

"It was my last chance to be a boy again."

The Tiniest Assassins

Okay, boiled down, it comes to this: the Martians come here, do a little serious devastation, scare the hell out of us, and then catch colds and die. Never gonna happen. For one thing, given the weaponry that H. G. Wells and the movie give them, they'll never have to emerge from their ships before they've destroyed every last one of us and the battle is over—and as long as they stay in their ships, they're immune to the one indefensible weapon we have: our peculiarly human viruses.

And there's something else to consider. Let's not forget that Wells lived before the era of modern medicine. I think it's only logical to assume that any creatures, benevolent or hostile, that can traverse the void and reach planet Earth have doubtless developed their science—and especially their medical science— to the point where they can pinpoint and identify any dangerous germs in our atmosphere, and either develop some form of immunization to them, or create some way to annihilate them at the source, which is to say Earth, before invading us.

It's just common sense. You wouldn't invade the waters off the coast of Australia unless you had some protection against the great white shark. You wouldn't wander through a pride of hungry lions without protection. Hell, we don't send our soldiers into battle these days without protection against bullets, chemical agents, biological agents, everything we can think of.

So I think it's fair to say that our germs are not going to kill any extraterrestrial invaders once they get here.

Nope. We're going to kill them long *before* they get here. And by the very same means that we (or Earth, if you prefer) used to kill Wells' Martian invaders.

How?

Well, as likely as not, it'll be by accident.

You see, in recent years NASA has been examining ships, rovers, orbiters, everything that we send into space.

And guess what?

Neither the cold of space nor the heat of re-entry nor the direct gamma radiation from the sun kills every living thing on those objects.

Oh, there's nothing there that'll bother *us*—at least not so far. But that doesn't mean an alien race with an alien physiology isn't looking down a barrel loaded with newly-identified microbes from good old Planet Earth.

We've even got names for them.

For example, there's *Bacillus Odysseyi*, which has been found on the Mars Odyssey orbiter. Why is this noteworthy? Because the damned thing has been orbiting Mars for close to four years. It survived the 40-million-mile trip, it survived three years in orbit, it survived gamma radiation, and it's doing just fine, thank you.

Now, no one's ever been killed by *B. Odysseyi*, and probably no one ever will be. But that's not to say that it couldn't wipe out a squad of Wells' Martians or Edgar Rice Burroughs' green Tharks in an afternoon, depending on what particular germs they're vulnerable to.

Then there's *Bacillus Safensis*. This baby is not only found in the Jet Propulsion Lab's Spacecraft Assembly Facility (known as SAF, which gave it its name), but it is alive and well today on Spirit and Opportunity, the current Mars rovers.

So what do these—and a dozen other viruses that have survived the heat and cold and radiation of spaceflight— actually do?

Nothing much. They tend to go forth and multiply, like every other living thing, but they're not harmful to us. Hell, they've even been found in the water supply of the Mir space station. Astronauts drank it. They all survived.

But they're human astronauts, not Martian or Centaurian or Antarean astronauts. Or citizens.

Right. Citizens. Don't forget: we've sent out a few deep space probes, and we'll send out more. A couple have already left the solar system. They're not traveling fast, not by galactic standards, and it could take them a hundred thousand or even a million years to make planetfall somewhere out there—but they're going to arrive with a zillionth generation of perfectly healthy microbes and bacilli ready to find new homes.

Maybe the planet they touch down on won't have any life on it at all. (Which is okay by the fellow travelers; they can wait a billion years until some comes along.) Maybe it'll have life that's as unbothered by exposure to them as we are.

And maybe it will have life that finds them to be pure poison—life that, unlike the hypothetical invaders we discussed, is totally unprepared for a visit by microscopic creatures than can wipe them out, that will never know what hit them, that might indeed have been the friendliest folk in the galaxy.

All right. That's the non-fiction side of it. Those bacilli are out there, some of them aren't coming back, and sooner or later they're going to make contact with *something*.

Now let's look at the possibilities, science fictional today, but perhaps less so in the future.

We've got a million dedicated computer hackers, plus some truly powerful equipment in the hands of experts, searching the heavens every night for signals from other worlds—SETI, the Search for Extra-Terrestrial Intelligence. They're probably not going to discover any in my lifetime or yours, but sooner or later they're going to latch on to some signals, because we're finding out that just about every star in the galaxy has planets, and with tens of millions of G-type stars out there, the odds are that an awful lot of them have, or once had, or someday will have life. And some of it will be sentient. And some of that will be searching the skies for signs of life just the way we do.

So eventually we're going to make contact with them. If we like what they have to say, fine. If we don't . . . well, if we can trace their signals back to their source, we can send them a little present. Not the microbes that are living on the Mars rovers today, but rather some of the most powerful stuff we can whip up (after we lie to them about our physiology and hope they're telling us the truth about theirs.)

And even if we don't know what their motives are, if meeting them at a neutral point in space is kind of like a blind date on a grand scale, it doesn't mean we won't go armed. Not with guns or lasers or any of that movie garbage; they'll be able to detect it from a light-year away. But with the most subtle weapons imaginable—Men, each carrying germs and viruses that we are immune to, each ready to transmit them by the simple act of breathing in and out.

Sounds pretty crude and heartless, I realize, and hopefully it will never come to that—but if your world is at risk, a visionary named Wells showed you that there is a far more efficient way of attacking the enemy than with a new generation of weapons, which history teaches us will be obsolete in a few years' time.

Much better to use a weapon neither Time nor heat nor cold nor radiation has been able to kill. There are going to be some alien immune systems that can't kill it either.

So how do we avoid killing off a friendly alien population?

We're working on it right now. NASA is aware that if enough of the bacilli I mentioned take root on Mars (or Venus, or Io, or any other world or moon in the solar system), we might one day discover life there, and if the bacilli have evolved or mutated enough, we'll never know that it came from Earth in the late 20th and early 21st Centuries. So some of the NASA scientists have been given the task of learning how to terminate these microscopic agents that space can't kill.

They already know that if they hit them with a few million degrees of heat they can't survive—but neither can the equipment they live on, and it's counter-productive to melt a spaceship before it ever takes off just to make sure that it doesn't take any microscopic travelers with it.

But they're learning, and before long they'll find a method. And that's absolutely vital, because although Wells didn't know he was telling the truth, we already have the ability to destroy the bad aliens. Now we have to make sure we don't kill the good ones by accident.

My Pal Ross

I'd like to tell you a little about my late friend, Ross H. Spencer, because his story is unique.

Ross loved his native Youngstown, Ohio, but he moved to the Chicago area to work in first a Studebaker and then a Ford plant. He took time off to help win the war in the Pacific, for which he was properly decorated and from which he made most of his lifelong friends. He fiddled a bit with poetry, but never wrote a word of fiction in his life, except maybe to the IRS. Then, in his early 50s, he had a serious heart attack, brought on by too many beers and too many cigarettes.

While he was recuperating in the hospital—and it was a long recuperation; he was never able to do physical work again—his wife bought him a couple of books to cheer him up. He was never much of a reader, and she didn't know quite what to get him, so she picked up two of Robert Parker's hard-boiled detective novels, solely because the hero, Spenser, shared an almost identical last name with Ross. Ross read them. He told me when I asked about his origins as a writer that he found the books so inadvertently funny that he wondered what would happen if someone tried to be that funny on purpose. I felt an instant kinship with him, because that was exactly how I had recently created my favorite character, Lucifer Jones, after watching Ursula Andress in the truly ridiculous *She*.

So, lying in a hospital bed, this man who'd never written more than an occasional poem, took pen to notebook and started writing *The DADA Caper*. It was an amusing book, but Ross was still teaching himself his craft. By the time he wrote the second one, *The Reggis Arms Caper* he was the funniest mystery writer in America . . . and by the time he finished the third, *The Stranger City Caper,* he was the funniest fiction writer alive. All self-taught in a hospital bed at the age of 50-plus, his only textbooks a pair of bestselling novels that he found too silly to be considered seriously.

And while he was learning to write fiction, he turned back to poetry as well. Most people didn't know that, because Ross was still an amateur and didn't know how to sell his poems. He produced one book of wonderful (and often hilarious) Robert Service-type poetry called *Welcome. Losers*—but it was published by a small press in an edition of 100 copies. I have one; I suspect Ross died with 75 of them in his basement. He kept writing poems—I have several that he jotted down in letters to me—but no more ever saw print; he simply didn't know how to market them. (And to tell the truth, I don't think he cared. He was more interested in writing them than selling them.)

Ross's Chance Purdue books hit the stands a couple of years before I finally got around to submitting the first Lucifer Jones novel. I had a feeling Lucifer would be a tough sell (he wasn't, but I was a little less confident back then), so I asked Ross what inside information he had about Avon, the house that published the Purdue books. How did he know to send such oddball humor there, and did he think they'd go for my pulp parodies?

His answer: he didn't know anything about Avon. He finished *The DADA Caper*, went to the library, picked up a copy of *Writer's Market,* and started submitting at the "A's," (Thank ghod Avon wasn't called Zeus, or he'd have given up long before he ever sold the book. I truly don't think any other publisher would have taken a chance on such an oddball off-the-wall comic novel. Later, after he'd established his reputation, they all did—but not in the beginning.)

I wasn't the only Chance Purdue fan. David Merrick optioned all 5 Purdue books for Broadway. He never did anything with them, but he sent Ross a $10,000 check every January for the better part of 15 years. (OK, Ross is dead, so I can tell you: Avon paid a less-than-earthshaking $2,000 apiece for the first 3 Purdue books, $2,500 for the fourth, and $3,000 for the fifth. He did a *lot* better after I finally helped him get an agent.)

I have written 3 fan letters in my life. One went to Ross, and we became friends for the last two decades of his life. He finally moved back to Youngstown about ten years before he died. He was a salty old guy who lived for the Three B's: beer, baseball, and broads. (He was happily and faithfully married, but he sure did like to look. I share both syndromes.)

I only met Ross once. We spoke on the phone many times, and since he hated to type we corresponded weekly by trading audio tapes, often reading the latest Chance Purdue and Lucifer Jones adventures to each other. Somehow I talked him into coming to the 1982 Worldcon (Chicon IV). He spent a few hours observing the microcosm, joined us for dinner at the Greek Islands, went home a couple of hours later, and never again complained to me about how strange mystery writers and fans were.

As I said, I've written 3 fan letters. One was to Barry Malzberg; he became my closest friend in science fiction, and I managed to bring most of his very best work back into print with the omnibus volume, *The Passage of the Light*. The second was to Alexander Lake, the hunter/ author who started me out on my lifetime love affair with Africa; he died a month before I wrote him, but 40 years later I was able to bring his forgotten classics, *Killers in Africa* and *Hunter's Choice*, back into print.

Ross was the third, and just a few months before his death I was able to edit *The Compleat Chance Purdue*, which if nothing else shows that when I write a fan letter to a writer, I'm sincere.

Anyway, this is the introduction I wrote for the book:

A couple of decades ago I went to the bookstore, looking for a nice, hard-boiled detective novel in the Raymond Chandler mold. I picked up *The Stranger City Caper*, primarily because of the cover art, which showed a private dick in a trenchcoat. I'd never heard of the author before, but I bought it anyway.

Well, let me tell you: covers can be misleading. I got home, opened the book—and twenty minutes later I was laughing so hard that I was literally gasping for breath. I knew long before I finished the book that Ross Spencer was a comic genius—an opinion that has only become firmer over the years—and I spent the next couple of days scouring the stores for any other Chance Purdue adventures that I could find.

Writers don't write fan letters to other writers, but within a week I had written one to Ross, a charming man who then lived about 40 miles away from me in Illinois. (We have both since moved to Ohio, though we're now a couple of hundred miles apart.) He responded not with a letter, but with an audio cassette—he actually hates to type—I responded in kind, and we've been friends ever since. When I finally met him, he turned out to be a fun-loving, white-haired, cigar-smoking gent with a twinkle in his eye—exactly the kind of person you would pick to be the creator of the immortal Chance Purdue.

Ross kicked off his late-in-life literary career by writing and selling five Purdue novels. He's since sold a batch more books, and has gone on to greater fame than Chance ever brought him—but to me Chance Purdue is classic, archetypal Ross Spencer, than which nothing is funnier. It's the kind of thing he does both effortlessly and better than anybody else.

Purdue is the perfect parody of the hard-boiled detective. He doesn't feel much pain, especially if you hit him above the neck. He's just about irresistible to women. He's so dumb that he can't even spell FBI. If there are twenty right ways to solve a crime and one wrong way, he'll invariably opt for the wrong way and solve it anyway. He is incapable of writing a two-sentence paragraph. (Footnote for historians: Ross once showed me the unfinished manuscript of his very first creation, detective

Clay Pierce, who is a clone of Chance Purdue in every way but one: Clay is incapable of writing a paragraph of less than two thousand words.)

Shortly after discovering Ross's work, I loaned a couple of the Purdue books to my friend, the award-winning science fiction writer Barry Malzberg. His comment upon returning them: "I never saw so many one-liners in my life. The man is the Henny Youngman of mystery novelists."

Actually, Ross isn't a mystery novelist at all. What he is is the funniest writer alive. I know this, because when I sit down to write humor I am the second-funniest writer alive, and I can't hold a candle to Spencer.

So what lies ahead of you in this five-in-one volume? Well, let me give you a very brief hint.

First there's *The DADA Caper*, in which we meet Chance Purdue, a detective so dumb that his IQ would freeze water, as he goes up against DADA, an enemy whose acronym stands for "Destroy America! Destroy America!"—which will show you how committed (and redundant) they are.

Next comes *The Reggis Arms Caper*, in which Chance saves the world from another Japanese invasion, and first meets the CIA's sexiest agent, Brandy Alexander.

Then there's *The Stranger City Caper*, in which Chance must ferret out mystery among the minor-leaguers—which in this case include a left-handed catcher with a wooden leg, a first baseman named Attila, and a shortstop who gets a triple hernia while pivoting to turn a double play.

After that there's *The Abu Wahab Caper*, a saga of gambling and corruption, in which Chance crosses paths with Quick Cash Kelly, Opportunity O'Flynn, Bet-a-Bunch Dugan, and a cud-chewing race-horse with two huge humps on its back.

And finally there's *The Radish River Caper*, which reunites Chance with Brandy Alexander and the infamous Dr. Ho Ho Ho, as he courts mystery and danger on the football field with such memorable characters as Suicide Lewisite and Zanzibar McStrangle.

If you've never read Chance Purdue before, I envy you, because you've got a few evenings of uproarious laughter awaiting you. If you *have* encountered him before, you'll be pleased to know that he hasn't changed one iota: he's still funnier than any of his competitors by quite a few levels of magnitude.

And, as editor, I will make a solemn pledge to you: if enough of you buy this book, I will harass Ross Spencer day and night until he completes that Clay Pierce novel and Alexander Books brings it to a helplessly laughing public.

Back to the present. I always check abebooks.com and bookfinder. com every couple of weeks to see if I can upgrade some of my too-often-read editions of some of my favorite writers—"M. E. Chaber" (Kendell Foster Crossen), Craig Rice, a handful of others—and of course Ross is always on the list. When I was checking in November, 2004, I came across a title I'd never heard of before—and that seemed passing strange, because Ross told me he'd sent me copies of every book he wrote, and he had discussed them all with me. The title was *Signifying Nothing*, and it came out from the same tiny press that did *Welcome, Losers . . .* so I figured it was another volume of poetry that he'd somehow neglected to tell me about.

Of course I ordered it, and gave it to myself for Christmas. And when I opened it up and looked through it, I realized that the introduction I'd written was wrong. Ross *had* written and published a Clay Pearce novel. I also realized why he'd never mentioned it. The copyright date puts it a year before the first Chance Purdue book. It's funny, but nowhere near as well written—and more to the point, all five Purdue plots exist as sections of *Signifying Nothing*; there would be no sense in ever reprinting it. Ross always knew what he wanted to do, and this was simply a first draft of it, a draft he didn't care to show people who loved his more professional work.

As for the Clay Pearce manuscript Ross showed me, I now realize that, at his higher skill level, he was re-imagining Clay Pearce. I don't have the manuscript, but I still have a number of audio cassettes, many of which were new and hilarious Clay Pearce adventures. I listened to them just before writing this, and it's like a totally different, far surer hand wrote these, as opposed to the book I bought for Christmas.

So now I wonder if there are any Chance Purdue manuscripts I don't know about, and who do I have to kill to get my hands on one?

But until one turns up, I'll settle for the ones that are in print, and for the pleasure of having known my funny and salty old friend.

The One Who Didn't
Direct Terrible Movies

The other day I mentioned Ed Wood to a couple of younger fans.

"The movie director?" asked one.

"The guy who did *Plan Nine From Planet X*?" asked the other, almost simultaneously.

"No, the fan," I replied.

"The movie director was a fan?" asked the first one.

Well, I was looking for something to contribute to this final issue of *Mimosa*, and that convinced me that someone had better write a little something about Ed Wood before fandom forgets him.

The first time I saw Ed was in the masquerade at my very first Worldcon, Discon I in Washington D.C., back in 1963. He was wearing about 75 membership badges from prior conventions and he walked across stage after being duly announced as "Superfan."

How true it was.

Ed's fannish exertions were legend. He edited the wonderful *Journal of Science Fiction*. He contributed to fanzines. He worked on conventions. Most important, he was one of the founders, and eventually the editor, of Advent Press, which was just about the only source of criticism and pro and fannish history in the field from the 1950s to the 1970s. This was the house that published everything from Knight's *In Search of Wonder* and Blish's *The Issue at Hand* to Bloch's *The Eighth Stage of Fandom* and Warner's *All Our Yesterdays*, as well as Proceedings (complete transcripts) of both Chicon III and Discon I.

He was also the most crochety, wonderful, ill-tempered, generous sonuvabitch I ever met.

Example: Right after Carol and I were married, we moved into a subterranean penthouse (read: basement apartment) at the corner of North Shore and Greenview in Chicago's Rogers Park area. We were the only two science fiction fans we knew—and unbeknownst to us, Chicago fandom met every month at George Price's apartment, which was perhaps 80 feet from our front door. It was Ed who befriended us at Discon, half a country away, and told us when and where to show up.

So we started attending the meetings. Like most newlyweds, we were broke, maybe a little more broke than most. I remember mentioning during a mid-December meeting at George's that Carol absolutely loved C. L. Moore's Northwest Smith stories (I hadn't read them yet, but I'm now their greatest fan), and I asked if there were any more beyond the two Gnome Press collections that she already owned. Someone, I think it was Alexei Panshin, said that yes, she'd written one for a fanzine that was never professionally published. I replied that I was going to start saving my money right then, and hopefully by next Christmas, 53 weeks off, I could find and buy a copy for Carol.

And that was that. The meeting broke up about midnight and we trudged back across the street through a heavy snowfall that was fast turning into a blizzard.

And at about 5:00 AM, the doorbell rang, and there was Ed Wood, covered with snow and ice. He had driven home to Milwaukee, maybe 75 miles away, in the blizzard, hunted up the fanzine with the Northwest Smith story, and driven all the way back to give it to me.

I overcame my surprise and began to thank him.

He snarled that only an asshole would want to give his wife a fanzine story for Christmas, turned on his heel, went back to his car, and drove home for the second time that night.

That was Ed in a nutshell.

Move the clock ahead a couple of decades. We had just had dinner with Ed and Jo Ann, his wonderful wife (and quite a fan in her own right, dating back to her CFG days). The talk turned to prozines, and he mentioned which ones he had complete runs of. I replied that I wasn't a completist, that the only thing I was even trying to get a complete collection of was Worldcon program books, and that I'd been within one of completing the run for a few years, but I'd been stymied—not by the first or second Worldcons, which produced more than ample numbers of program books—but by the 1948 Torcon, which seems to have produced only about 120 of them, all of which had been given out, and which were somewhat rarer than hen's teeth.

Two weeks later I get a manila envelope in the mail. I open it. Out falls a near-mint copy of the Torcon I program book. I look for a return address. There isn't any. I check the postmark. It says Hurst, Texas, which is where Ed and Jo Ann lived.

So I phoned him to thank him for such a rare and thoughtful gift— and spent the next 90 minutes listening to him harangue me, on long distance and at my expense, about the idiocy of collecting Worldcon program books.

Ed Wood—the pure quill.

Ed was a purist. By this, I mean he was Gernbackian in his tastes, rather than Campellian. He liked Tony Boucher and Horace Gold personally, but was sure their literary taste had contributed to the ruin of science fiction, which Campbell himself had seriously weakened when he gave up writing space operas and produced the Don A. Stuart stories such as "Twilight."

My first two science fiction novels were Edgar Rice Burroughs pastiches, and my third was a Robert E. Howard imitation. They came out in the late 1960s. I took a good hard look at them, appraised them honestly, then didn't write another word of science fiction for more than a decade, to give people time to forget those rather abysmal efforts. (They still return to haunt me at autograph sessions.) All of my friends understood and sympathized.

All except Ed, that is.

Until the day he died, he simply could not understand why I'd given up writing fabulous gems like *The Goddess of Ganymede* in favor of all that effete literary shit that kept winning Hugos. I can't tell you how many times he tried to talk me into giving up Kirinyaga and all this Inner Frontier crap and go back to writing what (he was sure) we both knew to be Pure Science Fiction.

I remember running into him at the 1976 Worldcon. He was sitting by himself in the lobby, a pre-publication copy of Dave Kyle's coffee-table book on the history of science fiction on his lap, looking like he'd lost his best friend. At first I thought Jo Ann must be critically ill. No, he said, she was fine. He held up the book. It was *this*, he explained.

He'd been doing some reviewing for *Analog*. I knew Dave was one of his oldest friends, and I knew that Ed was as honest as the day is long, and I naturally concluded that he hated the book and was filled with remorse at what he was going to write.

He was filled with remorse, all right—but only because he and Dave disagreed about various aspects of sf, and the book had no misstatements and only two typos, and he was going to have to give it a rave review. Which he did.

Other memories. People talk about Sam Moskowitz's voice. Yes, it was louder than Ed's, but not by much. Along with being a member of First Fandom and half a dozen other organizations, Ed was also a member of the Burroughs Bibliophiles. The BB met at Worldcons through 1978, and always held the Dum-Dum—their annual banquet—there. Usually Vern Coriell, the BB's founder, would announce the end of the banquet and the beginning of the speeches by screeching out a Johnny Weismuller cry of the bull ape to gently grab the diners' attention. One year Vern either wasn't there or had a sore throat, I can't recall which, and Ed gave the ape call—and it was so loud and so startling that one of the waiters dropped an entire tray of dirty plates.

Ed was a loving and doting father, and his son, Larry, was a bit of a prodigy. (He used to win long philosophical arguments with Phyllis

Eisenstein when he was three years old.) I remember at one Wilcon when Larry was still a pre-schooler, he asked Ed why the sky was blue. Ed began giving him a scientific explanation that was quite beyond my comprehension. I went away for a cold drink, chatted with a couple of old friends, and when I returned Ed was *still* explaining it to Larry.

(Laura once asked me why the sky was blue, and I came up with what I thought was a perfect 4-word answer: "Because it isn't green." Larry became a cipher expert for the Navy; Laura became an award-winning fantasy writer. I think both careers were inherent in the answers they received.)

Ed didn't care who he yelled at if he thought he was right. He once told me a story—and John Campbell himself corroborated it a year or two later—that Campbell, whose *Astounding* was regularly publishing Heinlein, Asimov, Kuttner, Leiber, de Camp, and that whole group, was prepared to reject Doc Smith's *Children of the Lens* back in the late 1940s, when Doc finally wrote and delivered the final novel in the series. It was just too crudely and clumsily written and characterized for what *Astounding* had become.

It was Ed who took Campbell aside and explained to him (as I'm sure only Ed could) that Doc had supported *Astounding* for years when he was the biggest name Campbell could put on the cover, and it would be the ultimate act of ingratitude to bounce the book now that Campbell didn't need him anymore.

(Now that I think of it, Ed was probably the only person who could win an argument of any sort with Campbell.)

Ed did something with atoms for his living—I have no idea what, but he was so highly specialized that only four or five places in the country were doing advanced enough work to hire him—and when computers came along, he wound up teaching computer courses in college.

And then one day he was gone—a heart attack while on vacation with Jo Ann in Las Vegas—and fandom lost the most intelligent, foul-tempered, passionate, growling, generous member it had.

And I lost a dear friend with exactly those same traits.

Memories of My Dad

My dad should have been born in New York. There is no question in my mind that if he had been, he'd have found and joined the Futurians, collaborated with Cyril Kornbluth, feuded with Don Wollheim, worked for Fred Pohl, and had affairs with Judy Merril and Virginia Kidd. They were his kind of people, but he didn't know it for more than 70 years.

As it was, he was born in Chicago on March 27, 1912, and grew up there. He was a young Communist, and took great pride in the fact that he didn't always vote a straight Democratic ticket, that indeed he had voted for Socialist Norman Thomas over FDR back in 1932. Even Bill and Hillary Clinton's abuses couldn't make him vote Republican, though they came closer than anyone else.

I remember that most of my baby sitters were young men who wore thick eyeglasses, spoke with Slavic accents, and thought the only way to entertain a 5-year-old was to read *Das Kapital* aloud or engage him in endless games of chess.

My dad lived and died with the White Sox, and since we lived on the South Side of Chicago—they had this strange team on the North Side that played in this place with lots of vines and no lights, but we never really acknowledged their existence—he must have taken me to over one hundred Sunday double-headers by the time we moved to a northern suburb in 1954. (Think of it. I got to watch Luke Appling and the Sox lose about 185 games. By the time they'd put together the Girl's Team—Nellie and Minnie and that whole crowd—we'd moved too far away to go to games, so we never saw their good teams.)

He tried very hard to talk me out of becoming a writer, not that he had anything against writers, but rather that, being a Depression kid, he had a lot against poverty. Once it was apparent that I was actually going to make a living at it, he became my biggest fan.

He attended only one convention while my mother was alive. (She was a bit of a literary snob, who had no use for science fiction and even less for fandom.) I was the Toastmaster at the 1976 Windycon—the one where the cops raided the skinny-dippers at the 13th-floor indoor pool—and that was it until my mother died. Then he decided to give conventions another shot, and drove to the 1984 Worldcon in Los Angeles (he was living in San Diego at the time), and suddenly found that he was having the time of his life. He made a ton of friends, hit more parties than I did, went to panel after panel, sat in rapt attention during the Hugo Awards, and decided that science fiction wasn't so bad after all.

He asked me for a list of books to read. I gave him about 30 authors and 150 titles. Within a year he'd read every one of them, and wanted more. He started coming to Midwestcon almost every year, and then he decided to strike out on his own, hitting a bunch of California cons by himself.

When I toastmastered the 1988 Worldcon, the committee gave me the Presidential Suite at the New Orleans Sheraton, which had a few extra bedrooms, so I invited both my dad and my daughter Laura (whose award-laden career as a romance and science fiction writer hadn't yet begun) to come on down and grab a bedroom apiece. Laura grew up in fandom, knew her away around a con every bit as well as Carol and I, and volunteered to act as my dad's guide. After three days she decided she couldn't keep up with him, and just pointed him toward the next two nights' parties.

By the early 1990s he'd discovered the pulps. In a year's time he read all 188 Doc Savage adventures, plus every Spider, Shadow, G-8, and Operator 5 that he could get his hands on. He is the only person I know who actually read all thirteen 60,000-word episodes of Operator 5's "Purple Invasion" epic, the *War and Peace* of the pulp magazines.

Along the way, he also finally got to see a bit of the world. One night he was telling me where to find all his papers and such if he died, and I mentioned that if he died the next day I would certainly take his money and spend it on a safari, and since that's where it was earmarked, why didn't he do the same thing with it while he was still capable of such an arduous trip?

So, at age 77, he met Carol and me in England during the 1987 Worldcon, and went on a 3-week safari in Kenya with us. He enjoyed it so much that, at 79, he joined Carol and me, Pat and Roger Sims, and my agent Eleanor Wood, on a lengthy safari that encompassed Egypt (including a Nile cruise), Kenya again, and Tanzania. At 80, he couldn't talk us into taking a trip to the Greek Isles—I had too many deadlines—so he borrowed my video camera, went alone, and loved every minute of it.

He moved from Caifornia to Orlando early in 1996, driving the whole distance at the ripe young age of 84. He already knew Dick Spelman, and Dick introduced him to Orlando fandom—the club, the reading groups, everything. And he became an active participant, constantly telling me how much he enjoyed the Orlando fan community. He flew to Los Angeles that summer for what was to be his last Worldcon.

His health started to fail in 1997, and by mid-year he had moved to an assisted-living facility, but he still read voraciously and attended meetings and cons whenever someone could drive him.

Then he moved into a full-care nursing home in 1999, and without any access to fandom, to the cons and parties and discussions he so loved, he lost most of the enthusiasm for life that had become his trademark. He didn't enjoy his last two years at all. His death was perfectly timed; he ran out of money and went onto Medicaid on July 1, 2001, and died on July 15. (Well, let me amend that: the body died then. The fan who was interested in everything had departed perhaps 20 months earlier.)

He wasn't a great man. He didn't leave his mark on any books or paintings or anything of lasting value. 20 years from now almost no one will know he ever existed.

But he was a good man, and a good father, and once he discovered fandom, a good fan as well. He left hundreds of friends behind, and no enemies. That's not a bad total for 89 years.

My Most Memorable Collecting Experience

My most memorable collecting experience didn't start out as one. We were living in Libertyville, Illinois in the early 1970s, about 35 miles north of Chicago, and I had just bought my daughter a horse. It came with a Western saddle, and since she was interested in dressage and jumping, she wanted an Eastern saddle (or whatever you call the damned things.) I priced out new saddles. They cost more than the horse did, so I picked up a couple of newspapers from the farming communities to the north of us, where I figured there were a lot of horses, and began looking at the classified ads. I never did find a saddle for sale, but I found the strangest ad: a young couple had just bought a century-old farmhouse and found that their attic was filled with boxes of books. They needed the storage space, and they were offering 25 cents per book—offering, not charging—to anyone who could cart a few boxes away.

I drove up that day, expecting to find a few moldering paperbacks and some hardcovers pulling away from their bindings.

I found them, but I also found two boxes filled with near-pristine first editions of Edgar Rice Burroughs books in dust jackets—maybe 35 in all.

I took them home with me—I still have about half of them; the rest I've traded for other wants—but I nobly told the nice people to keep their $8.75 and we'd call it square.

Me and The High Priest

I first met Anton LaVey, the founder and High Priest of the Church of Satan, back in August of 1968, long before I was a full-time science fiction writer. I'd sold a pair of pretty awful Edgar Rice Burroughs pastiches, but basically I was just a kid starting out, editing a couple of men's magazines and tabloid called *The National Insider*, which was like *The National Enquirer* only worse. The Worldcon was in Berkeley that year, and of course we planned to go.

Carol and I had never been to the Bay area, so I decided we'd go a few days early, spend them in San Francisco, and I'd line up a story or an interview each day to cover the expenses. During those four days I interviewed Carol Doda (the first topless dancer), the Low Moan Spectacular (a brilliant comedy group), and Anton.

I still remember taking a cab to his house, which was an old Victorian monstrosity painted black from top to bottom. There was a hearse parked in front of it, a lion roaming the back yard, and Anton answered the door dressed exactly like a priest, with one exception—instead of a cross, he was wearing a tiny coffin on a chain around his neck.

For some reason we hit it off. He had a huge collection of Arkham House books. I'd read a batch of them, and had actually known a handful of the authors, so we had something to talk about besides Satanism. After awhile I pulled out my camera, one of the girls shed her clothes, and Anton presided over a black mass.

It was dull as dishwater, and it's really difficult to be dull when you're chanting obscene spells over a gorgeous naked girl on a makeshift altar. I explained that the *Malleus Malicifarum* and the *Compendium Malificarum* were fine text books, but he was sitting on hundreds of wonderful (and occasionally Satanic) poems by Robert E. Howard, Clark Ashton Smith and H. P. Lovecraft in his Arkham collection, poems that had beat and meter—and eventually he did incorporate some of them into his ceremonies.

He was our guest at Baycon's masquerade, and I commissioned a regular column from him for the *Insider*. We became friends, in spite of the fact that I used to drive him crazy by calling him Anthony Levy (which seemed more likely to be his real name) and he was our house guest whenever a book-plugging tour brought him to our area.

Do I believe in Satanism? Of course not, no more than I believe in anything else. But let me tell you a little story, which happens to be true.

I used to phone him from the office whenever one of his columns came in, just to go over changes and corrections (this was many years before faxes, scans, and e-mails), and once I phoned him just after lunch on December 24. He mentioned that he'd forgotten to buy me a Christmas present (said the Satanist to the Jewish atheist), and was there anything he could get me? I said that it was starting to snow, and I'd sure love for him to use his Satanic connections to get me the hell out of there in the next ten minutes, since the city figured to be in gridlock by quitting time. It was just a thing to say, honest. I never expected what came next.

He mumbled some incomprehensible chant in an unknown language and told me it was taken care of, and I could go home in ten minutes. Then he hung up.

And 30 seconds later the power went off, and when it didn't come on again in five minutes, the publisher sent everyone home and closed up shop for the day.

Was it Anton? I sure as hell doubt it. Did it happen? Absolutely. Can I prove that it *wasn't* Anton? Nope. Did he take full credit for it for the next ten years? Of course. Could he do it again? I don't know; I decided never to ask for another favor. I mean, hell, if I was wrong and he *did* shut off the power from 3,000 miles away, I knew what church I definitely did not want to be beholden to.

Anton died a few years ago. We'd lost touch with each other by the late 1970s, and in truth we were never very close friends. But when I think back on all the colorful people I've known, he ranks right up there near the top.

When Funny Got More Laughs Than Dirty

I was re-reading a wonderful book that came out three or four years ago called *Seriously Funny*, by a man who, like myself, never thought much of the stand-up comedians of his/my youth, like Milton Berle, Henny Youngman, etc., who just stood there and told jokes that other people wrote for them—and who also find almost all the comedians of the past 20 years totally unfunny. (I'll include Saturday Night Live and SCTV in the unfunny group. The only two bright spots on the past quarter century, the only two I'd pay to see, have been Rita Rudner and, very occasionally, Dennis Miller.)

The book concentrates on the "new wave" of cerebral comedy that never played the big rooms, rarely made films, and have been pretty much forgotten these days . . . but they were the cream of the crop, and he's got long, thorough chapters on them:

> Mort Sahl (still the most brilliant of this bunch)
> Mike Nichols & Elaine May
> Tom Lehrer
> Lenny Bruce
> Ernie Kovacs
> Jean Shepherd
> Sid Caesar
> Bob & Ray
> Shelly Berman
> Jonathan Winters
> Woody Allen (before his movies)

maybe a dozen more.

Then there's *The Compass*, a book on the Compass Players, the most remarkable comedy group ever assembled. They started at Jimmy's, also called the Compass Bar, about two blocks from the slum apartment I lived in when I was attending the University of Chicago. Most (not quite all) were undergrad students at the U of Chicago, and in the three years they existed prior to moving to an abandoned Chinese laundry on Chicago's Near North Side and re-opening as The Second City in 1959, they numbered the following in their troop:

Mike Nichols & Elaine May
Jerry Stiller & Anne Meara
Alan Arkin
Severn Darden (far and away the most brilliant of them all)
Shelly Berman
Barbara Harris
Andrew Duncan
Ed Asner
Eugene Troobnik
Mina Kolb
Paul Sand
Del Close

That's a hell of a comic line-up. I actually belonged to a Second City workshop when I was in college, back in 1960 (before the original troop, which has never been equaled, moved to New York), and I got to do scenes with Barbara Harris, Andy Duncan and Gene Troobnik. The original Second City Players made three LP records—brilliant, cerebral, and long out of print—and I also have some audio tapes of them as they workshopped some of their improvisations. Never been anything like them for sheer talent.

Somehow the subject got around to this on New Year's Eve, at one of the CFG's rotating parties. Mark and Lynne Aronson, who also attended the University of Chicago before moving here, and are just a couple of years younger than Carol and me, remembered almost all the above. But the other 25 or 30 people, none of them culturally backward, knew only Nichols & May (most hadn't heard them, but knew they were a team), Woody Allen, Shelly Berman and Jonathan Winters—a tiny handful, and far from the best of them.

Are these guys all due to become nothing but historical feetnote, their brilliance piled onto history's junk-heap?

What about some of the others? The hottest ticket in London in 1961 and New York in 1962 was *Beyond the Fringe*, brilliant humor by four young Brits, two of whom became Peter Cook and Dudley Moore. I have a video of the performance . . . but except for Mark and Lynne, no one at the party had even heard of it.

And I remember going to Manhattan in the late 1960s, looking for writing assignments by day, and hitting the small clubs at night. We discovered the Ace Trucking Company (anyone remember them?) with Fred Willard, Stiller & Meara, a couple of others. We saw Gerry Matthews and Madeleine Kahn break into the biz with tiny, hilarious reviews at Upstairs at the Downstairs, where a lot of the songs were written by newcomers Cy Coleman, and the team of Tom Jones & Harvey Schmidt. Again, does anyone remember them, or are we doomed to watch HBO and Showtime comics who think endlessly repeating the word "Fuck" is both hilarious and cutting-edge?

Ghod, I hope not. I mean, I know each generation's growing up dumber than the last, but please tell me that Andrew Dice Clay is not the spiritual godfather of the next generation of successful comedians.

Homes Away from Home

Now that I just turned 65, I figure I've done, if not most, at least well over half of my traveling. And during those 65 years, I have been fortunate enough to stay at some of the more memorable hostelries on Planet Earth. Since I play to cut back on the traveling a bit during the next 30 years, I thought this might be a good time to share my memories of those accommodations with you.

We've stayed in places that were far more famous, but the most luxurious hotel accommodation we ever had was when I was Toastmaster at the 1988 Worldcon in New Orleans. The pro and fan Guests of Honor—Don Wollheim and Roger Sims—had first choice, and both chose suites in the Marriott, which was across the street of the Sheraton and hence 40 yards closer to the French Quarter . . . so we "settled" for the Presidential Suite in the Sheraton.

It had a living room with a 60-foot window wall overlooking the Mississippi, a dining room with a mahogany table and matching chairs for 24, the master bedroom had a gorgeous 4-poster king-sized bed on a raised platform and two walk-in closets, there were 3 other bedrooms (once we found out how many bedrooms we had, we filled them with Laura, a friend of Laura's, and my father). There were 6 bathrooms, each with its own phone and television. There was an express elevator that went from the lobby to our front door on the 49th floor and nowhere else.

I've stayed in my share of 5-star hostelries in the US, Europe and Africa (and the Sheraton isn't one; even before Katrina it only had 4 stars), but I've never experienced an accommodation like that one.

The contract between producers and the Writers Guild stated that we must be flown first class, driven by limo, all meals paid for, and housed in 5-star hotels. The most luxurious of them was the Beverly Hills Four Seasons. We had a penthouse suite, which is to say, a bedroom and a sitting room. (Well, once we had a penthouse; a couple of other times we had the same floor plan but not on the top floor.) It was spacious without being overwhelmingly so. What made it worth the money (not ours, thank ghod!) were the furnishings: a bed, chairs, chaise lounge, tables, desks, that must have cost upwards of $40,000 for the two rooms . . . and the wallpaper probably went $75 a square yard. Elegant bathroom, too.

That was the Capella International hotel.

The Miramax hotel was a little less in-your-face elegant but far more interesting. We had the same suite each time, at the Beverly Hills Nikko Inn. It was exceptionally high-tech. Every desk and table, even the nightstands, had rows of buttons that controlled everything in the suite. Push this button and the drapes would open or close; push that one and they'd open or close in the next room; push this other one and the water would start running in the bathtub; push another and room service would speak to you on the intercom so you didn't have to fumble for the phone. There were actually two bathtubs: a normal one, and one that was maybe three feet on a side and six feet high. Of course they had high-speed computer connections (before 99% of the hotels did), and state-of-the-art widescreen flatscreen TVs, stereos, DVD players, you name it, in each room. The furnishings and overall ambience were not up to the Four Seasons, and every time we had a business dinner they drove us to the Four Seasons' restaurant rather than eating at the Nikko, but as I say, it was a lot more interesting suite.

(We never saw anyone in the Four Seasons reading anything except *Daily Variety* and the *Daily Hollywood Reporter*; they were also the reading matter of choice at the Nikko, but at least a couple of people in the lobby were furtively peeking at the *Wall Street Journal*.)

When we went to Botswana in 1990 as part of a 6-week safari that included Zimbabwe and Malawi, we knew we wanted to stay at the luxurious Chobe Game Lodge when we visited the Chobe National Park, and we reserved a room. When we landed in London, prior to getting on a plane that would take us the rest of the way, the agent who had arranged the trip to our specifications was waiting there to greet us, and mentioned, in passing, that the honeymoon suite, the one where Richard Burton and Liz Taylor had spent a week after their second marriage, had just had a cancellation, and would we be interested? Ordinarily I'd have said no, but I'd just made a few foreign sales I hadn't anticipated, and we were only going to be at Chobe for 3 days, so I agreed.

By the time we got there two weeks later, we'd been staying in tented camps in the Okavango Delta (for "Delta" read "Swamp"), and some dry, dusty areas on the edge of the Kalahari, and we were ready for a little luxury. The suite was composed of a bedroom and a parlor, each about twenty by twenty feet. Beautiful tiled floors, lovely stucco walls, glass doors from each room leading out to a balcony. More important, the suite was air-conditioned—the only air-conditioning in the whole country other than in the capital of Gabarone. And it had a ceramic tile bath—the first enclosed, indoor bathroom we'd seen in ten days. Very comfortably furnished.

We walked out onto the balcony and saw that we were only about thirty yards from the Chobe River. We were also at the very end of the building. The balcony lead around to the side, and we couldn't imagine what there was to see there, but we walked around the corner and lo and behold, there was our own private swimming pool, built and positioned in such a way that no one not on our private balcony could see in. We used it maybe eight or ten times while we were there, and never wore a swimsuit.

Each morning we were served a huge breakfast on our deck, which we ate while watching maybe two hundred elephants drinking and frolicking in the river a short stone's throw away. (And when I wrote up my favorite meals in an article a few years ago, I stated that the best single dinner I've had in my life was at the Chobe Game Lodge.)

I know why Liz and Dick stayed there. What I don't know is why, with their money, they ever left.

We stayed in another luxury lodge on the same trip. About a week after leaving Chobe we found ourselves at Hwange, the biggest and best game park in Zimbabwe. I'd reserved a room at the Hwange Game Lodge, but instead we were given a huge suite, each room sporting numerous pieces of native Shona and Mtabele artwork and weaponry (spears, not AK-47s.) Had a private balcony overlooking a water hole, too. Not as luxurious as Chobe, but awfully good for Africa.

But I hadn't asked for it, and I didn't want to pay the thousand a day or so that it must cost, so I went down to talk to the manager about getting the room we'd reserved, and he said not to worry, it was a gift of the management.

Just out of curiosity I asked if the lodge was full and he had no choice but to give us a free upgrade, and he said no, the lodge was about half empty. Then why did he give us this gorgeous and obviously expensive suite at no cost, I asked. He grinned, pulled out a copy of *Paradise*, which was my science-fictional allegorical history of Kenya, and mentioned that when he saw my name on the guest list a few weeks earlier he'd decided that he wanted to make a good impression on me, that he never wanted me to say anything bad about him or the lodge if I ever wrote a novel about Zimbabwe. (Which I did—*Purgatory*—three years later. Actually, I never mentioned the lodge in the novel, not from any ethical concerns about my suite, but simply because, unlike Kenya's Norfolk Hotel, it played no part in the country's history.)

Still, it was a hell of a nice surprise, and a hell of a nice suite, too.

***

With one exception (Chobe), all the places I've mentioned so far, while luxurious, were paid for by someone else. But on our first trip to London, we stayed at the fabled Ritz, and paid for it ourselves.

(Why? Well, it was 1984, and a small suite—bedroom and "sitting room"—cost 150 pounds . . . and at the time the pound was worth $1.05. And since every room in or near Picadilly cost 90 to 100 pounds, we figured what the hell, why not splurge for a few days? I'm glad we did, That same suite today costs over a thousand pounds a night, which seems more that a little bit excessive.)

It was a nice, elegant suite, not up to the Four Seasons or a couple of others I'll get around to mentioning, but nice. But what made it memorable were the public rooms on the main floor. Of all the high teas we've ever had, at hotels, at Harrod's, everywhere, none ever approached the Ritz for quality. The lobby was as luxurious as you'd expect a Ritz lobby to be, the one dinner we had there was excellent, and they had a casino as formal and classy as one expects (and never finds) in Monte Carlo.

A hotel in Manhattan that was every bit as good as the Ritz, at least when we were going there, was the Plaza, where we stayed maybe a dozen times, back in the days when I had to travel to New York a couple of times a year to meet editors and solicit work. The rooms made you feel like a small child: the doors were ten feet high, the doorknobs were almost at eye level, every chair could easily have held a typical 450-pound fan, the bathtub almost needed a small ladder to climb over the side. It wasn't that expensive for a 5-star Midtown Manhattan hotel back then—maybe $150 a day throughout the 1970s; these days I'm told it's $600 for a room, $700 if you want a view of anything besides the brick wall of the adjacent building. (I can't remember the number of the room we always requested back then, but it overlooked Central Park.)

The lobby, like the Ritz, went out of its way to impress. Your pupils would contract from all the gilt on the furniture. They don't serve high tea in the States, but every night, on the way home from the theater (I don't think we've ever spent a single night in Manhattan without seeing a play), we'd stop in the lobby, sit down at a table, order coffee and a dessert (or sometimes Carol would order brandy or wine), and we'd be serenaded by a tux-and-tailed string quartet. Very nice way to end an evening.

* * * *

The Mount Kenya Safari Club is one of the three or four true luxury resorts in all of Africa. Initially a private club created by William Holden and some partners, the first few members included Lyndon B. Johnson and Winston Churchill.

It's at 8,000 feet altitude, not quite halfway up Kirinyaga (i.e., Mount Kenya). The sweeping lawns contain a huge swimming pool, a few ponds for water birds, and some bowling greens. There's an animal orphanage on the premises, and a private reserve, specializing in the rare bongo, within a mile. There's also a truly fabulous set of gift shops, which deal not only in the ordinary tourist items, but exquisite bronzes and paintings by East Africa's best. And there's a stable for those who like riding through wild mountain territory. Best of all, there's the main lodge, with a restaurant that's world-famous. Members in the private dining room (we had a few meals there with our guide, who's a member) order off a menu, and get a 7-course meal...but it's the general dining room that's garnered all the fame. It's an endless buffet—there are 6 meat tables, 4 dessert tables, 22 tables in all. If you choose to take your meal out to the patio, you'll be entertained by local dancers and drummers.

We've been there a number of times, and always stay in a private cottage—there are 8 of them, about 200 yards from the main building. Each cottage contains two large bedrooms, each with a walk-in closet and each with its own oversized bath, and a living room, complete with television (rare on the safari trail), wet bar (even rarer), and fireplace. Sliding doors lead from the living room to a patio with chairs, tables, and umbrellas, where you can sit and watch whatever's happening on the sprawling lawn, or just enjoy the peak of Kirinyaga in the distance.

A few miles around the mountain from the Safari Club, on the other side of the town of Nanyuki, is Ol Pejata, an elegant private estate formerly owned by Adnan Khoshoggi. It's 110,000 acres, filled with game—including the increasingly rare black rhino—and you either stay in Khoshoggi's main house (it's got four huge, elegant guest rooms plus an unbelievable bridal suite and bath), or, as we did, you stay in a private cottage that is even nicer than the one at the Safari Club. The food is excellent, served on a large dining patio, and there is a swimming pool available to all guests (which never number more than 12.) And of course you never have to leave the property to spend a couple of days driving around observing game.

And believe me, when you get to the Mount Kenya Safari Club or Ol Pejata after a couple of weeks of tents, outdoor bathrooms, and ostrich egg omelets, you think you've died and gone to heaven. There's not much in the States or Europe that can match either of them for luxury. (Though the Chobe Game Lodge in Botswana can, and I'm told that Londolozi, a private reserve in South Africa, also can.)

A few years ago we took a trip to Jamaica and stayed at the Royal Caribbean, which has since been sold to (yucch!) Sandals.

It had the nicest beach in the Montego Bay area, some 600 yards of white sand, plus a couple of swimming pools for those who didn't like the ocean. We stayed in a 3-room cottage, furnished in Island Expensive, with a shaded patio facing the sea. Breakfast was served on the patio every day, lunch—on days we were at the resort; we took a lot of day trips—was served right at the ocean. Dinner—and it was formal: tuxes and strapless gowns every night, just as Ian Fleming would have wanted—was served on a series of tiered patios and decks that surrounded a large dance floor. There was live entertainment every night, specializing in songs Harry Belefonte had made famous. (You wouldn't believe how quickly you can become sick of "Island in the Sun" and "Jamaica Farewell.") The clientele was about 1/3 American, 1/3 British, and 1/3 Canadian.

There were tennis courts and pool tables, with bars and bartenders everywhere, as well as wandering calypso bands everywhere. In the morning a staff of maybe 40 would scour the manicured grounds, picking up any leaf that had had the audacity to fall off a branch during the night. The place owned some glass-bottom boats, and rented sailboats of various sizes. You could also rent a van and driver and plan your own day trip to Dunn's River Falls, or Ocho Rios, or the rum distillery in the middle of the island, or the extensive nude beach at Negril, or even distant Kingston. At night, after the dinner and the dancing, you'd sit on your patio and watch the brilliantly-lit cruise ships passing by.

If there's a nicer way to spend a couple of weeks in January, we've never found it.

Down in the Grenadines, at the Southern end of the Caribbean, there's a little island, maybe 3/4 of a mile in diameter, called Petit St. Vincent.

It's not easy to get to. We flew from Cincinnati to Miami, changed planes, flew to San Juan, Puerto Rico, changed planes, flew to Barbados, changed to a little 5-seater, flew to Union Island, and from there took a motorboat to Petit St. Vincent.

Carol had read about it, but we didn't know anyone who had been there. Evidently some Cincinnati-based cargo pilot flew over it—it was uninhabited—weekly during World War II, and promised himself that when the war was over he'd buy it. And he did.

It's a very hilly island, surrounded by a coral reef. There's a main office/restaurant building in the center, and it's got the only electric power on the island. Scattered around the edges of the island are 11 luxurious villas, each two huge rooms, with an equally large bath, and with both covered and unshaded patios. Outside each villa is a flagpole, with two flags: raise the red flag and no one will approach the villa under any circumstance; raise the green one and someone will be there on a moped (a concrete walk for mopeds surrounds the island) within 2 minutes.

You have beautiful views of the sea, but you can't see any other villa from your own, which means they can't see you, either. You can wander around naked for a week, or sleep naked on your deck, and as long as you've got the red flag up no one will ever know. (Not that anyone cares in the first place.)

Great dining. They serve fresh shellfish—you can walk around and see them unloading the traps each morning—and there's filet and prime rib for those who don't want fish. I don't drink, but Carol assures me they have a top-of-the-line wine list.

Not much to do but relax and unwind. There's an obstacle course that no one uses, and there's great snorkeling, and that's it. You come home tanned, rested, and well-fed.

Some hotels were witnesses to history. A precious few, like the fabled Norfolk Hotel in Nairobi. were *part* of history. We've been to Kenya four times, and whenever we've been in Nairobi—the start and finish of each safari, and twice for a day or two in the middle—we've always stayed at the Norfolk, which, though far from large, has housed royalty from perhaps 50 countries, plus a goodly number of Presidents and Prime Ministers.

The main hotel has about a hundred rooms, but there are also a dozen two-and-three-room cottages on the grounds. At various times we've stayed in cottages that had been home to Robert Ruark, Elspeth Huxley, and Bror Blixen. (Never did stay in Teddy Roosevelt's cottage, damn it). Each cottage, in addition to its one or two bedrooms, tiled bath, and living room, has a shaded patio overlooking the two large, colorful aviaries. The hotel's restaurant, the Ibis Grill, is one of the three best in town, and the waiters are more than happy to serve you on the patio of your cottage.

Everywhere you look there are plaques commemorating some event that took place there, or some person who stayed there. In 1981 the main hotel was rocked by a fanatic's bomb on New Year's Eve; it was rebuilt in exactly the same style and colors, and by mid-1982 you couldn't tell there'd ever been an explosion. Unlike, say, the Mount Kenya Safari Club or the Chobe Game Lodge, the Norfolk wouldn't be a 5-star hotel anywhere else in the world; it might not even get 4 stars in the US, England, France, or Hong Kong. But it is so steeped in history and tradition that there is simply no place else to stay when starting or concluding your East African safari.

And a final batch of better accommodations:

• Chicago's Palmer House. We stayed there, in a small suite, after moving to Cincinnati. It's Chicago's answer to the Waldorf, and in my opinion is even nicer. (When I was a kid I used to go there all the time. There was a magician's supply shop on the second floor—I have no idea if it's still there; I'm talking half a century ago—and as long as you bought a trick, no matter how inexpensive, the guy who ran the place would dazzle you with tricks no kid could afford. It was a great way to see a half-hour professional magic show for maybe $1.25, and I never missed the opportunity when I was in the Loop.)

• San Francisco's Mark Hopkins. Nice, but not quite world class. Same with its famed restaurant, Top of the Mark; nice, but there are a lot better.

• Miami's Fountainbleu. They held the 1977 Worldcon here. It was in receivership at the time, and not at its best. Fabulous lobby, capable of seating 1,500 people in comfort, and a world-class swimming pool. Rooms and restaurant were nothing special.

• Orlando's Peabody. Not five stars, but as nice a four-star hostelry as you could want. Fine restaurant, great 24-hour coffee shop, wonderful lobby with its own 30-foot-high waterfall, large comfortable rooms. Home to the 1992 Worldcon.

• Nancy France's Grand Hotel. Every city in Europe's got a Grand Hotel (we hated Brighton's in England), but this one really *was* grand. Spacious rooms, huge bathrooms, excellent restaurant.

OK, so much for the good stuff. And just to show you I don't always luck out:

In the early 1990s, the Nebula Banquet was held in New York. I flew up alone. Just as well; Carol would have taken one look at the room and insisted that we move to the Plaza or the Waldorf.

Some genius booked us into the Roosevelt Hotel in Midtown Manhattan. At a time when the convention rate for most Midtown hotels was maybe $250 a night, the rack rate for the Roosevelt was $88.

It was overpriced.

The room was small. It smelled of mold. There were exposed wires along the baseboard on three of the four walls. The sink leaked. I killed a roach while I was unpacking. Never saw another roach; I think the rat I saw the next morning ate them all. Two of the three lamps had burned-out lightbulbs.

It's possible that the Roosevelt is still standing. If so, I don't know why.

Where Do You Get Your Crazy (Novel) Ideas?

It's hard for a science fiction writer to go anywhere without being asked, at least once, "Where do you get your crazy ideas?" The number of facetious and/or contemptuous answers, at least that I'm aware of, is nearing the thousand mark, and yet it seems to do nothing to discourage the endless recitation of the question.

Guy Lillian gently suggested that I answer them here once and for all. I agreed, and suggested he print 400 million copies of the fanzine so he can mail one to every English-speaking fan and then I'll never have to answer it again.

I'm keeping my end of the bargain. Now it's up to Guy.

The Soul Eater

I hate college. Always have, always will. But after we got married and I started making a living freelancing, Carol suggested that since I only needed something like 12 hours for my degree I go back and get it. (That was more than 40 years ago. I still need 6 hours, so you can tell how much a degree means to me.)

Anyway, I enrolled in an English course at night school. One week we were studying *Moby Dick*, and I'd been so busy delivering stories and articles that I didn't have a chance to read the required pages. But our professor was madly in love with the book (as I am, these days) and I knew if I got her talking she'd forget all about asking questions or making assignments. So I suggested, perhaps five minutes into the class, that Melville had begged the question, and the book would have been more interesting if we'd seen what happened to Ahab if, after a quarter century of megalomania, he'd actually killed the white while. What would he have done with the rest of his life, now that his only goal had been achieved?

The ruse worked. She and I argued it for two hours, and she never did ask me about the section I hadn't read yet.

But when I got home I started thinking about it, and eventually I decided that Melville had indeed missed a more interesting story, so I wrote *The Soul Eater*, about a hunter who is obsessed with killing a creature that lives in space and feeds on cosmic dust.

It was Carol who pointed out while I was writing it that I may have used *Moby Dick* as a jumping-off point, but by the end it owed at least as much to the legend of the Flying Dutchman. And it was Dick Geis who concluded that it was "the damnedest love story" he'd ever read.

Birthright: The Book of Man

This book was directly inspired, in an ass-backwards way, by a movie called *Alice's Restaurant*. Had to be the most incredibly boring film we'd seen in years, and after half an hour of this drivel, I muttered, probably more to myself than to Carol, "Why am I wasting my time with this turkey when I could be home doing something interesting, like writing the history of the human race from now until its extinction?"

And Carol whispered back, "So let's go home and get to work."

We walked out of the theater in the middle of the movie, and that night I plotted *Birthright: The Book of Man*, which not only sold here and in a few other countries, but created the future in which I've set perhaps 25 novels and more than a dozen stories.

Which just goes to show that you take your inspiration where you can get it.

Walpurgis III

I spent a couple of years during my starving-writer days writing a weekly article on the supernatural. I don't believe in it, of course, but by the time I was done I knew an awful lot about it.

One night Carol and I had one of our few major fights (we've had maybe three in 45 years). I stormed out of the room thinking she was the most evil woman in the Universe—and suddenly I had my plot. I went right back in, kissed her, and thanked her for giving me a novel.

What happens to a world populated exclusively by covens and Satanists who give sanctuary to a man whose deeds are far more heinous than Hitler's? What happens to people who give lip service to Evil when confronted by Evil Incarnate, a man who tortures and slaughters because the alternative to torturing and slaughtering never has and never will occur to him?

And just to make it interesting, I had the planetary government hire an assassin to take him off their hands before he kills every living thing on the whole planet. If the assassin can actually get to him, past his layers and layers of defense, it poses another problem: who is the more evil—a man who kills passionately, from compulsion . . . or a man who kills coldly and emotionlessly, from calculation?

Sideshow

I get a lot of my ideas from books, plays and screenplays where I feel the author has missed a better story than he told.

Like *The Elephant Man*, for example. Play (brilliant) or movie (a cut above mediocre), take your choice. They both got me interested in reading about John Merrick, the Elephant Man, and I finally came across his autobiography—and found something so unusual, so aberrant, that they left it out of both the movie and the play.

It seems that the carnival owner, the man who knew full well that Merrick was a sensitive and artistic soul but treated him like an animal for more than a decade, came by the hospital where Merrick had found sanctuary. He was dead broke, and asked Merrick to come on tour with him until he could put together a grubstake. Sir Frederick Treves and all the other hospital staff assured Merrick he didn't have to go—and yet Merrick *did* go back on exhibition, touring the freak shows of Europe all summer before returning to the hospital to die.

Now, that's the story that *should* have been told. The more I thought about it, the more I kept wondering: what hidden virtues were in that man to make Merrick willingly humiliate and endanger himself when he could have refused?

Finally, I decided the only way I could figure it out was to write the story, and since I'm a science fiction writer, I created Thaddeus Flint and *Sideshow*—and when I was finished, the grudging affinity between Merrick and the carny owner finally made sense to me.

It seems to have made sense to a lot of other people as well. My editor, Sheila Gilbert, asked me to turn it into a series, and while I was doing so, Signet published *Sideshow* in October of 1982. It went through four quick printings and got universally favorable reviews.

Eros Ascending
Eros at Zenith
Eros Descending
Eros at Nadir

One day in the early 1980s Carol and I decided to take a vacation up to the Lake Tahoe area. In preparation for it, I picked up a copy of *Nevada Magazine* in the hope of finding an ad for a nice resort. As I was thumbing through the pages, my attention was caught by a photo of a lovely naked lady, which on average is just about the very best way to catch my attention.

It turned out to be an ad for a limited-edition silver statue of a lady, leaning against a brass headboard. The plaque at the base of the statue said that this was Julia Bulette, who rose from the ranks of the working girls to become the madam of the biggest whorehouse in Virginia City, Nevada. She donated large amounts of money—*not* bribes and payoffs, since prostitution was legal—to the local police and firemen, and when a cholera epidemic broke out she turned the whorehouse into a free hospital. It wasn't until after a customer stabbed her to death that the local ladies decided she wasn't good enough to be buried in the local cemetery, so they planted her in Boot Hill, with only the brass headboard of her bed as a tombstone.

How could anyone read that and not want to write a book about it? So I proposed it to Sheila Gilbert, my editor at Signet, and she said she wasn't empowered to buy a mainstream or Western novel about a whorehouse, but she *could* buy a science fiction novel about one.

So I started working out stories to tell about an orbiting brothel called the Velvet Comet, and at some point Carol suggested that by that point in the far future we should be all through with sexism and the Comet had better appeal to *both* sexes. Furthermore, the cost of flying there from halfway across the galaxy would be prohibitive, so it made sense to make it the most luxurious location in existence, and make is a *complete* experience: not just a brothel with the most beautiful and best-trained prostitutes of both sexes (and a few aliens thrown in), but a two-mile-long shopping mall which would be the future equivalent of Rodeo Drive, a dozen five-star restaurants, and a lavish casino. No one would come to the Comet just for a roll in the hay.

I came up with four stories (the fourth after it is bankrupt and in drydock), and so I wouldn't feel I was telling the same thing over and over, I set each one about fifty years farther up the road, so the only continuing "character" was the Comet itself.

The Branch

The Branch came about because I had a broken chair when I lived in Libertyville, Illinois. I took it in to get it repaired, and was confronted by a shawl-wearing Orthodox Jew who got furious at me for some reason—maybe I was gnawing on a ham sandwich at the time; I honestly can't remember. At any rate, he started pointing out how all the non-pious Jews, of which I was a prime example, would suffer when the true Messiah finally arrived.

I was trying my best to be pleasant, since he was the only antique furniture repairman I could find in the phone book, so I suggested that things were looking up for him, since he was in excellent health and there was doubtless a very good chance that he'd live to see the Messiah and would he please give me a receipt for the chair? His eyes widened, his pupils dilated, and he explained to me that while he planned to live a long and happy life, he much preferred to be dead before the Messiah came, for—and he quoted chapter and verse to me—the Messiah of the Old Testament was not a prince of peace, but would come with sword and the fire to destroy civilization before building his new kingdom in Jerusalem.

And suddenly, instead of mollifying him, I began questioning him in earnest, and that night I began writing *The Branch*, the story of the true Jewish Messiah, who shows up about half a century from now.

Adventures
Exploits
Encounters
Hazards (in progress)

Lucifer Jones was born one evening back in the late 1970s. I was trading videotapes with a number of other people—stores hadn't started renting them yet, and this was the only way to increase your collection at anything above a snail's pace—and one of my correspondents asked for a copy of *She*, with Ursula Andress, which happened to be playing on Cincinnati television.

I looked in my *Maltin Guide* and found that *She* ran 117 minutes. Now, this was back in the dear dead days when everyone knew that Beta was the better format, and it just so happened that the longest Beta tape in existence at the time was two hours. So I realized that I couldn't just put the tape on and record the movie, commercials and all, because the tape wasn't long enough. Therefore, like a good correspondent/trader, I sat down, controls in hand, to record the movie (which I had never seen before) and edit out the commercials as they showed up.

About fifteen minutes into the film Carol entered the video room, absolutely certain from my peals of wild laughter that I was watching a Marx Brothers festival that I had neglected to tell her about. Wrong. I was simply watching one of the more inept films ever made.

And after it was over, I got to thinking: if they could be that funny by accident, what if somebody took those same tried-and-true pulp themes and tried to be funny on purpose?

So I went to my typewriter—this was back in the pre-computer days—and wrote down the most oft-abused African stories that one was likely to find in old pulp magazines and B movies: the elephants' graveyard, Tarzan, lost races, mummies, white goddesses, slave-trading, what-have-you. When I got up to twelve, I figured I had enough for a book . . . but I needed a unifying factor.

Enter Lucifer Jones.

Africa today isn't so much a dark and mysterious continent as it is an impoverished and hungry one, so I decided to set the book back in the 1920s, when things were wilder and most of the romantic legends of the pulps and B movies hadn't been thoroughly disproved.

Who was the most likely kind of character to roam to all points of Africa's compass? A missionary.

What was funny about a missionary? Nothing. So Lucifer became a con man who presented himself as a missionary. (As he is fond of explaining it, his religion is "a little something me and God whipped up betwixt ourselves of a Sunday afternoon.")

Now, the stories themselves were easy enough to plot: just take a traditional pulp tale and stand it on its ear. (The titles should give you a notion: "The Best Little Tabernacle in Nairobi," "The Insidious Oriental Dentist," "The Clubfoot of Notre Dame," "The Island of Annoyed Souls," and so on.) But anyone could do that: I decided to add a little texture by having Lucifer narrate the books in the first person, and to make his language a cross between the almost-poetry of *Trader Horn* and the fractured English of *Pogo Possum*, and in truth I think there is even more humor embedded in the language than in the plots.

So far Lucifer has made it through Africa (*Adventures*, 1985), Asia (*Exploits*, 1992), Europe (*Encounters*, 1993), and after an eleven-year hiatus is currently working his way across South America (when there are enough stories to collect as a book, it'll be *Hazards*; *Voyages and Intrigues* will take him to the South Pacific and Australia, just in time for World War II.)

If I could write only one thing for the rest of my life, it'd be Lucifer Jones stories.

Santiago

In his finest novella, *Space Chantey*, Ray Lafferty wrote the following:

"Will there be a mythology of the future, they used to ask, after all has become science? Will high deeds be told in epic, or only in computer code?"

It made me realize that I wanted to spend at least a part of my career creating myths of the future, peopled with larger-than-life characters possessed of colorful names and pasts—but I was stuck for a plot for the first one.

Then Carol saw a movie on television one night, a Sergio Leone film called *Duck, You Sucker!* (which is titled *A Fistful of Dynamite* these days), promptly rented it, sped ahead to a speech she wanted me to hear, and made me sit down and listen to it. James Coburn, playing a disillusioned IRA explosives expert who has been betrayed by those he trusted most and is now fighting as a mercenary in Mexico, gives a short speech about how once he believed in God and country and freedom and justice and nobility . . . and now all he believes in is the dynamite.

"Now go write the book," said Carol.

I did, and more than 21 years later it's still in print.

Stalking the Unicorn

In America, where the works of J. R. R. Tolkien have spawned literally hundreds of usually-dreadful imitations, the term "elf-and-unicorn trilogy" has become a pejorative among my fellow writers.

And, since I am a contrary kind of guy, when I finally sat down to write a fantasy novel after more than a dozen science fiction novels, I decided to write a book that featured both an elf and a unicorn, but had nothing to do with Tolkien or with anything else that was currently being written in the fantasy field.

I decided to set my fantasy in New York City, which is as bizarre as any mythical kingdom I've ever read about. My knight-errant is a private detective from "our" Manhattan, and his quest involves a stolen unicorn.

Since I didn't think the reader would willingly suspend his disbelief for any great length of time, the entire story takes place in the course of one evening, between nightfall and sunrise—and since fantasies tend to celebrate what is best and worst in us, I chose to have my story take place on New Year's Eve, perhaps the finest night of the year for celebration.

There is a great deal of humor and charm in *Stalking the Unicorn*, perhaps too much, because for some critics and readers it obscured the fact that, despite all the invention and surprises, this is a pretty bleak world that my detective has entered, certainly different and probably more interesting than his own world, but just as riddled with the effects of human frailty. The honorable people in this book are, alas, no more effective than the honorable people in Mallory's world; and while the dishonorable people may be charming and witty and engaging, that does not make them any the less dishonorable. When Mallory finally confronts his ultimate opponent, a demon known as the Grundy, he is also confronting the only explanation that I have for why our world is the way it is.

The book had a couple of printings, and Mallory has come back half a dozen times at shorter lengths. One of these days I'll put him in another novel.

Historical sidenote: This is the only title I've ever changed at editorial request. My original title was *Yes, We Have No Nirvanas*. My editor, Beth Meacham, convinced me that no one under the age of 40 would understand the reference, and I'm sure she was right—but I still prefer the original.

The Dark Lady

We were invited to the wedding of Dick Smith and Leah Zeldes up in Michigan. I don't remember my function—it wasn't Best Man and it wasn't just a member of the audience; I participated in some very minor way—and I needed a tux, and this took place before I owned one.

So the wedding party got my measurements and thoughtfully rented one for me—even the shoes.

As we were getting dressed for the wedding in our hotel room, I realized that while they got the tux right, they'd messed up the shoes. I wear a 13, and these were about a 10. And they hurt like hell. I kept trying to find a way to stand or walk comfortably in them, and I couldn't, and I guess I started muttering and bitching, and finally Carol said, "Stop growling at me. I'm not the Dark Lady."

I'd never heard of the Dark Lady before, and I found the term so evocative that I forgot all about my shoes and started writing notes on a hotel scratchpad so I wouldn't forget about it. Turns out it was from Shakespeare—count on Carol never to use a mundane reference—and by the time I got home I had the book pretty much mapped out.

Ivory

In 1984, in a security vault deep beneath the British Museum of Natural History, I was permitted to inspect the record tusks of the greatest mammal ever to walk the Earth, an animal known only as the Kilimanjaro Elephant.

Everything about this animal, from his life to his death, is shrouded in mystery and legend. His ivory was almost twenty percent heavier than the second-largest recorded set of tusks; he was a monster even among his own kind. No white man ever saw him. If any black man saw him during his lifetime, the fact is not recorded. Historians think, but do not know, that he died in 1898; they think, but do not know, that he died on the southeastern slopes of Mount Kilimanjaro; they think, but do not know, that he was killed by a runaway slave. And that is the sum total of their knowledge of this awesome creature.

The moment I first read about the ivory in the early 1980s I knew there was a story to be told—many stories, in fact; as many stories as there were people whose lives had been touched by the pursuit of the ivory. I became obsessed by it, and finally outlined a mainstream novel.

Then my agent, Eleanor Wood, always more level-headed than I, reminded me who and where my audience was, and suggested that I follow the tusks not just until they were locked away by the museum in 1937, but out into space over the next few millennia.

So I did. And got a Nebula nomination here and a Clarke nomination in England.

Paradise

I knew after I'd been to Kenya and had previously read a ton of books about it that I wanted to write a novel about its history—which in my case meant an allegorical science fiction novel. But the history I wanted to cover took place from about 1890 to the present, and the obvious choice was a "generations" book. I hate obvious choices, and besides, the early history was all made by whites and the more recent history was all made by blacks, and since whites and blacks don't intermarry in Kenya, I couldn't tell a generations novel even if I wanted to.

So I put off writing it. Then, on my next trip to Kenya, a 20-year-old white Kenyan girl that Carol and I were dining with offered the opinion that Kenya, pleasant as it was, was probably a much nicer place to visit just before her birth, when Britain still controlled it and government services were much more efficient and the poverty was, if not less widespread, at least less visible.

Perry Mason, our 52-year-old private guide, who was also at the table, said that no, she was mistaken. He had been in Kenya since 1952, having come there to fight the Mau Mau and stayed on to become a white hunter and then a safari guide, and in his opinion Kenya was probably at its best in the 1940s, the so-called Golden Age of East African hunting, before all the racial conflict began.

The next night, while visiting with Ian Hardy, an 80-year-old retired hunter who lived up in the Aberdares Mountains, the subject came up again. He had arrived in 1935, and thought Kenya must have been just about perfect a decade earlier, before the great herds were decimated and the farmers began fencing off the land and the hired help started getting notions of independence and equality.

But Karen Blixen had left Kenya in 1931, mourning the passing of her beloved country, which she felt must have been pristine and beautiful just before she arrived in 1912.

And, of course, F. C. Selous, Teddy Roosevelt's white hunter, left Kenya in 1910 because they had already ruined a once-perfect country.

Later in the trip, I spoke to a couple of black Africans, one a student and one a minor political office-holder. Both were sure that Kenya, although it certainly had its problems, was well on the road to becoming a Utopia.

And finally I had my fictional structure—the vision of a receding or forthcoming Golden Age that in truth never was and never will be.

Second Contact

There are not many authors that I'm addicted to, but one of them is Robert Ludlum. I love his intricate plots, and his unique brand of fictional paranoia. In a typical Ludlum book, by the halfway mark everyone is trying to kill the hero—the bad guys, the good guys, his friends, his enemies, his lover, his family, the government, everyone . . . and the second half of the book is a race to find out *why* before they can pull it off.

I decided that I wanted to try to bring that particular form of paranoia to science fiction and see how it worked. I was looking for a crossover audience, so my future of 2065 reads a lot more like 1990 with a few bells and whistles added, so as not to scare that hoped-for readership away. I like to think I pulled it off. I do know that halfway through the book only one person in the entire world *isn't* out to kill the hero (and pretty soon everyone's out to kill her too).

Soothsayer

One day I was being interviewed by some fanzine editor, and he was asking me who the most lethal character I ever created was—Jericho (from *Walpurgis III*) or perhaps the Angel (from *Santiago*)?

I don't remember my answer, but I know he started me thinking about who the most dangerous person in a fully-populated galaxy might be, and what skills might he possess? Would he be built like Arnold Schwarzenegger, or master his weapons like Clint Eastwood's Man With No Name? Or would he be as brilliant as one of A. E. van Vogt's mutants or supermen?

And the more I considered it, the more I kept thinking: wouldn't it be interesting if the most dangerous, lethal character in the galaxy wasn't a warrior or an assassin or a genius, but a very frightened little 6-year-old girl?

So I wrote the story.

And by the time I finished *Soothsayer*, I knew that I'd never be able to draw anyone more dangerous and deadly than little Penelope Bailey, whose greatest desire was to be anyone else.

The Widowmaker
The Widowmaker Reborn
The Widowmaker Unleashed
A Gathering of Widowmakers

One night I was in the conference room at the late lamented GEnie—there will never again be networks or conference rooms half as good—and people were discussing clones, and stories about clones, and it occurred to me that I was tired of clones coming off the table (or out of the vat, or wherever newborn clones come from) and functioning as if they'd had a lifetime of experience and knowledge.

So the framing device for the first three Widowmaker books was that the Widowmaker, a top-notch bounty hunter with scores of kills to his credit, able to defend himself better than anyone alive at the time, comes down with a disfiguring, debilitating and eventually fatal disease. And shortly before it can kill him, he has himself frozen in a cryonics lab/chamber until such time as they discover a cure for his disease.

But inflation eats away at his principle, and after a century he's out of money and it looks like they're going to have to wake him and toss him out—but then someone hears that he's still alive and offers enough money to keep him frozen for a few more years if they'll clone him and send the clone out to clean up a very hazardous situation.

They no longer have to grow them up from embryos and babies—who the hell wants to read about the Widowmaker wetting his diaper and learning to eat solid foods?—so the clone is created as a 22-year-old man with the Widowmaker's physical gifts, and after a month's intensive training he is as skilled on offense or defense as the original . . . but he's *not* a 22-year-old man. In terms of emotional maturity and experience, he's a 2-month-old child in a 22-year-old man's body, and as such he doesn't fare too well. He falls in love with the first woman he meets, he believes everything everyone tells him, and so on . . . and in the end it proves his undoing.

Well, I couldn't tell the same story twice, so for the second book I decided that cloning had progressed to the point where they could imprint all of the original's memories and experiences on his clone. This clone *is* the Widowmaker, cold, crafty, competent, and cunning, possessed of the original's memories—but the original has been in cold storage for 106 years, and those memories are a century out of date. Imagine an Abe Lincoln or a Doc Holliday trying to function in 2006.

For the third book, they developed a cure for the original, who is an old man and wants nothing more than to be left alone and tend to his gardening. But the two clones made hundreds of enemies, enemies the original has never seen and doesn't recognize, and they all want him dead.

Years later, I thought of another story. I think everyone assumes that if you could actually meet your clone you'd get along just fine with him. But when I got to thinking about it, I had to admit that I never saw siblings that didn't fight, regardless of their underlying love for each other—and when you're a trio of the most dangerous killers in the galaxy . . .

A Miracle of Rare Design

I find the story of Sir Richard Burton—the Victorian explorer, not the Elizabethian ex-husband (sorry about that)— fascinating. Here was a man who threw himself into his travels, totally assimilating the exotic cultures he visited. He was the first Christian to participate in Islamic services in Mecca, he lived with the Maasai and the Kikuyu, he and John Henning Speke had a race to discover the source of the Nile, he translated *The Arabian Nights* and a number of erotic Arabian works, he learned the languages and customs of every group of people he visited, and wherever he went he always lived like a native.

And each time he came back to England, he was less and less comfortable as a Victorian gentleman. He'd seen too much of the world, experienced too much, ever to be happy in his "own" millieu again. He wound up as the governor of an almost-unpopulated Caribbean island, translating works than no one else wanted to read.

And since I found his story fascinating, I decided to science-fictionalize it and put my own twist on it. My "Burton" is a man who undergoes cosmetic surgery to *become* each of the races he is studying. Each time he is changed back he is less and less human in his outlook and interests, until at the end there is nothing human left at all, just a unique creature that appropriates the most fascinating features of each race he has temporarily joined.

A Hunger in the Soul

I think I saw or read one too many heroic epics about Henry Stanley, intrepid journalist, finding Dr. David Livingstone in the dark heart of

Africa, and I finally lost my patience with this drivel.

Stanley, Spencer Tracy's saint-like film portrayal notwithstanding, was not a nice man. He was a glory hound who wantonly wasted more black lives than just about any hunter or explorer in African history, and his two major missions were both unnecessary.

David Livingstone wasn't lost. He was an explorer and cartographer who knew exactly where he was, and since he was also a doctor and a tireless campaigner against slavery, he preferred to stay where could do the most good. (Stanley may have found him, but Stanley couldn't convince him to come back to civilization.)

Then, having found a man who wasn't lost, Stanley went on another mission that cost hundreds of more black lives, this time to rescue Emir Pasha, a man who didn't want to be rescued.

Since no movie or literary popularization had ever felt compelled to make even the slightest genuflection toward the truth, I decided to tell the true story, thinly disguised as science fiction, in *A Hunger in the Soul*.

The Outpost

I had always wanted to write a book about a bar that was frequented by interesting people. Strange, perhaps, since I don't drink, but whenever I read the tales of Sprague de Camp's and Fletcher Pratt's Gavagan's Bar, or Larry Niven's Draco Tavern, or Craig Rice's Joe the Angel's City Hall Bar, or Ross Spencer's Wallace's, whenever I saw Rick's Cafe Americaine in film or the Gold Monkey on television (back in the bygone days when I actually watched television), it made me want to write about the kind of bar *I'd* like to hang out in.

And one day I finally decided it was time. So I populated it with bigger-than-life characters like Catastrophe Baker and the Reverend Billy Karma and Silicone Carny and the Cyborg de Milo and Hurricane Smith (and his insectoid bride) and a bunch of others. Each of them would tell heroic stories about themselves or some other equally colorful characters, with obvious embellishments, and there'd be a lot of fun poked at science fiction, from adventures such as "The Ship Who Purred" to such observations (this one graciously loaned to me by the late George Alec Effinger) as "Any sufficiently advanced technology is indistinguishable from doubletalk."

But along with all that I needed a unifying theme that made it more than a bunch of humorous tall tales and parodies held together because of the location. So I divided it into three sections. Part 1 is Legend, in which these heroes swap their difficult-to-believe stories at The Outpost while a war is getting closer and closer; Part 2 is Fact, in which they have to go out and fight the enemy, and most of them do not begin to fare as well as the stories in Part 1 would lead you to anticipate; and Part 3 is History, in which the war is over and the survivors gather again at the Outpost to exchange the tales of their adventures in Part 2, embellishing and editing like crazy, and since they are the survivors, you realize that of course their accounts will eventually be accepted as history. The point of the book is not only that history is written by the winners, as we all know; but also that the best history is written by the best embellishers and storytellers, and that colorful history, whether true or false, always forces out uncolorful history, whether true or false.

This is not my most important science fiction novel. It is not my best. It was not my best-received. But it is far and away my favorite science fiction novel. Except for Lucifer Jones (who isn't really science fiction), I never had as much fun writing anything in my life.

Lara Croft: The Amulet of Power

I wrote this because I owed a book to del Rey from an old contract, and this is the one they wanted. To this day I have never played any of the Lara Croft games or been able to sit through a Lara Croft movie all the way to the end without falling asleep despite Angelina Jolie's 40-inch bustline and tight t-shirts.

Del Rey had the game-book franchise; someone else had the movie-book franchise. They told me that the current game ended with Lara, who was kind of a female Indiana Jones (only prettier) buried in the rubble beneath the temple at Edfu, and the next game, which would come out shortly after the novel, would begin ten months later with Lara showing up alone and disillusioned in Paris. My job was to get her from the temple to Paris in the most exciting way.

Well, I've been to Edfu, and indeed I've been all the hell over Africa (and Paris as well), so I made it a mystical quest book—she's after an amulet with supernatural powers, and, in true Robert Ludlum style, everyone wants her dead. The guys who want the amulet think she has it and keep trying to kill her; the guys who don't want the amulet to ever be found think she's on the track of it and keep trying to kill her; the creatures produced by the amulet don't want her to learn how to control them and keep trying to kill her. Even her oldest African friend tries to kill her.

When all is said and done, the book is actually a Resnick travelogue. If she sleeps in a hotel or lodge or tented camp and no one tries to kill her, Carol and I stayed in that hostelry and enjoyed it; if they put a snake in her bed or threw a knife through the window, I'm gently suggesting that you *not* stay there on your next safari or trip to Paris or the Seychelles. Ditto with the restaurants: if she enjoys her meal, this is a Resnick-approved restaurant; if someone tries to poison her or shoot her, I am suggesting that when you're in that vicinity you give that particular restaurant a pass.

Hardly classic work, but it was a lot of fun.

Lady With an Alien

Watson-Guptill is a high-class outfit that publishes coffee-table art books and the like. Recently they realized that their readership was aging, so they decided to start a line of young adult novels, each about the creation of a famous painting, to interest the next generation in art.

My agent, Eleanor Wood, heard about it, and sent them a copy of *The Dark Lady*, which had recently won France's biggest prize—but more to the point, it's narrated by an alien art critic who is dubbed "Leonardo" by his human co-workers because they can't pronounce his name.

A couple of weeks later we heard from Watson-Guptill: they wanted a YA science fiction book about any of Leonardo Da Vinci's paintings.

I had no idea what to write about, so I began looking through Leonardo's paintings on the internet, and suddenly a science fiction story fell right in my lap. Leonardo created a famous painting titled "Lady With an Ermine" . . . but Leo's ermine didn't look like any ermine I've ever seen. So I wrote *Lady With an Alien*, which was well-enough received that I promptly signed for three more YA art novels. Added bonus: I got a great cover artist for free.

Starship: Mutiny
Starship: Pirate

One of the things I've noticed is that our greatest military men, men like Douglas MacArthur (I'm talking of skills, not personalities) and George

Patton (ditto) and Tommy Franks (who actually seems like a very nice guy), do not make history by toeing the company line or thinking in standard patterns.

. So when it came time to write a military book (*Starship: Mutiny*) I decided to make my protagonist a thinker rather than a standard hero type. In fact, I think maybe four shots are fired in the whole damned book, only one by him, and that one at a target which to this day he cannot identify. I also think the press is the greatest enemy our military has had for the past half-century, and I saw no reason to assume it'll get any better three millennia up the road. My protagonist is bright enough to use the media to his advantage whenever he can, but in the end it bites him in the ass, which is only to be expected.

For the second book, I came up with a real conundrum when reading some of Kendell Foster Crossen's old mystery stories that he wrote under the pseudonym of "M. E. Chaber," to the effect that even half a century ago the average price a jewel thief could get from a fence for stolen merchandise was about five percent of market value. Which gave me an interesting problem for *Starship: Pirate*: once you become a pirate, how do you support a starship and crew on five percent of market value for your plunder? Clearly you don't—so what *do* you do? Once I answered that, the book practically wrote itself.

LosCon Guest of Honor Speech
(November, 1991)

Usually, to warm the audience up, I tell some funny stories about the city in which I find myself. Unfortunately, I've never heard anything remotely funny about Long Beach, so I took a drive around yesterday to see what it was like.

It lacks South Brooklyn's *joie de vivre*, San Francisco's vegetable cults, Cincinnati's bold new approach to the First Amendment, or the asylum from which New Orleans draws its gubernatorial candidates. In fact, Long Beach's main accomplishment seems to be the creation of an entirely new mathematical concept: the shortest distance between two points is a construction zone.

Well, so much for Long Beach. Now it's on to the speech.

You know, giving a speech isn't as easy as it used to be. First, there is the matter of what you can and cannot say. The speaker's restrictions vary from one city to the next.

In New York, for example, you must tell a minimum of three Donald Trump jokes.

In my own home town of Cincinnati, which recently became the first city ever to sue an art museum for obscenity, you can say anything you want—as long as no one's listening.

In Washington D.C., you don't have to tell jokes at all. You simply point them out. Usually they can be found eating in the Congressional cafeteria.

Here in the Los Angeles area, I am free to discuss anything I want, with one exception: I've been informed that the locals are very sensitive about the fact that the rest of the NFL keeps beating the Los Angeles Rams like a drum—so I won't mention that at all.

Anyway, since I didn't want to offend anyone, I decided to solicit some suggestions for the topic of this speech. I went on the GEnie computer network, where most of SFWA hangs out, listed the topics I felt most comfortable with, and asked each of the pros to vote for one.

The topics I listed were:

A. My work as Enduring Literature

B. Bruce Pelz as a Hollywood Sex Symbol

C. East African fertility rituals

D. The Intricacies of the Cincinnati Bengals' No-Huddle Offense

E. Coat Color Inheritance in Collies

F. The true story about the night the L.A. cops arrested David Gerrold for frolicking naked in Griffith Park

The results of the poll were a little disappointing:
Jerry Pournelle voted for the no-huddle offense.
38 writers voted for Harold Stassen.
And 57 didn't understand the question.
So I decided that what I really ought to tell you about is what I did yesterday morning. And what I did was pay a visit to the La Brea Tar Pits and the Natural History Museum, an experience that would surely cause any Creationist to rethink his beliefs. The resemblance between a slavering, flesh-rending Tyranosaurus Rex and a science fiction publisher is simply too obvious to be denied.

I think the cyberpunks probably came from the pterodons, which made an awful lot of noise and commotion flapping their wings, but really didn't get anywhere.

Most of the smaller parasitical animals evolved into critics and academics. Those that lived exclusively on blood doubtless became agents.

I think fandom can find its roots there as well; there is no doubt in my mind that the primeval ooze evolved over the eons into corflu . . . and certainly the ferocious battles between the allosaurus and the triceratops resemble nothing more than a Worldcon business meeting.

I couldn't find anything that might have evolved into editors, but then, everybody knows that editors are aliens. The lack of human compassion gives them away every time.

I see I still have some time to kill, and since you're honoring the work more than the writer, I think I'll get serious for a moment and address myself to it.

Being a Guest of Honor at a science fiction convention is nothing new to me. But there is something this *is* new. For years, during autograph sessions, I would sit there and sign book after book after book. But for the last four years, it seems that I am sitting there signing magazine after anthology after collection.

Which leads me to a confession.

I feel like a fool making it—but what the hell, it's not the first time I've felt like a fool, and I'm reasonably certain it won't be the last.

Science fiction is a field which has produced at least 30 demonstrably great short stories, and, at best, two or three near-great novels. And yet, as recently as 1986, I held firmly to the conviction that short fiction was somehow trivial, that if an idea or a character was worth anything at all, then it belonged in a novel.

So I wrote novels. Some pretty good ones, if I say so myself. One was a national bestseller. Others came close. A few were optioned to Hollywood. Most of them sold to half a dozen or more additional countries, and were translated into any number of exotic languages.

The late Terry Carr, whose greatest fame was as a book editor, the creator of the Ace Specials, was the first to take me aside and gently explain that if I ever wanted recognition within the field, I was going to have to write some short stories, since most of my peers were too damned busy writing their own stuff to be bothered reading novels by an author with whose work they were unfamiliar. I thanked him for his advice, and explained to him that this was all well and good in theory, but short stories were pieces of fluff. Novels had *substance*.

He looked at me as if I was crazy. (I wasn't. Wrong, yes, but not crazy. Although in this case, that's merely a quantitative difference.)

I kept writing novels.

Then my friend Barry Malzberg, author of *Galaxies* and *Herovit's World*, probably the two finest science fiction novels of the 1970s, spent the better part of a year trying to convince me that short stories were predestined to be trivial only if you set out to write trivial short stories.

I listened politely, nodded sagely, and kept writing novels.

Finally my wife, line editor, and uncredited collaborator, Carol, took up the gauntlet. Carol doesn't lose a lot of arguments.

So I gave in. Officially. Just enough to obey the absolute letter of the law. I wrote one short story a year from 1977 through 1986. Sold most of 'em. Even won a couple of awards. Got picked up for a best-of-the-year anthology.

Trivial.

The awards were minor. The pay was minor. Even the year's-best anthology was minor; it appeared once and never again.

Then a strange thing happened. Usually, when I finished a novel, I would loaf for a week or two and then get right to work on the next one. But in the summer of 1987, I finished *Ivory* in mid-June, and the next novel on my schedule was *Paradise*, a science-fictional allegory of Kenya's past and future history. And since I was going to Kenya in September, it seemed counter-productive to start writing the book prior to taking a very expensive trip that had been arranged for the express purpose of researching it.

So I was looking at ten weeks of unproductive dead time, and I decided that I might as well finally give short stories an honest shot.

So I sat down, and before I left for Kenya, I had written and sold nine of them. Not only that, but even I had to admit they weren't all trivial. One of them, "Kirinyaga," was nominated for a Nebula, won a Hugo, and did more for my reputation than any novel I'd ever written.

Something else strange happened, too.

I found—to my absolute amazement—that I *enjoyed* writing short stories.

So after I finished *Paradise*, I took two months off and wrote another ten. And sold them all. And included in that batch was another Hugo and Nebula nominee.

And while the pay wasn't quite up to what my novels brought in, I found that if you sell enough short stories to enough major markets, it does a lot more for your bank account than sitting around the house watching the Reds and Bengals blow one lead after another.

My next novel after *Paradise* was *Second Contact*, and this time I didn't even wait to finish it: I wrote and sold seven more stories *while* I was writing it—and two of *them* were nominated for Hugos (and one of them, "The Manamouki," won my second one). More recently, while I was writing the Oracle Trilogy for Ace over a period of about fourteen months, I wrote and sold another twenty-two.

Some of them, admittedly, were good-natured pieces of fluff. I like humor, science fiction is one of the few remaining markets for it, and I've included some of the better ones here.

But a number of them *weren't* trivial. Some of them have substance I once thought impossible for works of short fiction (or at least for *my* short fiction) and I take an enormous pride in them. The Kirinyaga stories, the Teddy Roosevelt stories, such personal pieces as "Winter Solstice," are as ambitious and meaningful as any novels I have written.

Back in 1986, I seriously wondered if I would have enough short stories to form a respectable collection by the turn of the century. Now here it is, 1991, and my biggest problem in preparing the collection I just sold to Tor is which 30 stories to eliminate. Life just gets curiouser and curiouser.

So what you have standing before you is an avowed novelist who spent most of his life shunning short stories, and who has won two Hugos for short fiction and received eight Hugo and Nebula nominations in the past 30 months—seven of them for short fiction.

Go figure.

I have one last subject to address. Some few months ago, Harlan Ellison wrote an article entitled "Xenogenesis," which appeared in *Asimov's* and *Midnite Graffiti* and on a batch of computer bulletin boards.

The gist of it was a catalog of all the wrongs that fans have done to writers, all the hideous behavior we have to put up with not only at conventions but even in the sanctity of our homes, and it listed not only Harlan's grievances but those of a number of other writers as well.

I don't doubt for a moment the honesty of the accounts in that article—but I do think it's time for a member of the loyal opposition to speak up.

I have been attending conventions since 1963 and writing science fiction professionally since 1967, and in all that time I have never been treated with anything other than courtesy and consideration by fandom.

That's why I keep coming back to conventions, that's why I agreed to appear here, and that's why I look forward to my next convention, wherever it may be.

They say that you can choose your friends but not your family.

They're wrong.

I just gave a speech to *my* family.

Bravo Bevo!

Everyone knows that Wilt the Stilt was the greatest scorer in basketball history, the only man ever to score 100 points in a game.

There have been some great shooters since then: Michael Jordan, Julius Erving, Elgin Baylor, Kobe Bryant, and others — but no one ever came close to Wilt Chamberlain, right?

Actually, wrong.

Most people today have never heard of the greatest scorer in history, though he was playing when I was a kid. He was a nice, clean-cut boy from Ohio. He eventually stood six feet nine inches tall, and, hard as it may be to believe, he was white.

His name was Clarence "Bevo" Francis, the press lovingly called him "Little Bevo" as their notion of a joke, because six foot nine was about as big as people got back then, and for a two-year period he *was* the sport of basketball.

He came alone at a good time. College basketball had just been stung by a huge betting/point-shaving scandal in 1951. He soon made everyone forget all about it.

Let me tell you about him. He went to obscure little Wellsville High School in Ohio. Averaged 32 points a game, very good indeed, but no indication of what was to come. He gave a tiny hint of it when he scored 57 points in one game when he was a junior.

His coach moved from tiny Wellsville high school to an equally small college, Ohio's Rio Grande, and in 1952 Bevo followed him. It turned out to be the best thing that ever happened to Rio Grande.

Let's move the clock back to the evening of January 9, 1953. Rio Grand is playing against Ashland (Kentucky) Junior College, and Bevo has been lighting up the scoreboard all night. There are ten minutes left in the game, and he's already burned Ashland for 61 points.

Then he got hot.

Bevo Francis poured in 55 more points in the final quarter, and wound up with 116 for the game. That's right: 116 points. (The previous NCAA record was 87 points — 29 points less.)

The NCAA, in its infinite wisdom, decided not to allow it because it came against a junior college team, so you won't find it in the official record book.

But you'll find Bevo there as the greatest scorer in history anyway — because on February 2, 1954, he burned Hillsdale, a legitimate 4-year college, for 113 points.

And you'll also find that Rio Grande's record during Bevo's freshman year was 39-0. That's right; they went undefeated.

I think it's fair to say that Bevo had a little something to do with that: he averaged 48.3 points a game as a freshman. He slowed down as a sophomore, averaging only 46.5. (By comparison, neither Jordan, nor Bryant, nor the new superstar on the block, LeBron James, ever averaged as much as 40 points a game in high school, in college, or in the NBA.)

Suddenly, thanks to Bevo, little Rio Grande was the hottest ticket in the nation. They adjusted their schedule and played 17 road games in a row, all in huge arenas against formidable competition. Didn't bother Bevo. He just kept scoring, and Rio Grande just kept winning. In 39 games against 4-year colleges, including some powers like Miami, North Carolina State, Cincinnati, Villanova, Providence and Nebraska, he scored 50 or more points 14 times.

Bevo averaged 48.9 points for his entire truncated college career. And unlike Wilt, he could shoot the ball from anywhere on the court, and he could make free throws (including a record 37 against Hillsdale.)

Bevo was drafted after his sophomore year by the Philadelphia Warriors (the same team that drafted Wilt a few years later; they knew a scorer when they saw one.) Problem was, back then the superstars of the NBA made about $10,000 a year, a tad less than Michael Jordan's $30 million per. Basketball just wasn't the glamour sport it has become... and Bevo decided he could make more money working in the local steel mills.

He should have taken the offer, because what happened next ended his college career anyway. Rio Grande suspended him for skipping classes and exams after the 1953-1954 season, and since his campus job was paying a somewhat-less-than-munificent 50 cents an hour, he quit and took the best offer he could get, which came not from the NBA but from the Boston Whirlwinds, a barnstorming team that played (and made sure they lost to) the Harlem Globetrotters every night in front of packed houses. The Warriors knew what he could do and tried to sign him, but he had no interest in playing in the NBA, and after a few seasons touring with the Whirlwinds, then the Ohio Stars, and finally the Hazeltown Hawks — not quite the Balls, Celtics and Lakers — he turned his back on basketball, returned home, and went to work in the local steel mills. He kept at it until he'd raised his family, and never seemed to miss the fame and adulation.

He's still in Highland, Ohio, still living in contented obscurity, and still in the record books — the all-but-unknown greatest scorer of all time.

Music(als) of the Spheres

Guy Lillian tells me that the theme of this issue will be music. I don't know enough about music to set myself up as an authority, but if there's one thing I do know, it's the musical theatre—and you'd be surprised at how many musical plays are, by definition, either fantasy or science fiction. (You'd be surprised at this instant; hopefully when you finish the article you won't be.)

The list of shows and thumbnail sketches doesn't purport to be all-inclusive; I mean, hell, there are a lot of flops that I never got to see, hear, or even know about. But I'd say, in all immodesty, that it's about as complete a list as you're likely to find until Laura Turtledove, my long-time musical video/audio/bootleg trading partner, sits down and adds to it.

There are certain shows I'm not going to include, because they're just a little too marginal to claim they are true-blue science fiction or fantasy. Examples would be *Stop the World—I Want to Get Off* and *Tommy.* And there's another class of show I chose not to list, and those are musicals that accept the divinity of Jesus Christ and the truth of the Holy Bible, shows like *Jesus Christ Superstar*, *Godspell*, and *Joseph and the Amazing Technicolor Dreamcoat;* I'm going to proceed on the assumption that if you are a Christian you don't consider these shows to be fantasy, and to suggest otherwise would be offensive to your beliefs, a line of argument I'll leave to the Islamic Jihadists.

Okay, all that said, here is the list of musicals that can, by any reasonable definition, be considered fantasy or science fiction. I think you'll find some interesting surprises on it.

Aladdin. Hard to complain about a Cole Porter musical, especially with a libretto by S. J. Perleman. Originally produced for television, with a cast including Basil Rathbone, Cyril Ritchard, Anna Maria Alberghetti, and (o well) Sal Mineo, it was later mounted on the British stage.

Amour. Michel Legrand has scored over 100 films, and won some Oscars. He's done a lot less musicals, and for his first in decades he chose *Amour*, a brilliant and charming fantasy based on the French fable about a man who walks through walls. It ran for years in Paris, and to New York's everlasting shame, it ran for only three weeks back in 2002, despite a cast that included Tony-nominated performances from Malcolm Gets and Melissa Errico.

The Apple Tree, the first show written by Jerry Bock and Sheldon Harnick after their wildly-successful *Fiddler on the Roof*, this is actually three one-act musicals; the first ("The Apple Tree," from Mark Twain) and third ("Passionella" from Jules Feiffer) are fantasies. It made a star out of Barbara Harris in 1967, and reaffirmed star status for Kristen Chenoweth in a 2006 revival.

Bat Boy, a camp "sci-fi" piece of nonsense with songs by Laurence O'Keefe, is more bad parody than bad science fiction, but has just enough of the latter to qualify. And be instantly forgotten.

Beauty and the Beast. Unlike *The Lion King*, with its wildly creative costumes and sets, if you saw the Disney animated version of *Beauty and the Beast*, there's no reason to spend your money on the Broadway version. The Howard Ashman/Alan Menken score is fine, the actors were excellent, the story is classic—but the score was fine (and just about identical) in the movie, no one on stage was going to match the voice-overs of Angela Lansbury and Jerry Orbach, and the story was the same.

Big, the musical version of the less-than-brilliant film about a 12-year-old boy who suddenly finds himself in an adult's body, has a score by Richard Maltby and David Shire, every bit as unmemorable as the plot, and is yet another of those endless musicalizations of mediocre movies that makes you wonder why anyone bothered in the first place.

Brigadoon. Lerner & Loewe's first hit, it's a pleasant fantasy about a Scotch town than comes into existence once every hundred years. The movie was turned into a Gene Kelly vehicle, but the play, though not among the top rank, still holds up.

The Bone Room. Tom Jones & Harvey Schmidt's artiest play, this is about a *ménage a trois* at the Natural History Museum between a young girl, an old man, and Death. It was shown to invited audiences only, back in 1977.

Camelot. Anything that includes Excalibur and Modred has to qualify as a fantasy, including this Lerner & Loewe hit. Every scene was nice—but there were so *many* of them. I felt like I'd read all 250,000 words of the book when the play finally let out.

Carousel. Rodgers & Hammerstein's second major hit (after *Oklahoma!*), part of it takes place in Heaven, and Billy Bigelow comes back to Earth after his death to advise and guide is daughter, so it's clearly a fantasy.

Carrie. This is generally considered the single worst big-budget musical ever produced. Based on Stephen King's bestselling novel, it is so notorious that a book cataloguing the Broadway Musical Flop from the 1940s to the present is titled *Not Since Carrie*, because whenever a new turkey opens, the reviews tend to begin with "Not since *Carrie* (has there been such an abomination)". The wild part is two of Broadway's great divas agreed to play Carrie's mother. Barbara Cook created the part, realized just what she'd stepped in, quit, and they then hired Betty Buckley, who got to sing an aria and two reprises to snickering audiences while being drenched with blood from a severed carotid artery.

Cats. Every character is a cat, and one of them ascends to Heaven while onstage, so it's clearly a fantasy. Brilliant dancing, totally without any meaning. (What do I mean? Every dance in *West Side Story* furthers the plot. Every dance in *Cats* serves no purpose except to show you that the performers can dance.) Pedestrian score, mediocre lyrics.

Celebration, by the brilliant team of Tom Jones & Harvey Schmidt, is an allegory about the Winter Equinox, and about youth and age. It should have been performed on a small off-Broadway stage like the same team's *The Fantasticks*, rather than in a huge Broadway theater where it lost all its intimacy and charm. The play flopped—I blame the theater, not the cast or material—but all small-theater revivals have been successful.

Charly and Algernon. It's an easy argument to make that "Flowers for Algernon" is, if not the single greatest novella ever to grace the field of science fiction, surely one of the half-dozen best. But absolutely nothing about it lends itself to becoming a musical, even with that old Phantom of the Opera, Michael Crawford, playing Charly Gordon. It opened in London, flopped, got rewritten/revamped, came to the States, substituted P. J. Benjamin for Crawford, and flopped again.

Cinderella. Rodgers & Hammerstein created this for Julie Andrews as a television original, but because they were savvy marketers it didn't end there, and the play (without Andrews) eventually hit the New York and London stage, complete with fairy godmother.

City of Angels. A brilliant conceit, with libretto by Larry Gelbart and featuring Cy Coleman's finest score. This is the story of a mystery writer who is selling out to Hollywood, and it is also the story he's busily emasculating, told on one half of the stage in black and white, while his own story is told, in color, on the other half. It qualifies as fantasy, because at one point the private eye steps out of his own story to confront the author and castigate him for selling out.

A Connecticut Yankee is a 1927 play with a score by Rodgers & Hart, based on a 19th Century Mark Twain tale about a modern man who winds up in King Arthur's court, and proves that when you're good, it doesn't matter how old you are.

Damn Yankees. Pleasant show, pleasant score. History has come full cycle. This play, about a ballplayer on the Washington Senators making a deal with the devil, only works when you can hate the New York Yankees, so no one performed it in the late 1960s and the early 1970s. Then George Steinbrenner bought the Yankees and pours hundreds of millions into them, and it's been popular ever since.

Dandelion Wine. At least most of the flops listed here made it to New York, or at least into production *somewhere*. Not Ray Bradbury's *Dandelion Wine*, surely one of the most beautiful books to appear in the 20th Century. I have the studio demo tape, and there's a reason: not only are the songs completely unmemorable, but no boy whose voice is still a falsetto can carry a musical play for two hours.

Dracula—The Musical. About what you'd expect. Big budget, fancy costumes, unexceptional music, totally uninspired lyrics. Big yawn.

Evening Primrose. Not really a Broadway play at all, but a written-for-TV musical that was performed only once, back in 1967. By the brilliant team of Stephen Sondheim and James Goldman, it's based on John Collier's horror fantasy about people passing themselves off as manikins in a department store, then moving about at night. Fine songs, but totally unnecessary to the story. I include it because, despite its history, there are two different cast recordings.

The Fantasticks. A charming fantasy by Tom Jones & Harvey Schmidt, it plays games with time and with reality, it pulls actors it needs out of a stage trunk, it has a wall that looks and feels exactly like a yardstick—any way you analyze it, it's a fantasy. And since it's the longest-running play in the history of the musical theatre—42 years!—I'll be damned if I'm going to be the one to criticize it. (Besides, I love it.)

Finian's Rainbow. Burton Lane has some classics in this score, such as "Old Devil Moon," but the play *and* the score are pretty antiquated. Still, there's a leprechaun's role that actors from David Wayne to Fred Astaire to Malcolm Gets kill for, so I guess it'll keep getting revived, antique or not. And, thanks to the leprechaun and his magic, it's a fantasy.

Frankenstein—The Musical. This one had some promise, primarily because it followed the book and not the movie, and hence presented the monster as an object of sympathy—but the score and libretto just weren't good enough.

The Frogs. Stephen Sondheim's musical based on the play by Aristophanes, this one's lasting fame comes, alas, not from its quality (it hasn't got much), but because it was first performed in the swimming pool at Yale, with Meryl Streep and a couple of other future superstars in the chorus. It has singing, dancing frogs, it borrows characters from all over history, and is unquestionably a fantasy. Nathan Lane rewrote the libretto and starred in a Broadway revival; it didn't fare any better than the original.

Goblin Market was an avant-garde off-Broadway two-woman show, as strange as a musical version of *Waiting For Godot* would have been. It's based on a fairy tale in verse, more about sex and fear than fantasy, and it sank pretty quickly. I don't believe it's ever been revived, and I'm not surprised.

The Golden Apple, a lost classic (i.e., critics love it, audiences don't), this musical is based on *The Illiad* and *The Odyssey*, as is another further down the list. This one's by far the superior show, but it's pretty antiquated.

Greenwillow. The lovely fantasy novel by B. J. Chute was Frank Loesser's only flop, but it was the book that was weak, not the score. Tony Perkins starred as Gideon Briggs, the young man cursed with wanderlust, and while his voice wasn't much, he was well-trained and managed to hit all the right notes in a score that was written for a much better singer.

Grover's Corners. Tom Jones & Harvey Schmidt's musical adaptation of Thornton Wilder's *Our Town.* Probably their most brilliant work—and since everyone in Act 3 is dead, it certainly qualifies as fantasy.

High Spirits, a musical version of Noel Coward's comedy *Blithe Spirit,* with songs by Hugh Martin and Timothy Gray, was everything it was supposed to be: funny, witty, irreverent, sophisticated…and one thing it wasn't supposed to be: forgettable.

Into the Woods. Broadway's reigning genius, Stephen Sondheim, turns a bunch of fairy tales into a dark, grim, adult entertainment. Far from his best score, but so far above average as to put you in awe of what he can do when he's not at his sharpest.

It's A Bird, It's A Plane, It's Superman! Pay no attention to the horrible, emasculated version of this that played on late-night TV a couple of decades ago. The Broadway show was a delight, with a wonderful Strousse and Adams score, a pair of hilarious star turns by Jack Cassidy and Michael O'Sullivan, a proper Superman in Bob Holliday, and sets that looked like they were comic book panels.

Jekyll and Hyde—The Musical. Broadway just seems to love mounting big-budget turkeys based on great horror novels. This one was better than *Frankenstein* and *Dracula,* actually ran for over a year, was well-acted and well-sung, had gorgeous sets and costumes—but it had the usual problem: mediocre, unmemorable music and lyrics.

Kiss of the Spider Woman. Based on the straight play (and movie) of the same name, starring Chita Rivera, this qualifies as a fantasy simply because the prisoner spends half the play fantasizing about Rivera's singing and dancing Spider Woman.

The Lion King. Silly story, good but not outstanding music—but it also has the most imaginative costumes and sets ever seen on Broadway, and some wildly creative choreography.

Li'l Abner, the hit musical based on Al Capp's classic comic strip, isn't on this list because it's a comic strip. (*Annie*, you'll note, isn't here.) Nope, it's because at one point the women of Dogpatch pay some scientists to turn their men into gorgeous beach bums . . . but then the men just lay there, admiring their muscles, and the women have to come up with the money to put 'em back the way they wuz (to quote one of the songs).

Little Shop of Horrors may be the only science fiction (as opposed to fantasy) musical that was a bonafide hit. (Of course, playing in a very small off-Broadway house with a low overhead didn't hurt.) There's no getting away from its charm, most of which was supplied by the magnificent Ellen Greene, who reprised her role in the watered-down budgeted-up movie. Very witty score by Howard Ashman and Alan Menken.

Lord of the Rings. I haven't seen or heard it—it's still on its tryout tour somewhere up in Canada as I write these words—but it's clearly a fantasy, and given the popularity of the books and films, I'd have to say it's a cinch to hit Broadway sooner or later no matter how inept it is. Since we're going to be stuck with it regardless, let's hope it's a good one.

Mary Poppins. Another Disney movie turned into a Broadway musical—and as with most of them, if you saw the film, you already know the story and songs, and no one's going to perform them better than Julie Andrews and Dick Van Dyke, so why was this trip necessary?

Merlin was an interesting conceit. Veteran film scorer Elmer Bernstein moved to Broadway to create a musical about Merlin the magician. It starred (read: wasted) Chita Rivera and Nathan Lane, and existed only to let magician Doug Henning, who could neither act, sing nor dance, dazzle the audience with his tricks as Merlin. A two-hour magic show would have had a much longer run and more appreciative audience.

Metropolis. This travesty was based on the creaky old Fritz Lang silent movie, and starred Brian Blessed, who should have known better. We saw it during previews in London, and thought it surprising that 5th row orchestra seats were still available. It became a lot less surprising ten minutes into the play, when, to show the working conditions for the oppressed underground, the stage was flooded with smoke—which immediately turned left and spread out over the first dozen rows of the audience, choking and blinding us. And it did the same thing *four* times during the performance. So we had to rely on our ears, but the audience (those not yet overcome by smoke) was so busy laughing and snickering at all the tragic scenes that we never did find out exactly what anyone was saying. Probably just as well.

The Odyssey was one of Mitch Leigh's nine consecutive musical flops after he wrote *Man of La Mancha*. Based on *The Iliad* and *The Odyssey*, it starred Yul Brynner and Joan Diener, and it was *awful*. They re-wrote songs, they rewrote the libretto, they re-cast everything but the two leads—and it was *still* awful. And then one of the producers got a brilliant idea: okay, the play stinks, it'll never go in New York—but most of the people out there in Hicksville have never see Yul Brynner, so why don't we lengthen the pre-Broadway tour from six weeks to eighteen months? And they did, and they played to packed houses (and bad reviews) everywhere, and by the time they opened in New York under a brand-new name, *Home Sweet Homer*, they'd made their expenses. The play ran for a single performance—most Manhattan critics argued that it should have folded by the middle of Scene 3—and was never heard from again. But because there were Greek gods, at least when I saw it during its pre-Broadway run in Chicago—it's a fantasy.

Olympus on my Mind is a musical based on *Amphitryon*, or, to put it in more palatable terms (and I wish the librettist had), it's kind of a song-and-dance version of Thorne Smith's *The Night Life of the Gods*, but with maybe a tenth of the wit. Still, any play that's got Jupiter coming down from the mountain cruising for chicks has to qualify as a legitimate fantasy.

One Touch of Venus is the great Kurt Weill's one musical fantasy, with lyrics by Ogden Nash, about what happens when the statue of Venus comes to life. It was made into a rather dull film with Ava Gardner, but the play is actually quite a funny low comedy.

Out of this World, one of Cole Porter's few flops. This, like *Olympus on my Mind*, is based on *Amphitryon*. Didn't fare any better, though of course it has a far superior score.

Peter Pan. Everyone remembers Mary Martin "flying" on very visible strings in one of the many TV versions of this hit Broadway musical, but the play had a lot more to it than her Pan and Cyril Ritchard's

Hook. For one thing, it had fine lyrics by Julie Styne, Betty Comden and Adolf Greene, and excellent direction/choreography by Jerome Robbins. (Almost forgotten now is that Mary Martin didn't originate the part; the first, and longest-running, Peter Pan was Maude Adams.) (And another side note: the name "Wendy" didn't exist until James Barrie created it for the original play.)

Portrait of Jennie. This musical adaptation of Robert Nathan's fantasy novel, maybe the first and surely the most moving time-dilation romance, won the Richard Rodgers Award for best off-Broadway musical about a quarter of a century ago. The brilliant score consists of music by Howard Marren and lyrics by Enid Futterman.

Return to the Forbidden Planet. A totally unmemorable British musical (I don't believe it ever made it to America), it's got a derivative score and a silly script and, alas (or given its quality, maybe not so alas) has nothing to do with the classic movie, *Forbidden Planet.*

The Rocky Horror Show. It's a pretty silly play, with totally forgettable music, but there are enough references to science fiction, and enough out-and-out weirdness, that it qualifies. Too bad; I wish it didn't.

Seussical. Nice enough score by Stephen Flaherty and Lynn Ahrens, but that was close to the only nice thing about this fantasy musical based on the poems and stories of Dr. Seuss. Even Rosie O'Donnell's joining the cast couldn't save it; in fact, a considerable body of opinion feels that her performance hastened its death.

Shinbone Alley. Originally just a record featuring Carol Channing and Eddie Bracken, they finally turned it until a charming full-fledged musical play. It's based on Don Marquis' "archy and mehitibel" story-poems, and every character in it is a cat or a cockroach.

Spamalot, the Eric Idle-scripted musical based on *Monty Python and the Holy Grail.* The music is totally unmemorable, and the play is totally uncreative—by which I mean, the audience continually laughed *before* the punch lines. It was written for Python-worshippers, and while there were enough of them to put the show into profit, I don't think it's going to be revived very often, nor should it be.

Starlight Express, another of Andrew Lloyd Webber's mystifying hits (in England; he's only had three major hits here), every cast member in this one is a train engine or train car, and each of them is on roller skates for the entire show. A major race between Steam and Diesel takes place through the entire theater, with the performers skating on ramps just a few feet above the audience's heads. There was a certain charm to parts of it, but the overall impression you come away with is Silly.

Starmites. This one's almost forgotten today, though it got six Tony nominations just a few years ago. With a score by Barry Keating, it's a musical about a teenaged girl who builds a fantasy world populated by her favorite comic book characters.

Tarzan. It probably seemed a good idea. Disney created musical plays that were wildly creative, as well as a shade above mediocre in quality, with *Beauty and the Beast* and *The Lion King*, and came away with two long-running megahits. So why not do the same with *Tarzan*? Well, singing dancing apes, and a star fresh off *American Idol*, were two pretty good reasons why not.

Two by Two, written especially for Danny Kaye's return to Broadway, was the musical version of Noah (hence the title). Unfortunately, despite a score by Richard Rodgers, it didn't have a single memorable song or scene in it, and Kaye so offended the rest of the cast that no one worked very hard to keep the crippled ark afloat.

Urinetown. The play's an allegory, but since it's about a future in which an Evil Corporation controls every restroom in town, it qualifies as science fiction. And very witty science fiction, too, with a score by Mark Hollman and Greg Kotis that's almost *too* clever.

Via Galactia. Unquestionably the worst science fiction musical ever to make it to Broadway (*Carrie* was a fantasy), this hodgepodge was so confused and confusing that the producers attempted a never-before-tried innovation: they handed out a synopsis along with the Playbill, so the audience would have some slight notion of what was going on. It didn't help.

Weird Romance should be of special interest to science fiction fans, and I'll bet 99% of them have never heard of it. The score is by Alan Menken, and it consists of two one-act musical plays. One was adapted of a *Twilight Zone* episode; the other is a musical version of James Tiptree Jr.'s "The Girl Who Was Plugged In."

Wicked. A delightful, charming musical based on the bestseller about Oz's Good Witch and Bad Witch when they were friends back in school. Idena Menzel won the Tony as the Bad Witch, but it was Kristin Chenoweth as Glinda, the Good Witch, who charmed the sellout crowds and came away a superstar.

The Wiz. A hit all-black musical based on *The Wizard of Oz*, with songs by Charlie Smalls. Geoffrey Holder's direction, choreography and costumes (he's a man of many talents) helped audiences forget that they knew the story inside-out and that the songs in the MGM movie were better.

Zombie Prom. The title, alas, says it all. Dana P. Rowe and John Dempsey created a score that was too good for the plot, which is about a high school zombie who wants to attend the prom and reclaim the love of his popular girlfriend. Honest. So don't ever come up to me and tell me an idea is too dumb to make into an expensive musical flop.

One month later:

Well, like I said, the *real* expert is Laura Turtledove, Harry's spouse and the mother of all those beautiful and talented girls. I showed her the article this afternoon and asked if I'd missed anything. When you want to know, you go to The Source. Here's her answer:

All Shook Up. I hate jukebox musicals. This was the Elvis one from 2004, but it featured a magical jukebox. How else do you cram 20 Elvis songs into a show without actually having Elvis in it?

Assassins. Sondheim and Weidman's revue about successful and unsuccessful Presidential killers. Any show that has assassins from different centuries hanging out in a bar together deserves to be on this list, though my theatre major daughter vehemently disagrees with me.

Babes in Toyland. From '03. No, *1*903, as in Victor Herbert. The evil uncle of two tots wants to get rid of them, but they wind up in Toyland, where the toys and Mother Goose characters help them thwart the uncle. Some of these songs still get hauled out at Christmas.

By Jupiter. Rodgers and Hart's last original show, 1943, starring Ray Bolger. Queen Hippolyta and her gals hold the upper hand over their wimpy guys because the queen has a magic girdle that gives her strength. The Greeks, led by Theseus and Hercules, invade to help the males get the girdle, and they find their talents in the bedroom work better than those on the battlefield. It might have run longer, but Bolger left to entertain the troops.

Cabin in the Sky. Vernon Duke and John Latouche's 1940 fable of the battle between the forces of the Lord and those of the Devil for the soul of Little Joe Jackson (Todd Duncan). Ethel Waters' only book musical, this one produced the hit, "Taking a Chance on Love." Choreography by George Balanchine.

Chitty Chitty Bang Bang. 2002 British hit based on the Sherman brothers' movie (itself based on the Ian Fleming kids' book) about an inventor, his kids, and their flying car. Um, don't ask me for details about the plot since I last saw the movie in 1968. But the car flies!

A Christmas Carol/Scrooge. There are at least five versions of Dickens' tale, the significant ones being Leslie Bricusse's *Scrooge*, for which he did the music, book and lyrics, and was based on his film version. It ran in Britain in 1992 and 1996, then toured the US in 2003-2004 in versions with Davis Gaines and Richard Chamberlain in the leads. Mike Ockrent directed and Susan Stroman did the choreography for the Lynn Ahrens/Alen Menkin production that ran in NY every holiday season from 1994 through 2003. The Scrooges over the years included Walter Chalres, Terence Mann, Tony Randall, Hal Linden, Roddy McDowall, Roger Daltrey (!), Frank Langella, Tim Curry, Jim Dale and F. Murray Abraham. These shows packed the 5,100-seat theatre at Madison Square Garden.

Dance of the Vampires. The 2003 multi-million dollar flop based on Roman Polanski's film, *The Fearless Vampire Killers*. It started out a German production, and after heaps of revisions, lurched onto Broadway with Michael Crawford as Count von Krolock.

The Day Before Spring. Maybe this early Lerner and Loewe work (1945) is only a marginal fantasy, but it does feature the heroine getting advice from talking statues of Freud, Plato and Voltaire, as well as lots of speculation (through ballet) about alternate history. At a college reunion, a couple meet up with Alex, the guy the wife was going to elope with ten years ago, but his car broke down. Alex then went on to write a novel about what would have happened had it NOT broken down. At the reunion, the events of ten years ago begin to unfold again.

Doctor Dolittle. Leslie Bricusse's movie score about the doctor who could talk to the animals got revised for the stage in 1998. The Jim Henson workshop did the animals, and Julie Andrews was the recorded voice of Polynesia the Parrot.

Dorian/Dorian/Dorian Gray. There have been at least three attempts at doing Wilde's story of the fellow with the magic portrait. Doesn't seem to work.

DuBarry Was a Lady. 1939 Cole Porter hit show starring Bert Lahr as a washroom attendant who takes knock-out drops by accident and dreams he's Louis XV. Given that much of the show is a dream sequence, I think this should count as a fantasy. With Ethel Merman as Madame DuBarry and Betty Grable to flash those legs.

Dude. A weird allegorical rock musical (1972) from the creators of *Hair.* Dude (aka Everyman) wanders the universe in search of understanding, and good and evil battle over his soul. They performed this disaster in the reconstructed Broadway Theatre . . . with seat sections renamed "foot hills," 'trees" and "valleys."

A Fine and Private Place. Based on the Peter Beagle novel about the old man who lives in the cemetery and talks to the ghosts of the recently deceased. The songs are faithful to the story, but the music is unexciting and the characters don't generate the warmth they had in the book (though I know a guy who saw this show live and swears by its greatness). This ran at the Goodspeed back in 1989 and they reassembled the cast 15 years later to record the CD (music by Richard Isen, lyrics by Erik Haagensen). Gabriel Barre, a fine talent who has since turned to directing, was the Raven.

Flahooley. Yip Harburg/Sammy Fain fantasy satirizing American industry and greed. Debut of Barbara Cook, 1951. It's got a girl who can hear puppets talk, Arabs trying to get their magic lamp fixed (because they've run out of oil in Arabia; told you it was a fantasy), a genie that makes wishes come true, and many satiric shots at capitalism, which helped kill the show when it opened during the Korean War. It's been revised (cutting political/social commentary) as *Jollyanna.*

Follies. I wouldn't include *Grey Gardens* on this list, even though ghosts show up in the second act, but the ghosts of Sondheim's *Follies* are an integral part of the plot. Set in an aging theatre during a reunion of former showgirls, *Follies* focuses on two couples (Ben and Phyllis, Buddy and Sally). Ghosts of their past selves play alongside the contemporary characters, and everybody has a big breakdown near the end, performed as Follies numbers reflecting their mental states. Yes, *Follies* has a flawed libretto. That hasn't stopped me from seeing it every time I get the chance. One of the greatest scores ever written.

Forever Plaid. This was a smash hit off-Broadway in 1990. The Plaids were going to perform at a concert in 1964, but their car got hit by a bus of girls going to see the Beatles on the Ed Sullivan show. They are granted their last wish, to come back to earth to perform the concert they were about to give on the night they all died. Lots of tunes from the late 50s and early 60s.

Great to be Alive! A flop (52 performances) from 1950 about ghosts in a mansion (who can only be seen by virgins . . . and the audience, er, regardless of sexual status) who try to prevent a rich lady (Vivienne Segal) from buying the place from the descendant of the original owners. Book and lyrics by Walter Bullock, music by Abraham Ellstein and Robert Russell Bennett, who became better known for his great orchestrations.

Have I Got a Girl for You! A parody of the Frankenstein movies from 1985 (so they were probably stealing from Mel Brooks, whose *Young Frankenstein*, is about to open as a musical in November 2007— and not the other way around). It lasted a couple of weeks off-Broadway.

Happiest Girl in the World. Another musical set in ancient Greece, complete with gods. This one has a funny pedigree: it's based on Aristophanes' *Lysistrata* (where the women of Athens try to stop the war by refusing to have sex with their spouses), with lyrics by Yip Harburg and music by 19th c. French composer Offenbach.

Happy as Larry. Burgess Meredith directed and starred in this turkey (3 performances) from 1950 about an Irish tailor telling his pals about his grandpa, who had a good wife and a bad wife. Using witchcraft and "Three Old Ladies from Hades" (the Fates), they all go back in time to see the wives for themselves and help solve Grandpa's murder. What can you say about a show that lists among its songs, "The Flatulent Ballad?"

Here's Love. Meredith Willson wrote *The Music Man*, one of the classics. He also wrote *The Unsinkable Molly Brown*, a decent enough show. Then there was *Here's Love*, based on the movie, *Miracle on 34th Street*, which lasted for nearly a year, but just wasn't much of anything.. Maybe it was too hard to get excited over the mystery of whether the old man really was Santa at any other time than in December.

It's a Wonderful Life: The Musical/A Wonderful Life. As far as I can tell, there have been three efforts at turning the classic movie into a musical. Two never got beyond regional dinner theatre, but Joe Raposo and Sheldon Harnick's 1991 version was also done as a 2004 benefit for the Actor's Fund.

Just So. Cameron Mackintosh produced this 1998 take on the Kipling stories both in the UK and at the Goodspeed Theatre. Music by George Stiles, lyrics by Anthony Drewe, and it starred Gabriel Barre. But nothing ever came of it.

Ka-Boom! Okay, I know nothing about this show except what I ran across in one of my fat musicals books. The plot concerns the survivors of a nuclear attack . . . who decide to put on a show called "Creation, Part II." Music by Joe Ercole, lryics and book by Bruce Kluger. Somehow, it ran off-Broadway for 71 performances in 1981.

The Little Prince. Lerner and Loewe's last original score was for the decidedly peculiar movie version, but there have been three tries for the stage. John Houseman produced a version in 1993 starring Daisy Egan (from *The Secret Garden*) that ran a few months at the 28th Street Theatre. A. Joseph Tander's version lasted a week of previews at the Alvin in 1982. John Barry did the music, Don Black the lyrics, and Hugh Wheeler, the book; and Michael York as the Aviator. The early closure led to a court case in which the theatre owners (the Nederlanders) had to pay Tander a cool million.

Marie Christine. I've never seen this show, but the score is chilling (Michael John LaChiusa, with kickass orchestrations by Jonathan Tunick). I'm guessing it didn't succeed because the subject matter was simply too intense to bear watching. It retells the story of Medea, updated to late 19th century New Orleans. Marie Christine (the astounding

Audra McDonald), from well-to-do Creole family, falls for a white sea captain, Dante. She ultimately kills her brother to be with him and bears him two sons. When he begins to make a name for himself (partly thanks to her *voudon* magic in taking out his rivals), he dumps her for a white woman. She kills the woman through a cursed gift and then kills her own boys so Dante cannot have them. Buy the album and shiver.

Narnia. The NY State Theatre Institute tried adapting C.S. Lewis' *The Lion, The Witch & The Wardrobe.* It lasted two weeks.

Nightingale. Based on the Andersen fairy tale. This ran in London in 1983, with music an lyrics by Charles Strouse. It starred Sarah Brightman, who wasn't yet Mrs. A. Lloyd Webber. Or ex-Mrs. Lloyd Webber.

Once on This Island. Graciele Daniele (who also directed *Marie Christine*) had the honors of putting on this early Ahrens/Flaherty show based on a Caribbean fable of a peasant girl who is rescued from a storm by the gods. She then rescues the injured son of the landowner and makes a deal with the gods, giving up her life for his, since she thinks the power of love will help her overcome death. The rich guy lives, but spurns her, whereupon the gods turn her into a tree, which will live forever. It's charming, told in the format of a mother calming her own daughter during a storm through storytelling.

The Phantom Tollbooth. Arnold Black and Sheldon Harnick tried adapting Juster's kids' fantasy about Milo, who drives his car into the Land of Wisdom to save the two princesses, Rhyme and Reason. But Black died, so Harnick tried doing the music on his own, and the production never got beyond Cape Cod.

Raggedy Ann. Joe Raposo, who wrote so many great numbers for *Sesame Street,* wrote the score for a *Raggedy Ann* animated movie, which then got used in this piece that lasted five performances in 1986. Marcella (the little girl) is sick with fever and having strange dreams about her dolls. Raggedy Ann gives her heart to Marcella to save her life, whereupon Marcella wakes up and her doll is missing its heart. Apparently, this show went to the Soviet Union before the Broadway run (now *that's* playing out of town!) and the Russians loved it. Go figure.

Rainbow Jones. A one-night wonder from 1974, featuring a girl that can't connect in life, so she brings her magic book of Aesop's Fables to

Central Park, where her only pals, the critters in the tales, pop out and keep her company. Until she meets a jogger who helps her straighten out her head. Could I make this up?

Say Hello to Harvey. This version of *Harvey* (the invisible giant rabbit, remember?) ran in Toronto in 1981, but Washington and Broadway openings were aborted.

Shangri-La. As in James Hilton's *Lost Horizon.* Luckily for Hilton, he died two years before this clunker made it to Broadway in 1956. Yes, high in the Himalayas (constructed of Lucite), there's a place where no one ever ages. But without Ronald Colman, who cared? The talent for this was actually pretty damn good: Music by Harry Warren, lyrics and book by Lawrence and Lee, directed by Albert Marre, and starring Dennis King, Jack Cassidy, Harold Lang and Alice Ghostley. At the opening night party, Cassidy introduced Bock to Harnick, which was more important to showtune history than singing Lamas.

Steel Pier. An unsuccessful Kander and Ebb show from 1997, starring Karen Ziemba, Daniel McDonald, Gregory Harrison, and Debra Monk (with Kristin Chenoweth in a hysterical bit part, trilling for all she's worth). Ziemba plays Rita, a dancer who is secretly married to nasty, cruel Mick (Harrison), who runs dance marathons (it's set in 1933). Bill (McDonald) is a barnstorming pilot . . . who actually died three weeks ago, but is claiming the extra days since he got cheated out of his dance with Rita when his flight schedule got changed. She learns he's really a ghost at the end, but he gives her the courage to leave the abusive Mick at last. Susan Stroman's choreography was a tribute to all the dances of the 30s. For some reason, audiences didn't go for it. Me, I liked it, even if the hero was a dead guy.

Time and Again. Based on the Jack Finney novel about the man who goes back to the 1880s. produced by the Manhattan Theatre Club in 2001, with a score by Walter Edgar Kennon, it starred Laura Benanti, Lewis Cleale, and Christopher Innvar, which is a good cast. It had been in development for eight years and lasted three weeks at the City Center Stage

Three Wishes for Jamie. More Irish magic, but not enough (even with lead John Raitt at the top of his talents) to have a long run. In 1896, Una the Fairy grants Jamie three wishes: travel, the wife of his dreams, and a fine broth of a lad who will speak Gaelic. Naturally, there are complications on the way to getting the wishes to come true, including getting out of a pre-arranged marriage, ending up in America, and, since his wife is barren, adopting a mute kid, who miraculously says his first words in Bulgarian. I mean, Gaelic. Everybody said it was a rip-off of *Brigadoon* and *Finian's Rainbow,* which it was, though Raitt always felt it was one of his own favorites.

The Wind in the Willows. Based on Kenneth Grahame's classic kids' story of Toad, Ratty, Mole, and Badger. There have been several attempts to do a musical of *Wind,* mostly in Britain, but this one got briefly to NYC in 1985 and vanished under a heap of wretched reviews. The late David Carroll was Ratty, Vicki Lewis was Mole, and Nathan Lane chewed the scenery as Toad. Poop poop!

The Witches of Eastwick. Michael Crawford was supposed to do this one back in 2000, but Ian MacShane ended up stuck with it. Cameron Mackintosh sank heaps of pounds and endless revisions into this wreck. Maybe a magic spell might have helped. . . .

The Wizard of Oz. Aside from *Wicked* and *The Wiz,* the Baum novel itself was heavily revised into an early Broadway success in 1903: a puppet version (Bil Baird Marionettes) in the 1960s: and the classic Harburg/Arlen movie score was adapted for the stage in the late 1990s, with Mickey Rooney mugging as the Wizard and Eartha Kitt (later Jo Ann Worley) as the Witch.

The Woman in White. I don't know if this should be on this list or not, because I'm haven't seen/heard/read it and don't know if the woman really is a ghost. This was Andrew Lloyd Webber's latest catastrophe (2006 on Broadway), based on the Wilkie Collins novel. No doubt Sir Andrew has been looking for more Victorian horror novels to adapt. Michael Crawford, then Michael Ball, donned fat suits as evil Count Fosco, and Maria Friedman soldiered on as the female lead despite getting a diagnosis of breast cancer during rehearsals.

A Year With Frog and Toad. Far superior to *Wind in the Willows,* I urge all parents looking for good music for their kids to buy the album and see the show. Based on the books by Arnold Lobel about inseparable pals Frog (Jay Goede) and Toad (the endearing Mark Linn-Baker), Lobel's daughter Adrianne acted as one of the producers. Music by Robert Reale, book and lyrics by Willie Reale. It's sweet and funny and the score is adorable. I defy anyone to listen to the "Cookies" song and not smile. Alas, along with *Amour*, it got swallowed up at the 2003 Tonys by the juggernaut that was *Hairspray*.

Other bits: I know there's a *Ghost and Mrs. Muir* musical running around; it starred James Barbour, whose sexy baritone must have made a yummy ghost, and had a brief run out here in LA two summers ago, but I missed it. *Young Frankenstein* takes the Great White Way next month, as does Disney's *The Little Mermaid*. And Bruce Kimmel has a show that just got rave reviews at a festival for new musicals: *The Brain From Dimension X*. Apparently, the show's highlight is the solo by the disembodied brain.

Mike here again: I can't believe I missed some of those. I've seen *Assassins* and *Follies* over a dozen times each. I've seen a third to half of the others. But only the remarkable Ms. Turtledove could add them to the list. Is it any wonder that I plan to run off to Broadway with her the next time Harry and Carol go (yawn) bird-watching?

Lord of the (Show) Rings

Now that so many dog shows are turning up on product-hungry cable TV, I figure that *Challenger's* animal issue is a good place to explain just what a dog show is all about and how it works.

To begin with, a dog show is nothing more than a gigantic elimination contest. At the beginning of the day, there may be up to 3,000 dogs in competition; each continues going into the ring until he is defeated, and when only one is left, the show is over.

Now, the notion of having 3,000 dogs walk into a single ring at the same time is just a little far-fetched, so the competition is initially divided into breeds, and each breed is subdivided into various classes.

In collies (which are what Carol and I bred and exhibited for over a dozen years) — and indeed in all other breeds — the sexes are divided for all but the final class. Males are judged first, then bitches, and finally there is an intersex competition for the Best of Breed Award.

The classes are as follows: 6-to-9-month-old puppies, 9-to-12-month-old puppies, novice (for dogs who haven't ever won a class), bred-by-exhibitor (which should be self-explanatory), American-bred (also self-explanatory) and finally the open class (for which all dogs six months and older are eligible).

Where there are color differences the open class is frequently divided. Thus, in collies, there is an open sable class (sable being that "Lassie" color which can vary from lemon-yellow to rich mahogany), open blue merle (the gray or mottled collie that we had inadvertently specialized in), open tricolor (the basically black collies, with white collars and legs and tan facial markings), and the very rare open white (for collies which have colored heads but predominantly white bodies).

Thus, after the judging of the various classes in males, only the class winners are still unbeaten. They in turn come back into the ring for what is known as the Winners class, from which the judge will select one male as the best of the dogs he has seen thus far, an award known as Winners Dog. As a rather meaningless honorarium, he will select the second-best dog as well, an award known as the Reserve Dog and not at all unlike first runner-up in the Miss America pageant.

Of all the males entered in the breed on a given day, only the Winners Dog will receive points toward his championship. Based on the number of dogs he defeats, he will win from 1 to 5 championship points in a day, and he requires 15 points to become a champion.

And as if that is not hard enough, the American Kennel Club has placed two further stipulations on the attainment of a championship:

first, a dog must win at least two "major" shows, which by definition are shows that are worth 3, 4, or 5 points (which prevents him from beating a pair of stinkers fifteen times in a row); and second, he must win his two majors under two different judges, and must have won some of his remaining points under a third judge (which prevents him from following one judge who happens to like him all over the country and showing under no one else). The point scale varies from breed to breed and area to area; in the Midwest, where our collies did most of their campaigning from 1968 to 1983, a male had to defeat 2 other collies in order to win 1 point, 10 to win 2 points, 19 to win 3 points, 31 to win 4 points, and 53 or more dogs to win 5 points. The magic number was 19, since a dog cannot complete a championship without beating 19 or more dogs at least twice. The point scale was usually a little higher for bitches.

Once the points are awarded to Winners Dog, the same procedure is repeated in bitches. Then Winners Dog and Winners Bitch, representing the best non-champions in the breed that day, enter the Best of Breed competition against the champions, who compete only in this class since they have already amassed their 15 points and have no use for any more. One dog, usually but not always one of the champions, is chosen as Best of Breed, and a dog of the opposite sex is chosen as Best of Opposite Sex. If a male is Best of Breed, a bitch will be Best of Opposite Sex, and vice versa.

Finally, the judge chooses between Winners Dog and Winners Bitch and awards one of them Best of Winners. Best of Winners is occasionally a very important award, for it represents a way of picking up extra points without working very hard for them. Let us say that Winners Dog has won 3 points and Winners Bitch has won only 2 points. If the Winners Bitch is selected as Best of Winners, she has, by proxy, defeated all the males and is hence awarded that extra point that the Winner's Dog had won.

Once the Best of Breed Award has been given out in 100 or more breeds, the original 3,000 dogs have been whittled down to 100 or so who are as yet undefeated on that day. When we were showing, those breeds were now divided into six groups — Sporting, Hound, Working, Terrier, Toy, and the catch-all Non-Sporting Group — and very shortly only six dogs were still undefeated. (Since we retired from the game, they split Working into Working and Herding, so there are now seven groups.) These seven Group winners now enter the ring for the top prize of the day: Best in Show. Once that is awarded, the show is over, everyone packs up their dogs and grooming equipment, and the whole pageant moves on to the next day's show site.

Why do people who lose on a Saturday go right back against the same competition 20 miles away on Sunday?

Simple.

The judging of a dog show is entirely subjective. If Secretariat wins a race by 20 lengths and sets a track record in the process, no one can deny he was the best horse in the race; there is an official photograph of the finish that proves he was first across the wire, there is an automatic timer that proves he ran the distance 4 seconds faster than the second-place horse, and there are tens of thousands of spectators, each and every one of them ready to testify that he did indeed finish ahead of all the other horses. But a dog show depends on a judge's subjective taste. He may have an innate prejudice against the color of the dog you are exhibiting, or his own kennel may have been plagued by the very fault your animal possesses, or he may simply have gotten up on the wrong side of the bed. Or, in altogether too many cases, he may be licensed to judge 50 or 60 breeds, and is the equivalent to a man who is a jack of all trades and master of none.

On what does a judge base his decision?

Each breed has a written Standard, a verbalization of the ideal dog, and theoretically the judge selects those dogs that most closely approximate their Standards. To do this, he will have the handlers trot their dogs around the ring so he can evaluate their soundness, he will examine each dog's head and body individually so that he can determine its structure, and he will have each dog strike an alert pose so that he can stand back and evaluate the animal as a whole.

Dog shows are held almost every weekend of the year, all across the country, at sights ranging from Madison Square Garden (infrequently) to out-of-the-way fairgrounds that can be reached only by the most circuitous of back roads (altogether too frequently). The only stipulation placed on them by the American Kennel Club is that shows being held on the same day must be at least 250 miles apart.

Okay, you've got the basics. Now let me give you a typical day in the life of a show kennel — ours. And let me take a show from May, which is Desperation Month for collies, because once they shed their coats they can't be shown until the hair grows back five or six months later. This particular show occurred in May of 1974, and was a little more memorable than most.

On a chilly Saturday morning I packed three collies into my trusty Dodge minivan and headed north from Libertyville, Illinois to a pair of Wisconsin shows.

One of the three was Ch. (for "Champion") Gully Foyle. (Recognize the name?) Gully, a burly, big-coated blue merle, was the Eddie Stanky of the collie world. Leo Durocher used to say of Stanky: "He can't hit, he can't field, and he can't run. All he can do is beat you." The same was true of Gully. There were dogs with better heads, dogs with better bodies, even a few dogs with better coats — but Gully was the consummate show machine. He loved traveling (and a top show dog will log 30,000 miles a year or more), he loved strange surroundings, and he never relaxed in the ring. He knew exactly what was expected of him, and always did the job to perfection.

Around the house, Gully was a little on the dull side. All of his personality was channeled into his stomach (not necessarily a bad thing in a show dog, since they are "baited" with liver in the ring to make them look alert.) The best example came 1973, during the final days of the 17-year locust infestation. We had heard stories that 1973 was to be the "year of the locust", but laughed it off as merely leftover dialogue from an old Charlton Heston film — until the spring day the sky became black with them. They didn't exactly harm anyone, but for the better part of a month they were an incredible nuisance. Then, in midsummer, they began dying off by the millions. Every day I would go out to the dog runs, each of which was 50 feet by 15 feet, with my shovel, prepared to get rid of another 10,000 or so of the little insects — and never once did I find a single locust corpse in Gully's run. He was motivated entirely by his appetite, which exactly what was needed in a show dog. It was enough to make a man quietly proud — once he finished retching.

When Gully wasn't eating — and his diet consisted of anything smaller than himself (or larger if it was cut into pieces) — he spent his days and nights lying atop his dog house, very much like Charlie Brown's Snoopy. Once, after hearing one joke too many from a visitor, I decided to break Gully of the habit by erecting an A-frame dog house. The next morning, when I went out to clean the runs, I found Gully on the roof, his front feet wrapped over the top of the A-frame, his back legs suspended in space. At this point I gave up and gave Gully his old roof to lie on.

The second of the three dogs was Elf, a tricolor bitch who was fast closing in on her championship. Elf was an unusual case, the kind of dog Albert Payson Terhune would have loved to write about. Some dogs, like some people, try very hard to live; Elf, in her happy but empty-headed way, tried just as hard not to. She was one of the few collies on the grounds that we had bought rather than bred, and when she stepped out of the fibreglass airplane crate that brought her she was just about the prettiest puppy either of us had ever seen. She remained that way for almost three days. Then she got progressively uglier, and progressively bouncier, until it reached the point where she was offered as a pet, first for $100, then for $75, and finally for free. There were no takers.

So we decided to train her for the show ring, on the unlikely chance that she might some day look like a show dog again. Training Elf was not like training other dogs. She bounced. And bounced. And then bounced some more. At one point I recall suggesting, only half in jest, that we nail her feet to the floor until she learned what was expected of her. We never got around to it, and she never quite learned what was expected, either.

Finally, when she was seven months old, and bearing the official name of Nightwings (which made her Bob Silverberg's favorite dog), she was entered in a huge show in Cincinnati — and lost about as badly as a dog can lose. We decided that the competition might be easier further away from home, and she was sent to a handler in Texas. She was perfectly healthy when she boarded the airplane, and just about dead when she got off. No one knew what had happened during the flight. It took a veterinarian in Texas some two weeks to save her life, and she was then returned home.

She was entered in a show in mid-April of 1971, at which time she would be 10 months of age, but two weeks earlier, while Carol and I were away, she was the victim of the only serious dog fight the kennel had ever seen. (We never found out quite what happened, but we knew it had to be her fault. She just naturally got on people's — and collies' — nerves.) When we came home we found her lying on the ground in a state of shock. I immediately raced her to the vet's, where her front legs required 47 stitches — and while her legs were being sewn up, she began wagging her tail and finally jumped around so playfully that the vet was forced to anesthetize her.

Convinced by this time that the God of Dog Shows simply didn't want Elf to get into the ring as a puppy, we decided to breed her — just in time to discover a mild vaginal infection that made breeding her impossible at that time. Unbothered by all of this, Elf bounced her way to her first birthday, managing to sprain a leg while jumping up to visit Gully on his roof.

She was entered in another show in September, but when Carol was brushing her coat out prior to putting her in the car, Elf suddenly yelped — and blood began pouring down her leg. It turned out that she had done so much playful thrashing around while getting her stitches that one tuft of hair had been inadvertently stitched into a wound, and the brush had pulled it out, opening up the wound as well.

Elf bounced along for another three or four months, and was then bred. She whelped 8 puppies, three of them of unquestioned show quality. As each of the 5 pets was sold, Elf was offered to the prospective purchaser at the same price. There were no takers, and so the little tri-color bitch, still addle-pated and undaunted, remained in Libertyville.

In late August of 1972 we were preparing to go to California for a science fiction convention when we received a phone call from Stan Flowers, a professional handler who occasionally exhibited our dogs when we couldn't get to the ring ourselves.

"I've got a couple of nice judges coming up on Labor Day weekend," said Stan.

"Forget it," I said. "Everything is out of coat."

"Are you sure?" urged Stan. "These two have put your dogs up before. They like what you breed."

"No," I said. "The only thing I've got in coat is a pet bitch that nobody wants."

"Let me take a look at her."

So I packed Elf into the car, drove the five miles to Stan's house, and unloaded her.

Stan looked at her and grinned. "You think this is a pet, huh?"

"Yeah," I said. "Don't you?"

"I think she's the best collie in your kennel, including all your champions."

I did a double-take and looked at Elf again. Yes, she had a nice coat, and yes, she wasn't quite so ugly any more, but it was hard to think of her as anything but the resident kook. This was the bitch who, three days before whelping her litter, had climbed onto the kitchen counter, waited until I walked by, and then jumped into my arms, thereby causing me to slip a disk in my back. This was the bitch who, when singing, could reach K above high Q, usually at three in the morning. She had a lot of talents, but winning dog shows would never be numbered among them.

"I'm not going to pay you to take a pet in the ring," I said at last. "I could enjoy my money more by burning it on cold winter nights."

"Double or nothing," said Stan. "Pay me twice my fee if I win, nothing if I lose."

"Sold," I said.

A week later we returned home and found out that we owed Stan double his fee. Elf had won 4 points, 2 at each show.

"Luck," I said.

Two weeks later, at her next show, Elf not only won the points but went Best of Breed over champions.

She showed four more times in October, going Winner's Bitch at two of the shows for 4 more points and Reserve Bitch at the other two.

Then, as cold weather returned to the Midwest, she perversely began losing her coat, and we drove 500 miles to Nebraska with her, hoping to find a major before she was shed out completely. The Nebraska Collie Club, held the day after Thanksgiving, drew an entry of more than 40 collie bitches, quite enough for a major, and the judge was an old friend, Noel Denton, who usually liked our dogs.

Carol spent two hours grooming what was left of Elf's coat, applying chalk to the huge white collar to make it even brighter and then brushing it out, trimming feet and whiskers, making each hair on her body stand out proudly and beautifully.

"This is it," Carol announced when she was finished. "We won't be able to get her into another show for months." She pointed to the pile of hair, more than enough to fill a 50-pound grocery bag, that lay on the floor near Elf's grooming table.

I walked into the ring with her, and evaluated the competition. There'd be no sweat winning the class; all I had to do was keep her calm enough to take the Winner's Class as well.

Noel began walking around the ring, looking at each dog in turn, and I decided it was time for Elf to strike a pose and hold stock-still, displaying her body, neck, legs and expression to best advantage.

Look at me, boss! said Elf. *I'll bet I can touch the ceiling!*

The ceiling was 60 feet overhead. Elf made a valiant attempt to reach it.

When she landed, Noel was staring at her. "Okay, pose her later," he said. "Let's see her move now."

I began trotting across the ring, praying that Elf would run in a reasonably straight line.

You're O.J. Simpson and I'm Dick Butkus and I've got to stop you from scoring a touchdown, said Elf. She hurled herself happily against the back of my legs.

I finally made it around the ring and wound up in front of Noel again. He bent down to examine her head, checking to see if the sides of it were properly smooth and the teeth formed a scissors bite. Elf decided it was mountain-climbing time and just about got her back feet up to Noel's shoulders before she fell off. The crowd at ringside loved her. I began trying to remember any old recipes I might have seen for boiled dogmeat, while Carol covered her eyes with her hands and began walking, trancelike, back to the grooming table.

Elf was given a second-place ribbon and, having time of her life, bounced all the way back to the grooming area. When the show was over an outraged Noel Denton sought me out.

"Who taught you to handle a dog?" he demanded furiously. "You ought to be ashamed of yourself! This bitch might have won the points today if she had behaved!"

I handed the leash to Noel. "Show me how," I said, trying to hide a malicious grin of anticipation.

"I certainly will," said Noel. As he was speaking, Elf did a back flip.

Noel blinked once, handed the leash back, and walked away without another word.

She was bred to Gully a month later, aborted the litter with her usual good luck, and never coated up in time to find a major entry. Thus, when she came into season in the summer of 1973, she was bred to Gully again and produced a litter of five puppies. Once a bitch weans a litter she sheds down almost to the skin; with her usual over-enthusiasm, Elf had lost so much hair that she had once again been out of coat for most of the winter and spring shows. And now she was going up to Oshkosh with me, hoping to win one of those elusive majors before the size of the entries dropped off and she had to wait until autumn again.

The third of the dogs I packed into the van was Kim, Gully and Elf's 7-month-old blue son. Kim, officially The Gray Lensman, had been something special from the moment he was born. Very rarely can a breeder look at a litter of still-wet newborn puppies and spot a top-notcher, but Kim was one of those exceptions. He was simply the best male we ever produced, and we know it the second he popped out.

So much for beauty. Emotionally, he was even more scatterbrained than his mother. Physically he was stronger and bouncier. He outweighed her by a good 25 pounds, and was capable of doing far more damage with only half the effort.

Take, for example, dog crates. Almost all show dogs ride to and from shows in metal crates, and for a very good reason: if the car should have an accident, the crate will protect the dog and you won't have to spend the next few days scraping his remains off one of the windows. (And, in the case of Gully, it kept him from sitting on your lap and helping you read the traffic signs.)

Kim didn't like dog crates. Since his strength, even as a puppy, was measured in megatons rather than foot-pounds, getting him through the tiny door of a crate was usually a 10-minute undertaking. Once he was inside, however, the door was locked and he could be driven safely to his destination — until the day he became the first collie on record to break out of a locked crate. It occurred on the way to a handling class when Kim was five months old. There was a huge crash, and a moment later Kim trotted to the front of the van, proudly carrying a horribly misshapen metal door in his mouth.

The Oshkosh Kennel Club was Kim's first dog show and he acquitted himself well, winning a large puppy class. When three bitches didn't show up, the entry fell below the level of a 3-point show, and I withdrew

Elf, who didn't need any more minor points. Gully went Best of Breed again, for the 10th of some 22 such awards he was to win during the year.

Gully didn't win the Working Group, a loss which carried no disgrace with it, since there were some 30 Best of Breed winners competing, almost all of them champions, rather than the vast numbers of non-champion dogs involved in the individual breed competition, and I packed up the dogs and headed for the Oshkosh Holiday Inn. (Dog people soon become experts an the best motel chains, as well as individual motels within those chains: this one has enough room to set up three crates and a grooming table next to the bed, that one doesn't have enough grass to walk the dogs; another one has good food but lousy water, and so forth.)

The next morning I prepared to drive to Appleton, some 30 miles north of Oshkosh, for the Sunday show. I opened the door to the van, took Gully's leash off, snapped my fingers, and the big blue dog jumped into his crate. I repeated the procedure with Elf.

Then I brought Kim out to the van, absentmindedly unhooked the leash, and gestured to a crate.

I HATE CRATES! screamed Kim, and ran off in the general direction of the highway. He had gone about 50 yards when he spotted a puli practicing his obedience routine with his owner, and ran over to see if this was some game he could join.

The puli took one look at the 85-pound instrument of destruction bearing down upon him and didn't wait to find out whether or not it was a playful puppy. He took off like a bat out of hell, with Kim in hot and happy pursuit, and me and the puli's owner racing after the pair of them

Around and around the Holiday Inn we raced, through pass-throughs and under playground equipment. Then, as I was turning a corner, I stepped into a fresh pile of dog stool, slipped, and crashed foot-first into a glass wall with a bone-jarring thud. Thinking that I had invented a new sport, Kim raced up, tail a-wag, ready to participate. I grabbed him by the neck, limped painfully to the van, threw him bodily into a crate, and drove to Appleton.

By the time we reached the show site, my foot was swollen to almost twice its normal size from the collision, and I paid a group of helpful boy scouts to unload the dogs and grooming equipment and place them right next to the show ring. I then went around borrowing pain-killers from my competitors.

When asked why I didn't go home, I replied doggedly that Bernard Esporite was judging, and that Esporite had given Elf a Reserve three weeks earlier, and that the bitch that went Winners on that day had finished her championship in the interim and wouldn't be competing and that no goddamned little bruise was going to keep me out of the ring. (Well, nobody ever said dog breeders had to be smart.)

Kim was the first dog in the ring, and I hobbled around painfully, praying that we would be second so as not to have to return for Winners class. Esporite fell in love with Kim, giving him the first-place blue ribbon and gaiting him around the ring half a dozen times in Winners class before finally giving the points to a more mature sable dog.

At this point I considered taking my shoe off to relieve the pressure, but decided I'd never be able to get it on again over the swelling. An hour later I walked into the ring with Elf, who was bouncier than usual. She won her class, and returned a moment later in Winners class. Esporite had narrowed down his choice to two bitches, Elf and a lovely locally-owned sable. He decided to base his decision on proper movement.

We went around the ring once, then twice more. Then we ran in an L-shaped pattern, then a T-pattern. Then, just so he would be sure he was making the proper selection, Esporite ran the entire class around the ring twice more. Just as I was sure my foot wouldn't hold up for another step Esporite pointed to Elf, and the little black bitch celebrated winning her first major by jumping on me and knocking me down.

"Thank God that's over!" I grated as I hobbled out of the ring.

"What about Gully?" someone asked.

So it wasn't over after all. I sought out Jean Greenwood, a friend who had bought a number of dogs from us when starting her kennel, and asked her to take Elf into the ring.

"And remember," I said. "It wasn't a major in males, so do everything you can do to let the male beat you for Best of Winners. Don't take any liver into the ring, don't let her stand right, the whole bit."

"But why?" she asked

"It's a common courtesy," I replied. "She can't win any more points today, but the male can get a major if he beats her — and maybe someday, when we have to go Best of Winners for the extra point, somebody will do the same for us."

Then I was in the ring again. Gully tried his very best, but I simply couldn't keep up with him as we gaited around the ring. As for Elf, she evidently had decided to make a good impression on her new-found friend; everything that she usually did wrong for me she did right for Jean. A few moments later Esporite awarded her Best of Breed over Gully, who was Best of Opposite Sex. Best of Breed of course made her Best of Winners as well; I gave an apologetic look across the ring to the owner of the Winner's Dog, decided that I couldn't stay on my foot long enough to pose for victory photos with Elf and Gully, and hopped off to a telephone to tell Carol the news. Carol was properly overjoyed about the major, but a little too busy to celebrate. The milk had gone bad on the bitch who had whelped a few weeks earlier — the reason she had stayed at home — and she was being forced to wean the puppies earlier than usual.

I hunted up another batch of boy scouts, had them load the van, and stayed just long enough to watch Jean handle Elf in the Working Group. Elf was back to emulating a rubber ball again, and while the spectators loved it the judge had scant use for such antics and ignored her throughout the class.

Then came the 4-hour drive home. I had borrowed a knife, cut my canvas shoe off, and wrapped my bare foot in my coat. Since the temperature was about 70 degrees, I opened all the windows and pointed the van toward Illinois.

By the time we reached Milwaukee, it was 35 degrees out, and since I was driving in a short-sleeved shirt, I was damned near frozen. I pulled the car over to the side of the road in order to close the windows — and discovered that I couldn't walk. So I shivered for the final 90 minutes and at long last pulled into the driveway. I turned off the motor and began honking the horn, waiting for Carol to come out and help me make it to the door — but Carol was in one of the back rooms, teaching toothless puppies to eat raw hamburger, and didn't hear. Finally I got out of the van, hopped to the front door, and opened it, yelling for help.

Carol unloaded the dogs, put them in runs, and drove me right to the hospital, where the injury was diagnosed as a badly torn ligament complicated by gross stupidity, and I was fitted with a pair of crutches.

"That's about the dumbest thing I ever heard of," said the doctor as he finished applying an elastic bandage to the foot. "Why didn't you come home the minute it happened — or at least get someone else to show your dogs?"

"It was a major," I said, as if that explained everything.

"What the hell does that mean?" asked the doctor.

"Let me put it this way," I said. "if you were on the eighteenth tee, five under par, and you sprained an ankle, would you quit?"

"Hell, no!" came the explosive reply.

"This is the same thing."

Now that it had been explained in medical terms, the doctor's expression softened.

"Did you break par?" he asked.

"Yes."

"I guess it was worth it at that," said the doctor.

And, strangely enough, it was.

Bathrooms I Have Known

Back in the days when Carol and I were breeding and exhibiting collies—for the record, we had 23 champions, most of them named after science fiction stories and characters—we encountered some unusual bathrooms.

At the Springfield, Missouri Fair Grounds, the men's room consisted of a small building with a concrete floor. No matter where you stood, it sloped to a drain in the very center of the building. And that was it, in its entirety.

At the Wheaton, Illinois Kennel Club, the only way for 3,000 exhibitors to get from the parking lot to the grooming area was through—not around, not next to, but *through*—the women's bathroom.

There were a *lot* of bathrooms like that on the show circuit. We used to joke about them.

Then we started traveling around the world, and realized just how good we had it in Springfield, Wheaton, and the other show sites. One day, just for the hell of it, I put our experiences in a Toastmaster speech at Midwestcon, and it was so popular that I was flown to a number of other cons expressly to talk about bathrooms. Guy Lillian heard it at some con or other, and has prevailed upon me to resurrect the memories one last time.

The Matthews Range, Kenya. This is a mountain range in Northern Kenya that was only recently opened for tourism, and we were among the first to show up there. The tented camp's notion of a bathroom was a "long drop" (a toilet over a 30-foot-deep hole, common on the safari trail), and a shower consisting of a 5-gallon canvas bag that would be filled with hot water by what our guide liked to call "dusky handmaidens".

There were no car tracks in the Matthews Range—it was too newly opened for them—so all our sightseeing had to be done on foot. In the mountains. At 7,500 feet altitude. In the heat of the day. When we got back from a four-hour trek I was so exhausted I skipped the shower and went right to my cot for a nap. I awoke just after sunset and decided to bathe before dinner. So I duly removed my clothes, stood under the canvas bag, and pulled the cord that opened it—and let out such a scream that I scared away all the leopards they'd laid out bait for. Seems I'd forgotten what happens to hot water when it's left out for hours at 7,500 feet at nightfall—except that it wasn't hot water any more. I don't think I could have been any colder if you'd covered me with ice cubes.

* * * *

Jedibe Island, Botswana. It's not generally known, but hippos kill more tourists than any other animal in Africa. The reason's simple enough. Hippos have incredibly sensitive skin, so they protect it by staying in the water all day—but they don't eat in the water. After dark they climb ashore and forage inland for up to two miles to down their daily ration of 300 pounds of choice vegetation.

When they're in the water, all you can usually see are their eye sockets, their ears, and their nostrils, so naturally the tourist much prefers to photograph them on land, and the best time to do it is when they're coming back from a night's feeding.

Only one problem. Get between a hippo and water, and he panics. Every instinct tells him the water is safe, and he'll take the shortest route to it—which means he'll go *through* you, not around you.

So one day we're on Jedibe Island in the middle of the Okavango Swamp (I know, I know, I'm supposed to call it a Delta, but what it is is a swamp). Now, the more sophisticated tented camps usually supply a private bathroom, no matter how primitive, attached to each tent. Jedibe did not possess one of the more sophisticated tented camps. What it had was an ablution block, an area perhaps 30 feet on a side, surrounded by a 6-foot-high reed fence. Inside the block was a toilet (the long drop variety, of course) and a shower (the canvas bag variety, natch.)

At midnight I decide to use the facilities, so I wander over to the ablution block, maybe 40 yards from our tent—we were the only people in the camp that night, other than the couple who ran it—and in the fullness of time I prepare to unlatch the ablution block's door and return to my tent.

But just then a 3-ton hippo who'd been grazing in the area got an itch, and decided to scratch it by rubbing against the reed fence. And he rubbed, and he rubbed, and he rubbed, and that damned itch just wouldn't go away, and I knew how he felt, because I was being eaten alive by insects.

So I got to thinking, and I figured: Jedibe is a small island, maybe 300 yards in circumference, so if he sees me and he's got normal intelligence, he'll realize that all he has to do is turn around and trot off to the safety of the water.

Then I think a little more, and I figure: if, on the other hand, he's an exceptionally stupid hippo, wherever I stand he'll decide I'm between him and the water and will just lower his head and charge.

The scratching didn't sound very intelligent, and I decided not to chance it. Three hours later he satisfied his itch, grunted a few times, and went off for a swim. I got to the tent just in time to catch an hour of sleep before the sun came up and we were off to watch the very animal I'd been avoiding all night long.

Mana Pools, Zimbabwe. Another tented camp, this one on the Zambezi River. We arrived in late morning, were shown to our tent, and were left alone to unpack. Carol saw a movement overhead, looked up, and found that we were sharing the tent with a 5-foot long spotted bush snake. Of course, we didn't know what the hell kind of snake it was, so I sought out the camp manager, who explained that it was harmless to people, but would hold the tent's lizard and insect population down to zero.

I didn't think any more of it until we came in all hot and dusty from the afternoon game run. Carol decided to take a shower before dinner. It turns out that the snake had the same idea and got there first. She took a look at the snake. The snake took a look at her. She screamed in surprise. The snake hissed in terror. She took off to the east. The snake took off to the west.

Eventually Carol came back. The snake, poor distraught fellow, never did.

The Osiris. The Osiris is a ship, owned by the Hilton hotel chain, that travels the Nile from Cairo to Aswan and back again. We were visiting Egypt with Pat and Roger Sims, my father, and my agent, Eleanor Wood, and her kids.

Since I was the African expert, I did the booking. I choose the Ramses Hilton, because it was the only 5-star hotel in Cairo that had never had a reported case of botulism. I booked the tour company, which had enough clout to make a plane turn around and come back for us when we were late getting to the airport. And I booked the Osiris, supposedly the most luxurious ship on the Nile.

Well, two out of three ain't bad.

Pat and Roger had the room right above us. Every time Roger took a shower we had a driving rain in our cabin.

And Roger likes to shower.

I never saw a desert in Egypt, but I saw a *lot* of rain. All of it inside.

Malindi, Kenya. Malindi is a charming little town on the Kenya coast, halfway between Mombasa and Lamu. After touring the Gedi ruins, we checked in at the Sindbad Hotel, which looked exactly like something out of *Road to Morocco*, with its arched doorways and enclosed gardens and such. We had a nice dinner, watched some vigorous native dancers, and went to bed.

We awoke at six in the morning to find that our toilet, which had worked the previous day, was not functioning. We went down to the desk to complain, and the manager explained that there was nothing wrong with the toilet. To conserve water, he turned the toilets off at midnight and reactivated them at nine in the morning.

"But the shower and the sink worked," I said. "I tried them, just to see if the water had been shut off."

"Of course they work."

"Then why shut off the toilet?" I demanded.

He smiled. "Who takes a shower at four in the morning?" he responded.

Kenya may belong to the Third World. The Sindbad Hotel belonged to a world all its own.

The Sheraton Skyline Hotel, London. I'm including this just so you'll know that not all our bathroom experiences took place in Africa.

Carol suffers from jet lag, so we usually spend a day in London on our way to and from Africa, to give her system a chance to adjust. And the hotel we usually stay at by Heathrow Airport is the Skyline Sheraton.

So we land, and check in at the Skyline, and while I'm unpacking Carol walks into the bathroom. And a minute later I hear her calling me.

"What is it?" I ask.

"There's no knob or handle on this side of the door," she says. "Could you open it, please?"

I reach for the knob, and realize there's no knob or handle on *my* side of the door either. The entire mechanism is missing.

So I phone down to the desk, they send up a mechanic, he uses some tool or other to let her out, and admits that he has no idea what happened to the missing knobs.

Before we move our stuff to a new room, I look inside the bathroom. No windows. No phone.

If Carol had been traveling alone, she'd have been stuck there for maybe 22 hours until the maid came to clean the room the next morning.

* * * *

Maralal, Kenya. The Maralal Lodge is a convenient halfway point between the Samburu/Buffalo Springs reserves and the lakes of the Rift

Valley. (It's also the town where Jomo Kenyatta was imprisoned for 7 long years.)

The lodge has the most beautiful flower gardens. They're an odd sight in the middle of the arid Northern Frontier District.

It's a little less odd when you see the signs outside every cabin and in every bathroom, urging you not to drain the bathtub when you're through with it. With water at such a premium, they send a couple of attendants around every morning and afternoon. They fill buckets with dirty water from the tubs and empty them on the flower gardens.

The Mount Soche Hotel, Malawi. The best hotel in Blantyre, the former capitol of Malawi back when it was Nyasaland, is the Mount Soche Hotel, so that's where we stayed. The elevators semi-worked, which is to say they went up and down, but they never once stopped at our floor. That's a really trivial problem for African accommodations, so we paid it no attention.

While we were in Blantyre we went to the local museum, where the college-educated curator tried to convince us that witchcraft was a valid science, and we drove and climbed Mount Mulanje, which at 9,000 feet isn't much of a mountain, but it's the tallest one they've got.

And then we went back to the hotel. And I blew my nose, and tossed the tissue in the toilet, and forgot about it. And as Carol passed by, she saw it and decided to flush it away. And couldn't find the flushing mechanism. Finally she saw a little button on the wall, and realized that was it. And she pushed. And it didn't budge.

She pushed again. Nothing happened. Finally she braced her feet, threw her whole weight into it, and flushed the toilet just before her thumb was due to break.

Her comment: "I've walked maybe 20 miles yesterday, and today I climbed the tallest mountain in the country. And flushing that damned toilet is the most exercise I've had since we've been here."

The Maasai Mara, Kenya. So we're staying in a tented camp in the Mara, and after dinner we watch some dancing, and finally it's about ten o'clock, and it's time to go to bed, since we'll be getting up at six to go on a game run. (I'd much prefer to get up at a civilized hour, but in Africa the animals lay up in the heat of the day, and you tend to take your game runs from 6:00 to 9:00 AM, and again from 3:30 to 6:00 PM. In between, *everyone* sleeps.

Anyway, we get to our tent, and sure enough, the toilet in the attached bathroom isn't working. I report it to the camp manager, he sends a fellow over to repair it, and five minutes later it's working.

He announces that he's going to walk home now. I offer to hunt up the manager and get him a ride.

"I am a Maasai," he says with proper arrogance. "I have lived here all my life. I have no fear of animals."

Twenty minutes later a helicopter is rushing him to the Nairobi hospital a couple of hundred miles away. It seems he ran into an equally arrogant elephant who had lived there all her life and had no fear of Maasai.

Linyati Camp, Botswana. So we're in the Linyati area of Botswana, and it's another camp with an ablution block. And just before I turn off my reading lamp to go to sleep, I decide to pay the ablution block a visit.

I get out of the tent and take two steps toward the block.

"Hi, Mike," say three hyenas, who are posted halfway to the block. "We're so glad you came out to play with us."

They grin to show me how happy they are.

I go back into the tent.

Ngorongoro Crater, Tanzania. If you could spend only one day in Africa, you'd be well-advised to spend it in the Crater, a caldara (collapsed volcano) about 10 miles in diameter, with an enormous concentration of large mammals—and the walls are so steep and high that they have almost no poachers.

What they do have on the floor of the Crater is a lovely little lake where our party—Pat and Roger Sims, Carol and myself, and my father—all stopped to enjoy a box lunch. And about thirty yards away was an old-fashioned outhouse with an honest-to-ghod half-moon carved on the door.

My father announced his intention to pay it a visit. Moro, our native guide, recommended against it. My father decided he couldn't wait, so off to the outhouse he went.

"He is a very brave man, your father," said Moro.

"How brave do you have to be to enter an outhouse?" I said, assuming he had warned us off because it was filthy.

"Very," he said. "A black mamba"—the most poisonous snake in Africa—"lives beneath the little hole you sit on."

I had raced halfway to the outhouse to pull my father out of there when he emerged, looking much relieved and totally unbitten.

There are so many others. There was Island Camp on Lake Barringo, which seemed to have established an ant farm in our shower stall. There was another tented camp in the Rift Valley where we shared our bathroom with a pet waterbuck who came running every time he heard the shower going. There was a hotel in Nancy, France where every time you flushed the toilet the bidet shot water up to the ceiling.

But I'm going to close by telling you about the most memorable bathroom of all. The wild part is that I couldn't find it again if you paid me.

Maasai Mara, Kenya. It's 1986, our first trip to Kenya, and we're in the Mara, which is overflowing with animals and looks exactly like Hollywood's idea of Africa. We've been driving around watching them for a few hours, and Perry, our guide, and I decide that we have to answer a call of Nature. Carol, who has a bladder of steel, waits in the Land Rover while Perry and I go behind a likely bush.

And as we are doing what comes naturally, I look over, and there, about 20 yards away, is a 2,000-pound Cape buffalo doing exactly the same thing, and glaring at me as if I, and I alone, am responsible for his prostate problems.

So I alert Perry to our situation and ask him what to do.

His logical answer: "Finish before he does and run like hell."

We finished about ten seconds ahead of him, and beat him to the car by about three feet. The car proudly sported its scar from the buffalo's horns on our next two trips to Kenya, until it was replaced by a new Land Cruiser that soon displayed the gouge from a rhino's horn, which is an interesting story but has nothing to do with bathrooms, so I'll save it for another time and place.

I don't remember quite when I started writing up my Worldcon diaries, but they've become very popular. Most have appeared in Guy Lillian's *Challenger*, and over the years I seem to have written up a few other cons as well, such as DragonCon and the Nebula Weekend.

As I get older I find there's one kind of writing I do more and more often, and I like it less and less: obituaries for good friends who have left us. It seems like I'm doing more of them each year. Here's a small sampling (but too large anyway)

Part IV

Obituaries

Kelly Freas

Kelly Freas was one of the first pros I met when I entered the field 40+ years ago. I was in awe of him, but he went out of his way to put me at my ease. We quickly became friends, and remained friends for the next four decades, during which time he illustrated some of my books and some of my stories, and took it upon himself to bring me to the attention of more than one editor who might otherwise not have known I existed.

At the 1982 Worldcon in Chicago, we had lucked into a room on the 5th floor of the immense Hyatt, which meant we weren't at the mercy of the elevators. The con committee tried to get us out of there, since they felt that only committee members and the Guests of Honor should be there, but we knew the law and knew they couldn't force us out as long as we had a reservation and our credit card was good. We showed up a few days early, and on Friday morning Kelly arrived. The committee pounded on our door and demanded—for the fourth day in a row—that we leave the room. We wouldn't do it for the committee, but we were happy to turn the room over to Kelly. I told him he could hunt us up on one of the party floors—the 25th or 26th, as I recall—once we got a new room. His eyes lit up and he told the committee that, Guest of Honor or not, he'd much rather be on the party floor, which is precisely the kind of guy Kelly was: at least as good a friend to fans as he was to pros.

And those eleven Hugos are probably a few less than he deserved. He was as talented as he was friendly, and that's a *lot* of talent.

Jacques Chambon, 1942-2003

It's hard to believe he's gone. He contacted me just five days ago to ask about a slang word in a book of mine he was translating and editing, and he wanted to make sure he had it right. That's the meticulous kind of artist he was; one not-very-important word out of 150,000, and he had to make sure of it.

He published a dozen or more of my books at Denoel, then brought me over to Flammarion with him. On one of my trips to France, I thought I'd visit some other houses and see if I could get a little healthy bidding going. Silly notion. Every editor I met had been trained and brought along by Jacques, and their attitude was simple and straightforward: if Jacques wanted it, no matter what it was, no one would risk disappointing him by bidding against him and, ghod forbid, doing him out of a property he coveted.

Carol and I have been flown over to half a dozen French conventions in the past 5 years, and every time Jacques escorted us to his favorite restaurants, even took us to the Moulin Rouge (which is surely beyond the call of duty for an editor), and was a thoughtful and always-fascinating guide, host and raconteur.

He had a country home he loved, hours out of Paris, and some time back he moved there full-time, still running the Flammarion line but editing out of his house.

I hate it when friends die. I especially hate it when friends who are exactly my age die. And I hate it most of all when they are not just personal friends, but friends of the whole science fiction field. Jacques Chambon worked in the science fiction field for decades, and didn't have a single enemy on either side of the Atlantic. There are worse legacies.

Bill Bowers

Bill Bowers moved to Cincinnati at about the same time I did, some 29 years ago. He was already a Big Name Fan with a handful of Hugo nominations for fanzine publishing, and had indeed been selected to be Fan Guest of Honor at the 1978 Worldcon. Bill was one of the last of the people of whom it may truly be said: Fandom Is A Way Of Life. He published *Double: Bill* with Bill Mallardi, and *Stardust*, *Xenolith* and *Outworlds* on his own. As far as I could tell, all his friends were fans. His entire social life revolved around fandom,. He and another Worldcon Fan Guest of Honor, Rusty Hevelin, created and co-chaired a summer relaxacon, Spacecon, for the better part of a decade beginning in 1981.

Bill suffered from a number of debilitating ailments, not the least of which was emphysema; he was on oxygen the last few times I saw him (and like almost every other emphysema sufferer I know, it didn't stop him from smoking like a chimney.) Toward the end, when he was running low on money and realized that he wouldn't have time to read (or re-read) the tens of thousands of fanzines he had stashed in a rented storage wall, he asked me to start selling them for him on eBay, as he was too weak and too short of energy to do it himself. He practically wept every time I gave him a check, because it meant I had sold more of his cherished old friends.

Fandom will miss him.

Lee Hoffman

LeeH (her fannish sobriquet, which is pronounced the same as "Lee") was the first great femmefan, which is to say, the first to enter fandom and rise to the top on her own, rather than with/through a boyfriend or husband.

Her fanzine, *Quandry*, was probably the best around in the early and mid-1950s, and I still have, and cherish, every issue of her *Science Fiction Five-Yearly* (which gave birth to Bob Bloch's and Bob Tucker's one-shot, *Science Fiction Fifty-Yearly* a few years back.)

LeeH was as talented a writer as she was a fan writer and editor, and won the Spur Award from the Western Writers of America. She was a very deserving Fan Guest of Honor at the 1982 Worldcon in Chicago.

I can't remember where I first met her, but the last few times I saw her were at Tropicon in Fort Lauderdale in the late 1990s. She was always gracious, cheerful and witty. Science Fiction could do with a dozen of her clones.

LAN

His name was George Laskowski, and he was my friend.

I don't remember when we first met—probably a Midwestcon or an Octocon. He was pretty distinctive. Whether he was wearing a suit, a t-shirt, or a tux, he almost always wore this Davy Crockett raccoon hat. (I finally named it Cedric and began writing it up whenever I could, explaining that it was all that remained of the twin brother George always wished he'd had.)

I vaguely knew that he published a fanzine called *Lan's Lantern*, but I'd never seen a copy. One day he offered to send me one. I asked what was in it. He said the usual—reviews, articles, artwork. I said as long as he was doing reviews, why didn't he review my stuff?

Well, he'd never read me any more than I'd read him, so when I got home from the con I mailed him a few books—and damned if he didn't review every book I wrote for the next 15 years. And they were as thoughtful as any reviews I've received.

Any guy who likes my writing is aces with me, so I went out of my way to know him a little better, and then better still, and what I found was a man who exemplified everything that was best in fandom. He had a bright, inquisitive, probing mind. He was a voracious reader. He had no enemies that I could see. He had better manners than 98% of his contemporaries. He put out one hell of a fanzine, which got better each issue, and he was always open to (and even solicited) suggestions for improving it. In his mundane life, he was a teacher at a special school, and he was as dedicated to excellence there as he was in the *Lantern* or any other aspect of his life; he loved the kids, loved teaching them, and hated the politics that went along with it.

He won a couple of Hugos for *Lan's Lantern*, and deserved more. He also showed a couple of thousand members of the Hugo audience at Orlando what the word "class" is all about, when, back in 1992, Spider Robinson read off the wrong name—Lan's— and had to take back the Hugo and give it to Rich and Nicki Lynch. Lan stayed on stage to applaud and sincerely congratulate them. If they'd have taken a Hugo out of *my* hands and given it to Bob Silverberg or Joe Haldeman, good friends both, I'd probably have tripped them as they climbed up onto the stage to accept it.

Lan was so friendly, so interesting, so happy just to be part of fandom, that it seemed he'd go on forever. And then one day we got the word: he had cancer.

He fought it as bravely as anyone could. He put out another thick issue of the *Lantern*. I believe he even taught another semester. It was amazing, because the word was that this was one of the more virulent and incurable cancers. For a while it looked like he'd make it—and then he was gone.

I don't like it when anyone dies. I especially don't like it when they're younger than me. And I hate it when they're good and decent people who should still have had decades left. Lan departed much too soon, but there's one thing I know: he won't be forgotten too soon, or at all. As long as there are trufen in the Midwest and elsewhere, he'll be remembered, not for the *Lantern* and the Hugos, but for exemplifying all that was best in a fan—and a man.

Hal Clement / Harry Clement Stubbs R.I.P.

Harry was a sweet guy. Time and again I'd get up and give a GOH speech about science fiction, and he would seek me out later and gently explain why I was wrong on every point. Then two weeks later he'd give a GOH speech about the beauties of hard science, and I would seek him out and gently explain to him why his priorities and conclusions were totally wrong. We never agreed, and there was never had a harsh word between us.

I remember a few years ago we were talking over coffee, and he checked his watch and apologized but he had to leave. I asked if it was a panel assignment. He said no, that after years and years on diabetes medication, he was now on the needle and it was time to go give himself a shot. It was the only time he ever referred to his diabetes or his health in general.

He often looked a little lost at the dozens of smaller cons we found ourselves at. He was as approachable as any pro I ever knew, but he'd been around for so long that either fans were in awe of him and afraid to approach him, or else the newer few generations simply didn't recognize him or know who he was.

He wasn't wildly prolific, but there's no question that *Mission of Gravity* is a classic in the field, *Needle* comes close to classic status, and I was as thrilled as everyone else to see him win a retro-Hugo before he died.

I haven't checked, but I'm pretty sure the record will show that he's the only person ever to have been both a Worldcon Fan Guest of Honor (when Boston honored the Strangers Club in 1989) and a Worldcon Pro Guest of Honor (in Chicago in 1991). He became a Nebula Grandmaster in 1998. Not a bad trio of lifetime achievements to go out on.

Robert Sheckley

Back when I was learning how to write half a century ago, I had one role model—Robert Sheckley. Everyone knew he was the wittiest writer around, but to me he had an even greater quality: he was the most *accessible* writer around. Nobody ever made it easier to turn to the next page than the Sheckley of the 1950s and 1960s. (I also thought he must live an exotic, exciting life. When we became pen pals, his address was "Larry's Bar" in some little town in Spain.)

We'd been friends for years before we finally met in person, at a Windycon in the early 1980s, and over the years I must have bought eight or ten stories from him for anthologies I was editing. I also put together his three comic masterworks of the 1960s and edited them as *Dimensions of Sheckley* for NESFA Press.

As time went by I evolved from a hero-worshipping kid to a friend to an editor, and finally to a partner. We at long last got to collaborate on a story that came out a year before he died.

I only met him one more time after that long-ago Windycon. At the 2004 Worldcon in Boston, I got a call in my room. It was Bob, asking me to come down and have breakfast with him. It was eight in the morning, and I'd been asleep for maybe two hours. Probably no one else in the whole world could have gotten me to come downstairs and face food under those circumstances, but I didn't even think twice. I was dressed and down in the restaurant with him five minutes later.

To this day I think it was an insult when SFWA made him their Author Emeritus a couple of years back; Bob clearly had the credentials to be made a Grandmaster, and indeed was long overdue for it. I'm glad he was selected as a Guest of Honor at a Worldcon, another long-overdue honor, before he died.

He made it possible for humorists from Terry Pratchett to John Sladek to Esther Friesner to toil successfully in this field. He wrote what I consider to be one of the half-dozen finest books ever produced in the field, *Dimension of Miracles*. He was a pioneer who was late getting the acclaim he deserved, but he finally received it.

Mostly, he was my friend, and I miss him already.

Sir Arthur C. Clarke

As brilliant a scientist and science fiction writer as he was, there was far more to Arthur C. Clarke than that. For a serious Knight of the Realm, he had a truly offbeat sense of humor, and his *Tales From the White Hart* is an overlooked classic. (Who else could write about a cowardly man-eating plant?)

He was also an incredibly approachable man, in person or via correspondence. He wasn't above sending a few fan letters to encourage a writer (me) whose work he had just encountered, and he similarly had no problem letting me anthologize a story he'd written when he was simply a teenaged fan who called himself "Ego" Clarke and explain the origin of that name in the introduction.

His contributions to the field are manifest. His humanity was even greater.

Rev. Darrell C. Richardson

Just found out that an old friend died on Tuesday (September 19, 2006)—the Reverend Darrell C. Richardson, one of the first three or four fans Carol and I met when we entered fandom 44 years ago.

Darrell was a Baptist preacher, and a sincere one. He contracted cancer a quarter of a century ago. The doctors administered chemo, explained that it would cause his hair to fall out, and gave him 5 weeks to live. He had a pow-wow with Jesus that night, they decided he still had preaching to do, and the next morning he started growing a beard. He was out of the hospital and pronounced miraculously cured after a month (he knew why, even if medical science didn't), and he went on to spread the Word on 4 continents and maybe 50 countries, including just about every Third World hellhole there was.

The last time I saw him was at the 1998 Baltimore Worldcon, where he proudly told me that though he was in his 70s, he was exactly 2 pounds heavier than his playing weight when he was a starting guard for Georgia 50 years earlier. Darrell had one of the great pulp and pulp art collections. When he lived in the Cincinnati area (he was gone before I got here), he built an all-stone outbuilding to house his collection so that it could never burn down. He wrote a fine book on the work of J. Allen St. John, was a regular contributor to Bob Tucker's *Science Fiction News Letter* 55 years ago, co-published a small specialty press, and was a decent man and a good friend.

Memories of Tucker

Bob Tucker was my friend for 43 years.

He was fandom's friend for about 30 years longer than that.

He was a professional writer, of course—Hugo nominee, probably an even better mystery writer, always willing to give a newcomer the benefit of his wisdom. But it's for his undisputed position as the best-loved fan in science fiction's history that he'll be remembered the longest.

They'll be reminiscing and telling Tucker stories for decades to come. Here are a few of mine:

When Lou Tabakow was dying in a Cincinnati hospital, Bob asked if he could stay in our guest room at nights while he visited Lou by day. Of course we said yes. Now, it was generally considered that despite his love of Beam's Choice, and his leading everyone in a series of "Smooths" at every convention (I'm sure someone else will explain that reference), he just took a small sip and passed it around, that he wasn't really a heavy drinker after all. Well, we bought a bottle of Beam's Choice just before he arrived. Neither of us drinks; when he left two days later it was empty. So much for small sips.

The first night he spent with us, he got up at about three in the morning to use the bathroom. I was writing—I usually write from about 10:00 PM to maybe 5:00 AM, when there are no phone calls or visitors to disturb me. Bob saw the light in my office, stopped in the doorway, and asked where the bathroom was. I replied that I'd tell him as soon as he scribbled down a cover quote for my current book. He explained that he was desperate for a bathroom. I explained that I was desperate for a cover quote from Wilson Tucker. We each won; I got my quote, and ten seconds later he got his bathroom.

Then there was the Resnick/Tucker Award. We were the judges for the first few Windycon masquerades back in the mid-1970s, and we duly gave out Most Beautiful and Most Humorous and all the other categories, but we decided there was one category that was missing, so we invented the Resnick/Tucker Male Chauvinist Pig Award, which was given to the nakedest girl in the masquerade. The prize was a drink in the hotel bar, paid for by the two judges. Well, nothing untoward happened for a year or two, but at one of those early Windycons, and I can't remember the number or year as I write this, the winner of the award had a costume composed entirely of transparent plastic. She duly won, we duly took her down to the hotel bar for her prize, and the Chicago cops duly arrested her for indecent exposure. (Yes, we managed to talk them out of it.)

I'll miss him. I hope he's busy right now, giving his pal Bob Bloch a preliminary tour of the Tucker Hotel. (I'm sure someone will explain that reference, too.)

A good man, a better writer, a still better fan, and a fine friend.

And I am getting goddamned sick and tired of writing obits and reminiscences of fine friends. It'd be nice if the Star Maker would just look the other way for a few years.

R.I.P. — The Dean

It happened again. No sooner do we get over mourning the loss of one giant when the Star Maker grabs another, and this time he took the unquestioned Dean of Science Fiction.

Jack Williamson was among the first science fiction writers to befriend me when I was breaking into the field almost 40 years ago. He was definitely the first to treat me not only as a friend, but as an equal and a peer, which made me feel he'd made a terrible mistake (and, in truth, *still* makes me feel so.) He was so friendly, so giving, so approachable, that he always seemed to be completely unaware of the fact that he was, well, ***Jack Williamson***.

He won the Hugo in 1984 for *Wonder's Child*, the first writer ever to win that most coveted award with an autobiography. One of my proudest editing achievements is that I got him to expand it, add another two decades to bring it up to date, add his diary from World War II, and also include a batch of photographs. It came out a few months ago, and I'm grateful that he was able to see it before he died.

Like many of Jack's friends, I was flown out to Portales for a Williamson Lectureship. What impressed me the most was not the beautiful buildings, or even the outstanding science fiction collection in the library, but the credentials of many of the professors and assistants I met there. They were from Harvard and Yale and Columbia and Stanford and the like, and when I asked them why they'd chosen to work in a little out-of-the-way place like the University of Eastern New Mexico, the answer was always the same: they'd been reading Jack Williamson all their lives, and they'd have gone to New Mexico, or Burkina Faso, or to any place short of Hell Itself to work with him.

When it came time to do a "tribute volume," a collection of stories set in Jack's various universes and futures, I was one of those Jack invited into *The Williamson Effect*. I did a humorous little piece, a takeoff on his classic *Darker Than You Think*, in which the narrator winds up eating Jack Williamson. He got a real kick out of the fact that from that day on, I always introduced him to audiences as a man of exquisite taste. Which, all humor aside, he was.

I think the greatest compliment I could pay him—and I've said it a number of times in a number of venues—is that he remains the only author in my experience who continued to improve with every decade. I can't think of any higher praise than that.

When you're 98 years old, your death doesn't come as much of a surprise, but that doesn't take the sting off it. Jack embodied just about all of science fiction's history in a single man and a single lifetime, and we're going to miss him for a long time to come.

Algis Budrys

Algis Budrys and I lived about a dozen miles apart for more than a decade, when I was first starting out in science fiction. He was one of the reigning giants, I was just a kid who wanted to write the stuff, but he always found time to talk to me and teach me.

He was the Guest of Honor at the 1976 Windycon, the first time I'd ever been asked to be a Toastmaster. And since it *was* the first time, I did my homework and stockpiled about two hours worth of Budrys zingers. I only spoke for about ten minutes — but every time I saw him in an audience for the next two decades, I unloaded more of the unused Budrys jokes on him. Finally one day I ran out, and he sought me out later and asked, with genuine hurt in his eyes, what he had done to so offend me that I stopped insulting him in public.

Which is exactly the kind of guy my pal Ajay was. I'll miss him. We'll *all* miss him.

As with Once a Fan..., this book will wind up with a section devoted to the Resnick Lists. I find that they, like the author, are in a constant state of change, which I hope is a good thing showing growth and development, rather than a bad thing showing indecision and fuzzy thinking. But I wouldn't bet on it.

Part V

The Resnick Lists

My 50 Favorite Movies:

1. *Lawrence of Arabia*
2. *They Might Be Giants*
3. *The Maltese Falcon*
4. *Mask of Dimitrio*s
5. *The Flame Trees of Thika*
6. *The Quiet Man*
7. *Casablanca*
8. *L. A. Confidential*
9. *Zulu*
10. *Field of Dreams*
11. *The Wind and the Lion*
12. *Les Demoiselles de Rochefort*
13. *The Magnificent Seven*
14. *Black Orpheus*
15. *The Ritz*
16. *The Wonderful Ice Cream Suit*
17. *The Bridge on the River Kwai*
18. *The Day of the Jackal*
19. *The Third Man*
20. *Treasure of the Sierra Madre*
21. *Marilyn Hotchkiss' Ballroom Dance and Charm School*
22. *Always Outnumbered, Always Outgunned*
23. *The Good, The Bad, and The Ugly*
24. *Farewell, My Lovely*
25. *The Great Escape*
26. *The Guns of Navarone*
27. *Lili*
28. *The Gods Must Be Crazy*
29. *A Beautiful Mind*
30. *Shaka Zulu*
31. *The Human Comedy*
32. *Prince of the City*
33. *1776*
34. *Seven Brides for Seven Brothers*
35. *The Man Who Would Be King*
36. *The Sundowners*
37. *King Solomon's Mines*
38. *The Professionals*

39. *The Umbrellas of Cherbourg*
40. *Tim*
41. *Fantasia*
42. *On the Waterfront*
43. *Topkapi*
44. *The Year of Living Dangerously*
45. *Bang the Drum Slowly*
46. *Duck Soup*
47. *Sunset Boulevard*
48. *The African Queen*
49. *Trader Horn*
50. *Sinbad the Sailor*

(*sigh* Not a single science fiction film on the list)

My 25 Favorite Musical Plays:

1. *Sweeney Todd*
2. *Falsettos*
3. *Amour*
4. *City of Angels*
5. *Grover's Corners*
6. *Ain't Supposed to Die a Natural Death*
7. *1776*
8. *The Fantasticks*
9. *Pacific Overtures*
10. *Man of La Mancha*
11. *Portrait of Jennie*
12. *Follies*
13. *Baker Street*
14. *Sunday in the Park With George*
15. *Celebration*
16. *A Little Night Music*
17. *West Side Story*
18. *110 in the Shade*
19. *Carnival!*
20. *Sophisticated Ladies*
21. *Take Me Along*
22. *It's a Bird, It's a Plane, It's Superman!*
23. *Fiorello!*
24. *The Threepenny Opera*
25. *Philemon*

My favorites among my own characters:

1. Lucifer Jones
2. Harry the Book
3. John Justin Mallory
4. Jake Masters
5. Thaddeus Flint
6. The Valkyrie
7. Catastrophe Baker
8. Jefferson Nighthawk
9. Eli Paxton
10. Wilson Cole

The 50 Greatest American Race Horses of the 20th Century

1. Seattle Slew
2. Citation
3. Man o' War
4. Dr. Fager
5. Kelso (g)
6. Swaps
7. Native Dancer
8. Colin
9. Count Fleet
10. Ruffian (f)
11. Forego (g)
12. Secretariat
13. Buckpasser
14. Affirmed
15. Damascus
16. Cigar
17. War Admiral
18. Sysonby
19. Alydar
20. Tom Fool
21. Landeluce (f)
22. Graustark
23. Bold Ruler

24. Spectacular Bid
25. Round Table
26. Equipoise
27. Armed (g)
28. Phar Lap (g)
29. Sunday Silence
30. Assault
31. Easy Goer
32. Personal Ensign (f)
33. Twilight Tear (f)
34. Whirlaway
35. Tim Tam
36. Gallant Fox
37. Discovery
38. John Henry (g)
39. Busher (f)
40. Majestic Prince
41. Arts and Letters
42. Twenty Grand
43. A. P. Indy
44. Grey Lag
45. Allez France (f)
46. Stymie
47. Galorette (f)
48. Exterminator (g)
49. Regret (f)
50. Devil Diver

(g) gelding
(f) filly

My All-time NFL team:

Offense:
    QB: Joe Montana (49ers)
    RB: Gale Sayers (Bears)
    RB: Jim Brown (Browns)
    WR: Jerry Rice (49ers, Raiders)
    WR: Randy Moss (Vikings, Chargers, Patriots)

TE: Kellin Winslow (Chargers)
T: Forrest Gregg (Packers)
T: Anthony Munoz (Bengals)
G: Jerry Kramer (Packers)
G: Larry Little (Dolphins)
C: Mike Webster (Steelers)

Defense:
E: Bruce Smith (Bills)
T: Alex Karras (Lions)
T: Merlin Olson (Rams)
E: Reggie White (Eagles & Packers)
OLB: Ray Lewis (Ravens)
MLB: Dick Butkus (Bears)
OLB: Lawrence Taylor (Giants)
CB: Night Train Lane (Lions)
FS: Deion Sanders (Falcons, Cowboys)
CB: Herb Adderly (Packers)
SS: Ronnie Lott (49ers)
Punter: Ray Guy (Raiders)
Placekicker: Lou Groza (Browns)
Coach: Vince Lombardi

My All-time NBA teams:

1st team:
Center: Wilt Chamberlain (76ers/Lakers)
Forward: Julius Erving (76ers)
Forward: LeBron James (Cavaliers)
Guard: Michael Jordan (Bulls/Wizards)
Guard: Oscar Robinson (Royals/Bucks)
Coach: Red Auerbach

2nd team:
Center: Kareem Abdul-Jabbar (Bucks/Lakers)
Forward: Karl Malone (Jazz)
Forward: Tim Duncan (Spurs)
Guard: Jerry West (Lakers)
Guard: Magic Johnson (Lakers)
Coach: Phil Jackson

3rd team:
  Center: Bill Russell (Celtics)
  Forward: Elgin Baylor (Lakers)
  Forward: Bob Petit (Hawks)
  Guard: John Havlicek (Celtics)
  Guard: John Stockton (Jazz)
  Coach: Jerry Sloan

All-time baseball team:

1B — Lou Gehrig (Yankees)
2B — Rogers Hornsby (Cardinals)
SS — Ernie Banks (Cubs)
3B — Brooks Robinson (Orioles)
RF — Babe Ruth (Red Sox/Yankees/Braves)
CF — Ty Cobb (Tigers)
LF — Ted Williams (Red Sox)
C — Johnny Bench (Reds)
P — Sandy Koufax (Dodgers)
P — Walter Johnson (Senators)
P — Roger Clemens (Red Sox, Blue Jays, Yankees, Astros)
P — Allie Reynolds (Yankees)
RP — Hoyt Wilhelm (Giants/Orioles/White Sox)
Manager: Dick Williams (A's)
General Manager: Branch Rickey (Dodgers)
Owner: Bill Veeck (White Sox)

All-time Best Jockeys:

1. Bill Hartack
2. Angel Cordero, Jr.
3. Eddie Arcaro
4. Jerry Bailey
5. Laffit Pincay, Jr.
6. Pat Day
7. Bill Shoemaker
8. Ishmael Valenzuela
9. Braulio Baeza
10. Russell Baze
11. Chris McCarren
12. George Wolfe
13. Garrett Gomez

My favorite songs from Sondheim plays:

ANYONE CAN WHISTLE — "It's Always a Woman"
ASSASSINS — "The Ballad of Booth"
BOUNCE — "My Two Young Men"
COMPANY — "Sorry-Grateful"
EVENING PRIMROSE — "When?"
FOLLIES — "The Road You Didn't Take"
THE FROGS — "Instructions to the Audience"
A FUNNY THING HAPPENED ON THE WAY TO THE
    FORUM — "Bring Me My Bride"
INTO THE WOODS — "Agony"
A LITTLE NIGHT MUSIC — "Now"
MERRILY WE ROLL ALONG — "Like It Was"
PACIFIC OVERTURES — "A Bowler Hat"
PASSION — "I Read"
SATURDAY NIGHT — "Saturday Night"
SUNDAY IN THE PARK WITH GEORGE — "Finishing the Hat"
SWEENEY TODD — "A Little Priest"

My favorite songs from Jones & Schmidt plays:

THE BONE ROOM — "Come to Life"
CELEBRATION — "Survive"
COLETTE COLLAGE — "Be My Lady"
THE FANTASTICKS — "Try to Remember"
GROVERS CORNERS — "Time Goes By"
I DO! I DO! — "Nobody's Perfect"
MIRETTE — "Keep Your Feet Upon the Ground"
110 IN THE SHADE — "Evening Star"
ROADSIDE — "Smellamagoody Perfume"

My favorite songs from other musical plays:

AIN'T SUPPOSED TO DIE A NATURAL DEATH — "Just
    Don't Make No Sense"
AMOUR — "Painter's Song"
THE APPLE TREE — "What Makes Me Love Him?"

ASPECTS OF LOVE — "Love Changes Everything"
BAKER STREET — "Letters"
THE BAKER'S WIFE — "The Meadowlark"
BALLROOM — "Who Gave You Permission?"
BIG RIVER — "River in the Rain"
BRIGADOON — "Come to Me, Bend to Me"
BY JEEVES! — "That Was Nearly Us"
BYE BYE BIRDIE — "One Boy"
CABARET — "What Would You Do?"
CAMELOT — "Camelot"
CAN-CAN — "Allez-Vous En"
CANDIDE — "Glitter and Be Gay"
CARNIVAL — "Mira"
CAROUSEL — "Soliloquy"
CATS — "Memories"
CHICAGO — "All That Jazz"
CITY OF ANGELS — "You're Nothing Without Me"
CRY FOR US ALL — "Veranda Waltz"
DAMN YANKEES — "Whatever Lola Wants"
DESTRY RIDES AGAIN — "Rose Lovejoy of Paradise Valley"
DIRTY ROTTEN SCOUNDRELS — "All About Ruprecht"
DRESSED TO THE NINES — "Portofino"
DO I HEAR A WALTZ? — "Do I Hear a Waltz?"
DONNYBROOK! — "Sez I"
ELEGIES — "Anytime"
ERNEST IN LOVE — "The Hat"
EVITA — "High-Flying, Adored"
FALSETTOLAND — "The Baseball Game"
FIORELLO! — "Politics and Poker"
FIDDLER ON THE ROOF — "If I Were a Rich Man"
FINIAN'S RAINBOW — "If This Isn't Love"
FLOWER DRUM SONG — "You are Beautiful"
FLOYD COLLINS — "The Call"
FUNNY GIRL — "People"
THE GOLDEN APPLE — "Lazy Afternoon"
GREENWILLOW — "Faraway Boy"
GUYS AND DOLLS — "My Time of Day"
GYPSY — "Rose's Turn"
HELLO, DOLLY! — "Elegance"
HOW TO SUCCEED IN BUSINESS WITHOUT REALLY
    TRYING — "I Believe in You"
IN TROUSERS — "The Rape of Miss Goldberg"

IRMA LA DOUCE — "Valse Milieu"

IT'S A BIRD, IT'S A PLANE, IT'S SUPERMAN — "You've
 Got Possibilities"

JACQUES BREL IS ALIVE AND WELL AND LIVING IN PARIS
 — "Amsterdam"

JESUS CHRIST, SUPERSTAR — "I Don't Know How to Love Him"

THE KING AND I — "Shall We Dance?"

KING OF THE WHOLE DAMNED WORLD — "King of the World"

KISMET — "Baubles, Bangles and Beads"

KISS ME KATE — "Brush Up Your Shakespeare"

KWAMINA — "One Wife"

LA CAGE AUX FOLLES — "Song on the Sand"

THE LIFE — "It's My Body"

LI'L ABNER — "Namely You"

LITTLE SHOP OF HORRORS — "Somewhere That's Green"

LOST IN THE STARS — "Big Mole"

MACK AND MABEL — "Movies Were Movies"

MAN OF LA MANCHA — "I, Don Quixote"

MAN WITH A LOAD OF MISCHIEF — "Hullabaloo Bulay"

MARCH OF THE FALSETTOS — "Marvin at the Psychiatrist"

MARGUERITE — "China Doll"

MERLIN — "It's About Magic"

MINNIE'S BOYS — "Mama, A Rainbow"

THE MOST HAPPY FELLA — "Mama, Mama"

THE MUSIC MAN — "Rock Island"

MY FAIR LADY — "On the Street Where You Live"

A NEW BRAIN — "And They're Off!"

NEW FACES OF 1952 — "Penny Candy"

NEW GIRL IN TOWN — "Flings"

NICK AND NORA — "Boom Chicka Boom"

NIGHT OF THE HUNTER — "The Lord Will Provide"

NINE — "Guido's Song"

OKLAHOMA — "Oh, What a Beautiful Morning"

ON THE TOWN — "Some Other Time"

ON YOUR TOES — "There's a Small Hotel"

ONCE UPON A MATTRESS — "Normandy"

PAINT YOUR WAGON — "Mariah"

PAL JOEY — "Zip!"

PETER PAN — "Never Never Land"

PHANTOM OF THE OPERA — "The Music of the Night"

PORTRAIT OF JENNIE — "Alhambra Nights"

THE PRODUCERS — "The King of Broadway"

PROMISES, PROMISES — "She Likes Basketball!"
RAGTIME — "Ragtime"
REDHEAD — "I'm Back in Circulation"
THE RINK — "Aw, Mom!"
RIVERWIND — "Pardon Me While I Dance"
1776 — "He Plays the Violin"
SHENANDOAH — "Meditation
SHERLOCK HOLMES — "Without Him There Can Be No Me"
SHINBONE ALLEY — "My Friend Mehitibel"
SMILE — "Disneyland"
SONG OF SINGAPORE — "Foolish Geese"
THE SOUND OF MUSIC — "Edelweiss"
SOUTH PACIFIC — "Younger Than Springtime"
STARLIGHT EXPRESS — "Uncoupled"
SUNSET BOULEVARD — "New Ways to Dream"
SWEET CHARITY — "Hey, Big Spender"
TAKE ME ALONG — "Staying Young"
TENDERLOIN — "Little Old New York"
THE THREEPENNY OPERA — "The Ballad of Mack the Knife"
TOM JONES — "How Can I Thank You?"
THE 25TH ANNUAL PUTNAM COUNTY SPELLING BEE —
   "Six Languages"
WE TAKE THE TOWN — "Silverware"
WEST SIDE STORY — "Maria"
WICKED — "Popular"
WONDERFUL TOWN — "My Darlin' Eileen"
ZORBA — "Life Is"

My favorites (not necessarily my best) among my own work (through 2009):

Novels:
   The Outpost
   Hazards
   Adventures
   The Soul Eater
   Santiago

Novellas:
 "Seven Views of Olduvai Gorge"
 "Hunting the Snark"
 "Kilimanjaro"
 "Honorable Enemies"
 "Keepsakes"

Novelettes:
 "Alastair Baffle's Emporium of Wonders"
 "For I Have Touched the Sky"
 "Soulmates" (with Lezli Robyn)
 "All the Things You Are"
 "A Little Knowledge"

Short stories:
 "A Princess of Earth"
 "Travels With My Cats"
 "Article of Faith"
 "The Elephants on Neptune"
 "Robots Don't Cry"
 "The Bride of Frankenstein"
 "The 43 Antarean Dynasties"

Series:
 Lucifer Jones
 Starship
 John Justin Mallory
 The Widowmaker
 Tales of the Galactic Midway

My Favorite Comedians:

1. Severn Darden
2. Mort Sahl
3. The Original Second City Players (1959-1961)
4. Tom Lehrer
5. Low Moan Spectacular
6. Rita Rudner

7. Benny Hill
8. Stiller & Meara
9. Nichols & May
10. Sid Caesar
11. Jean Shepherd
12. Dennis Miller

My Favorite Mystery Writers:

1. Raymond Chandler
2. Dashiell Hammett
3. James Ellroy
4. M. E. Chaber
5. Rex Stout
6. Fredric Brown
7. Ross MacDonald
8. Leigh Bracket
9. James T. Cain
10. Arthur Conan Doyle

(Ross H. Spencer wrote humor disguised as mystery novels; if he counts as a mystery writer, put him second.)

My science fiction collaborators over the years:

1. Nick DiChario
2. Lou Tabakow
3. Barry N. Malzberg
4. Barbara Delaplace
5. Lawrence Schimel
6. Linda Dunn
7. Jack L. Chalker
8. George Alec Effinger
9. Lyn Nichols
10. Susan Shwartz
11. Jack Nimershein
12. Louise Rowder
13. Josepha Sherman
14. Ann Marston
15. Ron Collins

16. Adrienne Gormley
17. Kristine Kathryn Rusch
18. Catherine Asaro
19. Tom Gerencer
20. B. J. Galler-Smith
21. Robyn Herrington
22. M. Shayne Bell
23. Tobias S. Buckell
24. Mark Stafford
25. Dean Wesley Smith
26. Janis Ian
27. Michael A. Burstein
28. Ralph Roberts
29. B. D. Faw
30. Robert Sheckley
31. Kay Kenyon
32. Susan R. Matthews
33. Paul Crilley
34. Linda Donahue
35. Harry Turtledove
36. Nancy Kress
37. James Patrick Kelly
38. Kevin J. Anderson
39. Bill Fawcett
40. David Gerrold
41. Eric Flint
42. Pat Cadigan
43. Lezli Robyn

The 5 Best SF/F magazines:

1. *Unknown*
2. *Astounding*, 1939-1944
3. *Galaxy*, 1950-1956
4. *Asimov's*, 1992-2002
5. *Weird Tales*, 1930-1939

LaVergne, TN USA
05 April 2010
178239LV00002B/8/P